MW00452505

PRAIRIE NIGHTS TO NEON LIGHTS

The

Story

Of

Country

Music

In

West

Texas

PRAIRIE NIGHTS TO NEON LIGHTS

JOE CARR & ALAN MUNDE

Texas Tech University Press

Copyright 1995 Texas Tech University Press

All rights reserved. No portion of this book may be reproduced in any form or by any means, including electronic storage and retrieval systems, except by explicit, prior written permission of the publisher.
This book was set in Berkeley Oldstyle and printed on acid-free paper that meets the guidelines for permanence and durability of the Committee on Production Guidelines for Book Longevity of the Council on Library Resources.

Printed in the United States of America

Library of Congress Cataloging-in-Publication Data
Carr, Joe.
Prairie nights to neon lights : the story of country music in west Texas /
Joe Carr and Alan Munde.
p. cm.
Includes bibliographical references and index.
ISBN 0-89672-349-6 (cloth) — ISBN 0-89672-365-8 (paper)
1. Country music–Texas, West–History and criticism. I. Munde, Alan. II. Title.
ML3524.C328 1995
781.642'09764–dc20

94-48096
CIP
MN

97 98 99 00 01 02 03 / 9 8 7 6 5 4 3

Design by Kerri Carter

Texas Tech University Press
Box 41037
Lubbock, Texas 79409-1037 USA
1-800-832-4042
ttup@ttu.edu

West Texas
Where you can go farther and see less,
Where there are more creeks and less water,
Where there is more climate and less rain,
Where there is more horizon and fewer trees,
Where there are more cows and less milk,
Than any other place in the Union.
Leona Mae Austin, age 14, Childress, Texas, 1922

In West Texas you can look in any direction and see
for fifty miles, and if you stand on a tuna fish can,
you can see for a hundred miles. *Butch Hancock*

West Texas is the only place in the world where
you can be up to your butt in mud and have dust
blowing in your eyes. *Jimmy Dean*

CONTENTS

ACKNOWLEDGMENTS

The authors wish to thank the many West Texas musicians and our friends and family members who shared stories and photographs. Many took the time to respond in writing to a questionnaire, and others allowed taped interviews in their homes by telephone or in person. Without these people this book could not have been written.

This project was conceived and directed for much of its first three years of development by Susan Miller of the University of Nebraska. Susan approached the authors about the project in 1989, and it was her gentle but insistent prodding that kept it on track. Her insightful suggestions and editorial input are reflected on every page of the work. Editor Carole Young helped keep the project on track, and copy editor Judy Sacks introduced several format changes that vastly improved the manuscript.

The Southwest Collection at Texas Tech University and the research library at the Panhandle Plains Museum at West Texas State University were excellent sources of material, and their helpful staffs often led to important material that we otherwise might have overlooked.

Ronnie Pugh and Bob Pinson of the Country Music Foundation in Nashville were extremely helpful and provided discographies and historical information on several subjects. Pete Curtis, Dutch LaRue, Jack Douglas, Keith Ward, Tom Forsel, Charles Hunter, Larry Richardson, Lloyd Maines, Wally Moyers Jr., The Hale Center American, and many others provided rare documents and photographs.

English music historians A. J. Turner of The Hillbilly Researcher and Howard Cockburn of Now Dig This provided information about Charline Arthur.

The Abilene Reporter News's impressive "morgue," with its files of newspaper clippings, provided a wealth of information, and the paper's photo file produced some of our favorite photographs. The staff there was very helpful and knowledgeable. Hank Harrison of San Antonio freely provided rare materials from his extensive country music collection. He was particularly helpful with information and pictures of Slim Willet, J. R. Chatwell, and Floyd Tillman. Mr. Dub Rogers, the West Texas television pioneer, graciously allowed use of photographs from his impressive collection housed at South Plains College. John Sparks of the Communications department at South Plains College brought this collection to the authors' attention and helped research the photographs. Rick and Mary Gardner of Gardner Photography in Houston made beautiful prints of a large group of the photographs. Their generous work always exceeded expectations. Jeff Whitley of the College Relations

Department at South Plains College copied many of the rare photographs (some in poor original condition) found in this work. He graciously gave of his time and talent. Dennis Harp of Texas Tech University helped with photographic advice and resources.

With only the crudest of instructions from the authors, Steve and Jackie Garner produced the map of West Texas designed to orient readers to the region. We sincerely appreciate their beautiful work.

We thank Anne Solomon for her help with the manuscript and Paula Carr for being a sounding board and her photographic work. Our families showed incredible patience and understanding during this project as it took time from lives and room from homes.

PRAIRIE NIGHTS TO NEON LIGHTS

INTRODUCTION

The arid plains and rugged ranch land of West Texas has been fertile soil for the growth and development of country music. Permanent Anglo settlement in the area began in the 1880s.[1] Blistering heat, numbing cold, persistent winds, and lack of water made West Texas an inhospitable environment for any but the heartiest residents. Into this land came people of many descriptions: cowboys, farmers, and entrepreneurs.

Hardly more than a hundred years has passed since the beginning of this settlement. Indeed, many West Texas communities were formed during the first three decades of the twentieth century. So new is the country that at early settlers' celebrations held annually throughout West Texas in the early 1990s, it was not unusual to find the honored settlers present and in many cases still active in the community. In this brief time, modifying the musics they brought with them and absorbing influences from every possible direction, the early West Texas Anglo musicians developed a rich regional music that continues to evolve today.

No regional music is completely free of outside influence. The European ancestors of country music have intermingled with and influenced one another since their arrival in America. Since the turn of the twentieth century, the phonograph and, later, the radio, have accelerated this process. Exchange occurred among the various musical heritages of Texas. Anglo-Celtic settlers, for example, brought a rich tradition of fiddle music, balladry, and church music inherited from their European ancestors. The blues and field songs of African Americans in East Texas, the polkas of Czechs and Germans in South Texas, the Louisiana Cajun French music of deep East Texas, and the rich musical heritage of Mexico and the hybrid "Tex-Mex" music all served to shape and alter the sound of Texas's country music.

No clear consensus defines the boundaries of West Texas. We have chosen the 98th meridian as the extreme eastern boundary of West Texas, centering most of our discussion on the area west of the 100th meridian. The 100th meridian marks the eastern boundary of the Texas panhandle and forms the north-south boundary with Oklahoma. The area to the west of it includes the metropolitan and rural areas surrounding Amarillo, Lubbock, Abilene, Big Spring, Pecos, Midland, Odessa, and San Angelo. A few miles east of this line lies Wichita Falls. Discussed only peripherally is El Paso, as far removed historically and culturally as it is geographically from the rest of populated West Texas. Also omitted are the vast, sparsely populated expanses of West Texas that include the Big Bend area, Marfa, Alpine, Van Horn, and Fort Davis.

The 98th meridian marked the approximate western extent of Anglo settlement reached on the eve of the Civil War. The area west of this line was occupied until late in the nineteenth century by various tribes of nomadic Plains Indians, most of whom were hostile to the presence of whites. The gentle, rolling plains around Abilene extend west until they are suddenly broken by the Caprock Escarpment, the edge of the *Llano Estacado* or Staked Plains, which includes much of the Texas panhandle. South of the caprock, the rolling terrain slowly becomes drier and flatter, opening into the Permian Basin around Midland, Odessa, and points west.

On early maps of the American West, this region was represented as part of the Great American Desert. West of the 100th meridian, the annual rainfall is generally less than twenty inches. Of the striking climatic contrasts between East and West Texas, West Texans will tell you that during Noah's flood, their region got only a quarter of an inch of rain.

Many of the hundred or so people we spoke to believe that a common thread runs through the music of West Texas, but few could identify specific attributes of the regional style. The land is often mentioned as a shaper of the music, as in this romantic excerpt from the liner notes of a Bob Wills album: "The vast silences of the Texas plains have produced more than their share of American minstrels. Perhaps it is the great emptiness of the prairies that prompts men to lift their voices to dispel the silence, perhaps it is the simple pleasure of living freely under changing skies."[2] In this view, the stark nothingness of the country imparts some message to the inhabitants of the region, a message they reflect in their music and other creations. The climate, characterized by sharp contrasts of heat and cold, periods of drought, relentless winds and blowing dust, is also often credited as an influence. The great distances that separate populated areas and a sense of isolation and independence derived from the big spaces are cited as contributing factors. A Texas Tech University museum exhibit on West Texas music was simply entitled "Nothin' Else to Do." One might conclude that the sum of these natural environmental forces molds the residents' creations, and that in the music can be heard the echoes of the wind and the rhythm of life on the prairie. As romantic and attractive as these ideas may be, they are difficult to support.

One element uniting much of West Texas country music is that it was intended for dance. While the music of cowboy singers, religious music, and the poetry songs of the recent era do not fit this model, dance has certainly been one important factor in West Texas's musical development. Cowboy musicians often played for dancers, as did the early fiddle bands in the first decades of the twentieth century. The birth of Western swing music in the 1930s can be described as the blending of American popular dance music and the regional dance music of the American Southwest. After World War II, electric honky tonk music, the descendant of Western swing, provided an even more danceable beat. Rock and roll music, appearing in the 1950s, has a heavy dance beat at its core.

In the modern era, most West Texas country music bands perform primarily for dances. The relative rarity of regional bluegrass music performances can partially be attributed to the fact that it is not dance music.

Many West Texas musicians feel there is something unique about the music of the area. The West Texas Music Association was founded by such performers. Many artists from the region, such as Jimmie Dale Gilmore and Joe Ely, continued to identify themselves as West Texas musicians long after they left. Public television's music series "Austin City Limits" devoted an hour-long program to West Texas songwriters, and an Austin night club featured a weekly "Lubbock night" starring performers from West Texas. One wonders why other musically productive regions of Texas have not been spotlighted in this way when they may, in fact, have produced more musicians than the relatively small output of West Texas. Part of the answer may lie in the mystique that surrounds West Texas and its music.

When the popular imagination is captured by anything labeled as Texan, the images evoked are likely to be West Texan. Endless plains, big sunsets, cattle roundups, cowboys and Indians—these are all images of the western part of the state. Dallas, Fort Worth, Houston, Galveston, and Austin, all located in the eastern areas of the state, have strong Texas myths connected to them, but the names "Abilene," "Amarillo," "El Paso," and "Pecos" conjure up the popular idea and legend of Texas. The popularity of the romanticized West during the 1930s is illustrated by the Girls of the Golden West, a yodeling sister duet from Illinois. Millie and Dollie Good dressed in cowgirl attire and publicized that they were from exotic-sounding Muleshoe, Texas.[3] Films and novels such as *Giant*, *Red River*, *The Last Picture Show*, *Texasville*, and *Lonesome Dove* all project the images of West Texas as the image of Texas in general. Texas itself, of course, has a larger-than-life image throughout the world. The "first," the "biggest," the "best" are superlatives constantly used by and about Texans. The field of country music is an area where this giant reputation is deserved. Music has been one of the major cultural exports of West Texas, including the likes of Bob Wills and Buddy Holly; it is understandable, therefore, that music comes to mind when people think of the region and its contributions to the world.

This work discusses Anglo country music primarily, although the rich musics of other ethnic and racial groups have heavily influenced Texas country music and will be discussed as they relate to our topic. We address not only folk musics, such as cowboy songs and fiddle music, but also commercial expressions. Much of what is considered country music exhibits substantial amounts of noncountry influence. In Texas, perhaps more than in other parts of the country, the lines between musical styles have been blurred by musicians who combine many influences to create new and often exciting musical forms. Western swing, for example, incorporates many characteristics of jazz and popular music. The music of Buddy Holly and other 1950s rock and roll musicians is another example of the way several musics can be molded into a new form. Similarly, the West Texas songwriters of the 1970s and 1980s do not all fall neatly into the country music category. We will discuss them as they relate to country music.

Through profiles and interviews with selected musicians who have helped to shape the sound of West Texas country music, printed sources, and photographs, a picture of the music emerges as a unique regional expression that borrows freely from many musical sources and yet retains an essence that is West Texas.

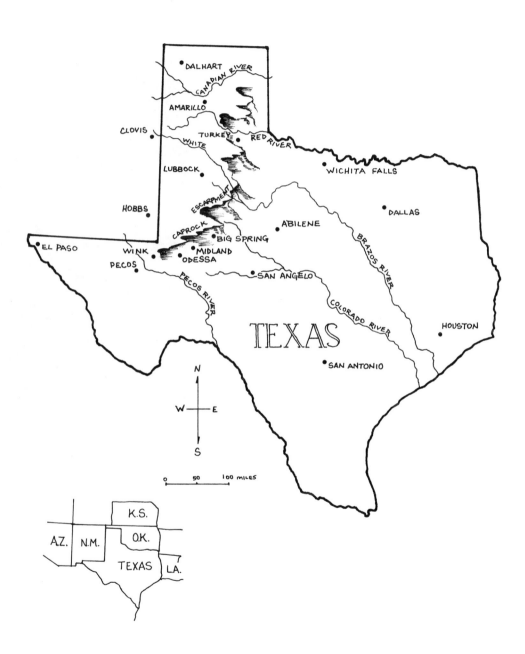

DALHART

CANADIAN RIVER

AMARILLO

CLOVIS

TURKEY

RED RIVER

WHITE

WICHITA FALLS

LUBBOCK

ESCARPMENT

HOBBS

DALLAS

CAPROCK

ABILENE

BIG SPRING

WINK

EL PASO

MIDLAND

ODESSA

BRAZOS RIVER

PECOS

SAN ANGELO

PECOS RIVER

COLORADO RIVER

HOUSTON

TEXAS

SAN ANTONIO

N

W ——— E

S

0   50   100 MILES

K.S.

AZ.   N.M.   O.K.

TEXAS   L.A.

COWBOYS, SETTLERS, AND FIDDLERS

The story of country music in West Texas begins with the cattle industry. As early as the 1860s, while Indians still roamed freely throughout much of the region, the first cattle trails had been blazed. Most of the important cattle trails of the 1870s and 1880s began in southern and western Texas and developed northward to major railroad centers such as Denver, Cheyenne, and Dodge City. Trail names such as the Goodnight-Loving and Chisholm are familiar even to the casual observer of the American West. The cattle drives employed cowboys who worked and lived with cattle on their long and sometimes dangerous journeys north.

The age of the cattle drives was relatively short. By the mid-1880s, barbed wire fencing closed the open ranges forever. Cattle could now be kept inexpensively in enclosed spaces. Fences and expansion of the railroads made the trail drives obsolete. Despite their short lifespan, however, trail drives left a Texas-sized legacy: The American Cowboy.[1]

Romanticized and idealized by writers from the beginning, the cowboy rapidly became an American hero, a symbol of the human qualities Americans held most dear. Even after fences closed the range and changed the cowboy lifestyle, the public remained enamored with those rugged sons of the West. The national fascination with cowboys and the American West was so great that many easterners were inspired to come out west for a taste of cowboy life.

Country music in West Texas originated with cowboy song. It is fortunate that several insightful men heard the songs of the cowboys and recorded the words. The first of these was Jack Thorp. Thorp, born in 1867, was an adventurer from the northeast who eventually lived as a cowboy. In 1889 and 1890, he traveled throughout eastern New Mexico and the Texas panhandle collecting cowboy songs— the first such project completed in the country where cowboys lived and worked.[2] *Songs of the Cowboys*, published in 1908, included twenty-three of these songs, five written by Thorp himself.[3] Thorp published his work at Estancia, New Mexico, and only two thousand copies were printed. Of these, it is estimated that only twenty copies have survived, and they are highly prized collectibles.[4] Although flawed–Thorp did not document the sources of the material or record any melodies–Thorp's work is important because it provided the earliest view into the music of West Texas and the American Southwest.

The first scholarly collection of cowboy songs was made by John Avery Lomax (1867-1948). Lomax was born in Mississippi, two years before his family moved to Bosque County, Texas, in 1869. Lomax began to collect ballads and folk songs as a childhood hobby. He later completed B.A. (1897) and M.A. (1906) degrees from the University of Texas. It was not until Lomax attended Harvard in 1907, however, that he received encouragement to collect western ballads and folk songs.[5] As is still often the case, Lomax found enthusiasm for Texas music stronger abroad than at home.

After three years of collection and several rejections by publishers, *Cowboy Songs and Other Frontier Ballads* was published by Sturgis and Walton in 1910. With larger circulation than the Thorp opus, it introduced many readers to authentic cowboy music. As a scholar, Lomax risked ridicule collecting the "low folk poetry" of frontier Americans. In his introduction to the 1910 edition of the work, Lomax's Harvard professor Barrett Wendell almost apologized for the lack of "beauty and power" in the verses.[6]

The Lomax book included several of Thorp's songs. In the period from 1907 to 1910 Lomax collected "Little Joe the Wrangler," written in 1898, according to Thorp, and published it without mentioning Thorp.[7] In later editions of the Lomax book, however, Thorp is fully credited for the song.[8] Lomax's interest in this material and its publication were important milestones in the legitimation of American folk music as a subject for serious academic interest. In fact, *Cowboy Songs and Other Frontier Ballads* has been termed "a landmark that compared with the publication in the previous century of Francis James Child's ballad books."[9]

Many of the songs in these two volumes are variants of older songs from other parts of the United States. An explanation of how these songs may have traveled and evolved is given in the notes to the Library of Congress recording *Cowboy Songs, Ballads, and Cattle Calls from Texas.*[10] In the cited example, "The Buffalo Skinners," an English love song published before 1800, provided the basis for the English sea song "Canada I O," published in 1847. Ephraim Braley, a lumberjack in Maine, in turn composed a song in 1853 based on "Canada I O." This song later appeared, in altered forms, in the oral traditions in Pennsylvania as "Colley's Run I O," in Michigan as "Michigan I O," and in Texas as "The Buffalo Skinners." No doubt other songs in the cowboy tradition traveled to Texas in similar fashion.

The songs concern a range of subject matter. "The Buffalo Skinners" tells of a buffalo hunting trip from Jacksboro to West Texas in 1873. Also included are songs about trail drives and roundup time, such as "The Old Chisholm Trail," "Whoopee Ti Yi Yo, Git Along, Little Dogies," and songs about notorious outlaws like "Sam Bass" and "Jesse James." The cowboys who did sing, and not all did, sang for their own and one another's enjoyment, as a simple way to pass time during a lonely and sometimes boring job.

The popular notion that cowboys sang to calm the cattle at night has some detractors. Thorp reported the following in his autobiographical *Pardner of the Wind:*

It is generally thought that cowboys did a lot of singing around the herd at night to quiet them on the bed ground. I have been asked about this, and I'll say that I have stood my share of night watches in fifty years, and I have seldom heard any singing of that kind. What you would hear as you passed your partner on guard, would be a kind of low hum or whistle, and you wouldn't know what it was. Just some old hymn tune, like as not—something to kill time and not bad enough to make the herd want to get up and run.[11]

In his notes to the 1910 edition of his work, Lomax announced that "a number of the most characteristic [songs] cannot be printed for general circulation."[12] Bawdy songs, representing a considerable portion of the cowboy repertoire, went largely undocumented until quite recently because of the conservative moral climate of the early part of this century. For decades, numerous underground publications circulated among college students and a few commercial collections were published, but for the most part, this body of songs was transmitted solely through the oral tradition. The serious collection and study of "dirty" cowboy songs was finally established with the publication in 1989 of *The Whorehouse Bells Were Ringing* by Guy Logsdon.[13] That these songs and others survived so many years without publication is testimony to their lasting appeal. It also points to the fact that the oral tradition is still an active way of passing information from person to person and from one generation to the next.

Cowboys often were single men without homes or family, but permanent white settlement in West Texas increased in the late 1800s, once the region was considered safe from hostile Indians. Settlers were attracted for many reasons. Some came to start businesses, while others came to establish farms or ranches. Many must have sensed the space and opportunity this new land seemed to offer. Ross Edwards's family was perhaps typical of this breed. Edwards, a fiddler and one-time mayor of Lubbock, related the story of his family's move to West Texas from Granbury (near Forth Worth) in his autobiography, *Fiddle Dust*:

> As a young man Dad was a buffalo hunter, and when the game was over he came home, married, and started farming and stock-raising. . . . Now the country was getting too thickly settled for Dad, and he was preparing to go west and grow up with the country. He had a family consisting of a wife, three girls, a boy, a mother, and about one hundred head of cattle and horses. I remember some of the preparations. Fixing up the chuck wagon, getting together outdoor cooking utensils, ropes, tents, etc. . . . I was fitted out in a new saddle, bridle, blanket, and all the accouterments necessary for producing a real cowboy. Dad hired the man who broke my horse . . . to help me "slow track" that herd of horses and cattle. We rounded up and set sail sometime in the fall of 1891. Mother drove one of the wagons and Dad the other. [14]

At age seven, Ross helped drive the herd at the rate of ten to twelve miles a day, toward Foard County in twenty-one days. The family moved into an old, unused dugout home located twelve miles outside Crowell. Ross's Uncle Rube had moved to the area earlier and helped the family get settled. After sinking a water well, they went to Vernon, fifty miles northeast, to get lumber for a house. Ross's father and Uncle Rube built two fourteen-foot rooms and hauled rock from a nearby canyon to build a chimney.[15]

Through efforts such as these, West Texas was settled. Due to the vast distances between settlements and sparse population, West Texans were isolated and therefore welcomed any opportunity to socialize with their neighbors. During the 1880s and 1890s, dances were the most important social events connected with ranch life.[16] Until as recently as the 1940s, barn dances and house parties continued to be important sources of entertainment. Mrs. Jack Miles, whose family settled on the Concho River in Tom Green County "when San Angelo was a mere village of picket houses and adobe huts," remembered, "Jack and I attended many frontier socials, picnics, fish fries, races, and glorious old-time square dances, where fiddle, banjo, and guitar made 'Sally Gooden,' 'Turkey in the Straw,' and 'Pop Goes the Weasel' famous. Thirty or forty miles was not considered a long distance to go on horseback to a dance."[17]

The music most often featured a fiddler and perhaps an accompanist, often on guitar or, if it was available, piano. Lizzie Campbell, wife of Matador Ranch superintendent Henry Campbell, hosted an annual Christmas party and dance beginning in 1883. She recalled, "Music for the first [Christmas party in Motley County] was provided by one of the cowboys who had a very small selection of tunes. He was usually accompanied by some other boy who beat the wires on the strings of a fiddle. These old timers would play all night, seemingly with as much enjoyment after the sun was up next morning, as when they began at sundown."[18]

Elijah Cox, a black soldier at San Angelo in the 1870s, fiddled for dances at Fort Concho.[19] He related the following in a 1924 newspaper interview: "Folks danced the schottische, the polka, the square dance, and the quadrille. I'll bet I can play 300 waltzes, all different without stopping."[20] Rollie Burns, who worked as a cowboy on the "22" ranch in Crosby County during the 1880s, recalled two dances held during the winter of 1881-82. The events were anticipated for months. The first dance, held at Will Slaughter's home, attracted around thirty cowboys. Women were scarce in this frontier region and in demand at social functions. Fifty years later, Burns still remembered the nine women at this dance and their names:

> Three nights and two days—quadrilles, waltzes, schottisches, and polkas. I wondered how the women stood it. With the men it was different. There were three times as many of them as women; consequently they got to rest about two-thirds of the time. When one of the boys got tired and sleepy, he could go out to the half

dugout used as a bunk house and get a nap, but the women were not given a chance to rest. However, they danced with minimum exertion. The men swung them so lustily that little effort was necessary on their part. Before daybreak of the third morning, however, their feet got tired and sore.[21]

With so few women at these early West Texas dances, the men would have to wait a long time between turns. Often, selected men would be designated a "heifer branded" or a "lady fair" to be marked with a handkerchief tied on their arm or by some other means. These men would then be dance partners for the other men.[22]

One of the most elaborate dances in this early period was a three-day event organized by Bill Richards, who owned the 3D Ranch in Cottle, Foard, and King Counties. Western writer John Hendrix described the event, which was held to honor cowboys who had come to that section before 1879: "It was held in late July, 1903, in a hackberry grove of thirty-five or forty acres, eighteen miles southeast of Paducah in the old Moon Pasture which Richards had acquired. From Quanah, fifty-five miles away, the nearest railroad point, wagon freighters hauled material for a dance platform, large enough to accommodate four sets of square dancers at a time. They also hauled out twelve hundred loaves of bread, two barrels of pickles, fifteen bushels of onions, and a *baby grand piano*." Twenty head of cattle were butchered and barbecued for the dance, which began at noon on a Friday. Hendrix continued: "From the first music on Friday afternoon until 12 p.m. [midnight] Saturday night, there was not a moment that dancing was not in progress, except for a short period during Friday night, when by general consent everyone 'took out' for about three hours to let the piano cool off. One young lady, now a portly matron, still boasts that she never missed a set nor waltz during the three days."[23]

Country fiddler Bob Suggs of Welch related a tale from when his father was a boy about the fun that children and teenagers had at the dances. Many times, the young people would congregate outside while their parents danced to the music. As the evening progressed, mothers would bring their infants and place them in their horse-drawn buggies, where the babies would sleep peacefully through the night. The mothers would then return to the festivities inside. The mischief began when the young people switched the babies around in different buggies. When the dance broke up in the early hours of the morning, the parents, satisfied that their infants were sleeping soundly, would start their journey home. The mixup often was not discovered until the families were many miles from the ranch, and, in a day of horse-drawn transportation and few telephones, it could take a week to return the infants to their respective homes.[24]

One of the most pervasive images of early western music is that of the guitar-playing cowboy singer. Often, he is depicted sitting by a campfire, calming the "dogies" with his prairie lullaby. This image, however, is largely a creation of Hollywood western movies of the 1930s and 1940s.

Such stars as Gene Autry and Roy Rogers are the models upon which the popular image of frontier cowboy music rests. Cowboys did play the guitar, but the favored musical instruments were the harmonica, the banjo, and the fiddle. These instruments had the advantage of being smaller than the guitar and therefore easier to carry on horseback. Of these instruments, the fiddle has had the strongest and most lasting influence on the music of Texas.[25]

The fiddle suited the cowboys' and early settlers' musical needs in several ways. Fiddles were small and portable, and some violin cases were designed to be strapped to a saddle like a saddlebag, although probably few could afford such a luxury. Bulkier guitars were less likely to survive the rigors of travel on horseback or in a wagon. Fiddle music, too, was the most popular rural dance music of the period. A fiddler was a prerequisite for a square dance, one of the most popular social gatherings on the range. According to Thorp, "the people of Texas didn't know the National Anthem, but they all knew 'Turkey in the Straw.'"[26] This story from the days of the Texas Republic illustrates the pivotal role of the fiddler at early Texas dances:

An Army captain, according to his own account, had found dancers in an East Texas tavern attempting to revive the only available fiddler, victim of an overdose of inspiration from his whiskey bottle. "The dancers . . . rolled the drunken man upon the floor, they stirred him up, they rubbed his head with vinegar, and they crammed an entire jar of Underwood's pickles down his throat—but all would not do." Although the captain had never played any sort of musical instrument, he offered to substitute for the drunken musician. When the dancers accepted enthusiastically, the captain took his place in the violinist's chair, picked up the fiddle, and made a few musician-like flourishes and preliminary motions. "At length, . . . he drew the cork by giving every string on the violin a general rake with the bow. Away they went like mad, Captain H. still sawing away, stamping his right foot as if keeping time, and calling the figure. . . .

It may be readily supposed that the dancers had but a limited knowledge of music; but they could tell, in their cooler moments, a tune from a tornado. The first two couple[s] had by this time finished, and the second had commenced, when one of the former addressed his partner with:

"Eliza, did you ever hear that tune he's aplaying afore?"

"Can't say that I ever has," was the response, and this within hearing of Captain H. who was still punishing the violin as severely as ever.

"Does it sound to you like much of a tune . . . any how?"

"Well it doesn't."

"Nor to me either," said the first speaker, who all the while had his head turned to one side after the manner of a hog listening. "My opinion is that feller is naterally jest promiscuously and miscellane-ously sawin away without exactly knowing what he's doin."[27]

The fiddler held an unusual position in West Texas society. Fiddle music was prized as one of the few social diversions available. The fiddler however, was often characterized as lazy, hard drinking, and generally worthless.[28] This duality existed before Anglos arrived on the Texas plains. Christian folk tradition held that the fiddle was the instrument of the devil and that a talent for playing the instrument was gained through a bargain with the devil. Some Protestant denominations on the frontier forbade dancing, putting the fiddler on the fringe of proper society, the purveyor of a desirable but forbidden entertainment. Old-time fiddlers sometimes came up with their own solutions to this dilemma. Bud Browning, a Matador ranch cowboy and fiddler at the turn of the century, was "too religious to dance, but not too religious to fiddle for the better part of two nights and one day while others danced."[29] J. R. Craddock, an observer of Texas folklife, commented, "When a church member took part in a dance he was said to have 'danced himself out of the church' and he had to be 'saved' at the next revival. With some persons it was a habit to 'dance out of the church' in the winter and to be 'saved' at the 'camp meeting' the following summer when dancing was not in vogue."[30]

The music these fiddlers played must have been similar to that played by fiddlers from the southeastern states. Many titles appear in both traditions, and large numbers of Texas settlers and cowboys came from the South. Within a short time, however, Texas fiddle music began to change. The earliest recordings of Texas fiddlers, made in the 1920s, show that tunes like "Sally Johnson" and "Sallie Gooden" had taken on new personalities in the West.[31] According to fiddle music authority Earl Speilman, Texas "is the one area which has evolved an utterly unique and distinctive fiddling style, a style which is almost immediately identifi-able."[32] The post-frontier style featured slower tempos than those typi-cally found in comparable fiddle music of the eastern United States. More emphasis was placed on melodic invention and variation than on the rhythmic bowings found in eastern styles.[33] It is uncertain why these changes occurred. Perhaps the adventurous spirit of these settlers was reflected in their music: the West offered a chance for a fresh start, and the fiddlers made the most of it.

In the era before radio and recording, fiddling and fiddle tunes were passed directly from one generation to the next through an oral tradition, just as storytelling and ballad singing were. Small inaccuracies and embellishments were part of this process, as fiddlers relied on memory to recreate tunes taught to them note by note. Texas fiddlers, however, began to change the tunes in more overt ways. An excellent example of this evolution appears in the early recordings of fiddling legend Eck Robertson, the first and most important early recorded musician of West Texas. Born Alexander Campbell Robertson on November 20, 1887, in Delany, Arkansas, he moved with his family to the Texas panhandle in

1900 and settled on a farm near Amarillo.[34] Both Eck's grandfather, Joe Robertson, and his father, T.L. Robertson, a Disciples' minister at Henryetta, Oklahoma, were fiddlers of note.[35] Eck remembered being surprised to discover that his father played the fiddle, for the elder Robertson had stopped fiddling upon entering the ministry and before the birth of his children.[36] Eck's brother Quince, who died at the age of thirty-six, was also a noted fiddler.[37] Eck related that when he was eight years old, he made his first fiddle by stretching the hide of the family cat over a large gourd. Later he traded a pig to a neighbor for a $3.25 Sears Roebuck fiddle. Eck eventually joined his brother and cowboy fiddler Pat Hooker in a small dance band. Since Eck's father did not approve of young Eck's performing, his brother would slip him out the back window of the house. Eck explained, "We'd play for a whole dance, they'd slip me back into the window, and my father would never know I'd been gone."[38]

At sixteen, Eck left home to perform in traveling medicine shows in Oklahoma. Undoubtedly, it was here that he began to develop the sense of showmanship that characterized his performances throughout his long career. In an early promotional photo, Eck posed with an American flag attached to the scroll of his fiddle. In another, he posed with his fiddle bow tucked behind his knee, demonstrating some fancy "trick" fiddling. With two landmark recording sessions in 1922, Eck Robertson earned his place in American folk music history. That session produced the first recordings of American country music.[39]

Much of the lore concerning early Texas fiddlers can be traced to the writings of Dr. J. B. Cranfill, a fiddler who recorded with Eck Robertson in 1929. In one of several newspaper articles about fiddling in the 1920s, Cranfill discussed Matt Brown, a contemporary of Eck Robertson.[40] Raymond Brown of Lubbock is the nephew of Matt Brown and a champion fiddler in his own right. He remembered both his uncles, Alf and Matt Brown, as master fiddlers. The Brown family had moved from the Goldthwaite, Texas, area to West Texas sometime after the turn of the century.[41] Hugh and Karl Farr, who played hot swing fiddle and guitar, respectively, with the Sons of the Pioneers during the 1930s and 1940s, knew Brown. Their brother, Glen, asserted that Matt Brown had a big influence on all three brothers: "During our childhood, [Matt Brown] was the most popular violinist, I guess, anywhere in the country. Everybody who played anything, you know, looked up to Matt Brown. He was a middle-aged man when we were kids."[42]

Texas fiddlers acknowledge Brown as the composer of "Done Gone" and "Brown-Kelly Waltz" (now known as "Kelly Waltz"), both standards in the contemporary Texas fiddle repertoire. Eck Robertson recorded "Done Gone" in the landmark 1922 New York sessions and "Brown-Kelly Waltz" in Dallas in 1929. Robertson obviously thought a lot of Brown's compositions, as he recorded "Brown-Kelly Waltz" in two parts, filling both sides of a 78 rpm record. Cranfill related this anecdote about the composition of "Done Gone":

Some years ago there lived in the Panhandle country of Texas a wonderful fiddler named Matt Brown. He was left afoot some miles from Amarillo and started to walk to that town. After negotiating half the distance he was tired and weary, so he sat by the roadside waiting for an automobile to come along. Finally he saw one of those machines—automobiles were so new to all of us then—approaching him and traveling in the direction of Amarillo. He jumped out into the road and attempted to flag this wild-eyed driver down so that he might get a ride into Amarillo. The automobile paid no mind to him and after Brown had jumped aside to save himself from injury, he sat down all disconsolate and composed "Done Gone," one of the greater of the fiddle pieces and it is rendered with the artistry, a skill and a perfection of execution by Eck Robertson that would warm your heart if you could hear him play it.[43]

Unfortunately, there are no recordings of Matt Brown's fiddling and no way to judge how skilled a musician he was. The tunes credited to him, however, give us reason to suspect he was quite accomplished. "Done Gone" is performed in the key of B flat, an unusual and more difficult key than the typical fiddle keys of A and D. According to Raymond Brown, in 1924, while performing with a traveling medicine show, Matt Brown drowned in a fishing accident near Spur, Texas. It was Matt's brother Alf, therefore, who had the larger impact on young Raymond's fiddling.[44] Perhaps Matt Brown's modern impact would be as strong as Eck Robertson's had he lived to record his compositions.

Jess Morris, born June 12, 1878, in Williamson County, Texas, was a noted fiddler in the western Panhandle region.[45] In 1890, his father moved the family to a ranch near old Tascosa, in the northwest panhandle. The family lived for a time in the Casimero Romero home, built in the 1870s by some of the earliest settlers of the area.[46] By 1894, at age sixteen, Jess formed his first musical group, which played for dances and balls throughout the region. Reportedly, it was not unusual for Morris's group to receive one hundred dollars for an evening of music. He is said to have studied violin both in Austin, Texas, and at Valparaiso, Indiana, but he claimed he would never be anything but a cowboy fiddler.[47] Morris competed in Amarillo's Tri-State Old Fiddlers' Contest in 1928 and 1929 but did not place. The newspaper account of the 1928 contest, however, singled him out for his rendition of "Goodbye Ol' Paint." According to the article, "the audience forgot all dignity and joined in a hearty, lusty yell on the chorus." In the 1931 contest, Morris placed second behind A. E. Rusk of Canyon, who won the event, and ahead of Eck Robertson, who took third.[48] Besides fiddling, Morris worked as a cowboy and a wolfer on the XIT, LS, and LIT ranches.[49]

In the early 1940s, Morris registered several of his original songs and fiddle tunes with the Library of Congress, including "El Rancho Grande XIT Schottische," "XIT Ranch Cowboy Polka," and "Ridin' Ol' Paint an' Leadin' Ol' Ball."[50] After receiving the certificate of registration for "XIT Ranch Cowboy Polka," Morris sent copies of his works to the Fort Worth

Star Telegram to promote his new composition. In a letter dated July 18, 1940, Morris commented, "I gave you folks, that Schottische & Polka—Manuscripts—and I wish you would get some real good musician, to play them over for you, and if they don't sound right, then get another musician." In another letter to the paper, dated July 24, Morris added, "Please let the musician have the Manuscript to practice on some, before he plays it, because, that manuscript, is hard to read like all manuscript[s]."[51]

Morris's best known work was the popular cowboy ballad "Goodbye Old Paint."[52] In 1942, folk music collector John Lomax recorded Morris's performance of that song for the Library of Congress Archive of Folk Song. It was later released on the Archive of Folk Culture album *Cowboy Songs, Ballads, and Cattle Calls from Texas*. According to Morris, he learned the song from Charley Willis, a black cowboy who in turn had learned the song on a cattle drive in 1871: "Charley played a jews-harp, and taught me to play it. It was on this jews-harp that I learned to play 'Ol' Paint,' at the age of seven [about 1885]. In later years I learned to play the fiddle and played 'Ol' Paint' on the fiddle, in my own special arrangement—tuning the fiddle accordingly." Morris noted, "Many publishers swiped my song and had it published, and many old maverick 'Paints' were running wild and unbranded."[53] Jess Morris died in 1953.

The people who came to settle and work in West Texas brought with them the musical seeds that would grow and bear fruit after the turn of the century. Just as their traditions and culture changed to fit this new setting, so the music evolved. By 1900, a unique musical expression had developed, especially among fiddlers, that was to shape the musical output of West Texas for decades to come.

Elijah Cox, fiddler at Fort Concho (San Angelo, Texas) during the 1880s. Courtesy Fort Concho National Landmark, San Angelo, Texas.

Pioneers Dance Party, circa 1890, site unknown. Courtesy Panhandle Plains Museum, Canyon, Texas.

Lubbock, Texas, 1891. Courtesy Southwest Collection, Texas Tech University, Lubbock.

Cowboy "Stag" Dance. All male dances were not uncommon on the frontier. Courtesy Panhandle Plains Museum, Canyon, Texas.

Frying Pan Ranch Dance Party, 1897. Courtesy Panhandle Plains Museum, Canyon, Texas.

O.B. Ranch cowboys returning from cattle drive, June 26, 1906, Tahoka, Texas. Courtesy Southwest Collection, Texas Tech University, Lubbock.

2

FIDDLE BANDS

AND

MEDICINE

SHOWS

The 1920s was an explosive decade of change throughout the United States. In West Texas, country music enjoyed an exciting period of development. Fiddlers and guitarists formed bands to play a popular form of country dance music at house parties and ranch dances, and traveling shows brought country music entertainment to the region and offered employment to young musicians. By the end of the decade, radio had become an important new entertainment medium and performance venue for West Texas country musicians.

By the 1920s most of West Texas was slowly entering the modern period of settlement; it was the last area in Texas settled by Anglos. Dirt roads and streets were the norm, and settlers often lived in dugout homes until they could build more permanent housing, just as settlers had done before the turn of the century.[1] The major cities of the region were at least several decades old and were growing. Most secondary population centers such as county seats were very young, and many were not established until the 1920s.[2]

As was true elsewhere in the United States, radio had little impact on West Texans at the beginning of the 1920s, but by the end of the decade it had become part of daily life for many. Musician Henry Lester, born in 1909 in Memphis, Texas, heard champion fiddler Eck Robertson over Dallas's WFAA radio station in 1923 and 1924. Lester caught the daily program at 12:30 pm on an Atwater-Kent battery-powered radio for which he had traded a mule. Lester's older brother, who lived across the road, ran a cable along the telephone line and connected it to a speaker so he could listen to Henry's radio in his own home. Disputes arose because Henry had control of program selection.[3]

Raised in central Texas, Sons of the Pioneers fiddler Hugh Farr listened to the family's battery radio in the early 1920s. Every night, after the family was asleep, Hugh put on the radio earphones and listened to the Carleton Coon/Joe Sanders Orchestra, also known as the Kansas City Nighthawks, from Kansas City. Throughout his professional music career, Farr credited the Nighthawks as a major early influence on his own jazzy fiddle style.[4]

House and ranch dances continued to be popular throughout the twenties. Musician Bob Kendrick, who grew up near Cisco, remembered these events as the biggest entertainment in the community. The man of the house hosting the dance collected a fee from the male dancers and pinned numbers on them. The numbers served the two-fold purpose of identifying who had paid to dance and giving turns to the dancers. In the limited confines of a house, only a few couples could dance at a time, so they rotated in shifts. The band, often a fiddler and accompanist, located in the doorway between the two largest rooms in the house where the most couples could dance at a time. At the end of a set of dancing, the organizer called out the numbers for the next set and asked them to get their partners. In this way, the next group of dancers would get a turn.[5]

Ranch dances have become rare, but fiddle contests are as popular now as they were in the early decades of this century. The tradition of fiddle contests is an old one. In Texas, perhaps more than in other areas, contests served to shape and define fiddling. Impromptu gambling and gaming were popular pastimes in the early days of the state, and whenever a new fiddler entered the territory of a local favorite, a contest might be organized to determine the better fiddler. These earliest contests must have been quite informal, with few rules governing selection of tunes and audience reaction determining the winner.

By the 1920s, contests had become more formal. They were entertainment for the public as well as opportunities for musicians to gather and exchange musical ideas.[6] Fiddle contests gained national popularity in the 1920s, owing partly to the promotion and support given by automobile manufacturer Henry Ford, who in the mid-1920s sponsored traditional musicians and fiddle contests throughout the United States in an effort to revive old-time fiddling and dance.[7]

One of the largest West Texas contests of that period was the first Tri-State Old Fiddlers' Contest held March 20, 1928, in Amarillo. The Amarillo *Daily News* published a specific list of rules:

> 1. Each contestant will draw place by lot, giving him his order on the program.
>
> 2. Each contestant shall be forty years old, but not over one hundred ten.
>
> 3. Each contestant shall play one piece only, unless requested by the judges to play more, but shall be required to have ready at least five selections for emergencies.
>
> 4. Each selection offered shall be not less than three minutes, nor more than five minutes.
>
> 5. Each contestant is to play old fashioned music, preferably quadrilles, as this is more closely associated with the old breakdown dance.
>
> 6. Each contestant to be allowed not to exceed two accompanists [*sic*].
>
> 7. In forming conclusions of the merit of each contestant, the judges shall pass on a percentage basis, taking 100 per cent of course as perfect, and that no man is perfect. They shall judge each separate selection under its column, giving it the percentage that in their judgment it is entitled and the final total of these added percentages will show the winners in order. If any ties should develop, and the judges require, then those who are tied for place shall play another selection, or until such tie is settled.

8. The judges at their discretion may use the applause of the audience in reaching a decision if it is declared necessary.

9. Being an Old Fiddler's contest, credit shall not be allowed to the modern jazz.

10. Contortions of the body of the artist shall not be given undue credit, patting of the feet justified.

11. Each contestant shall furnish, by March 16, information giving his birth place, date of birth, incidents of his life, and his picture, late photo if convenient.

TRI-STATE FAIR ASSOCIATION Dr. O.H. Lloyd, director[8]

Advertised with at least four articles in the Amarillo *Daily News*, the event drew a crowd estimated at more than two thousand persons, who paid from fifty cents to one dollar for admission. The first prize of one hundred dollars went to Louis Franklin of Wilbarger County. Milt Trout of Dimmitt and H. E. Whelchel of Amarillo placed second and third, respectively.[9] The sixteen other contestants included Jess Morris of "Goodbye Old Paint" fame and Pat Hooker of Shamrock, the panhandle cowboy who had taught Eck Robertson the basics of fiddling.[10]

Robertson, billed as the "world's champion fiddler and Victor recording artist," competed in several fiddle contests held in Amarillo.[11] At the 1928 All Panhandle Old Fiddlers' Contest, he arrived too late to compete but was allowed to perform. Eck Junior accompanied his father and after the performance used the open back of his own banjo to collect money that was raised from the listeners.[12] The next day, the two Robertsons and Pat Hooker performed at the Amarillo sheriff's department and jail. Nine-year-old Eck Junior "made that banjo do everything but shed tears," wrote the reporter for the *Amarillo Sunday News*: "[Sheriff Wiley Pollard] threw his new stetson on the floor and in a shaking and trembling voice said: 'Eck, if you play that "Done Gone" anymore, I'm going to turn every prisoner in this jail loose.' And all the rest of the listeners felt the same."[13]

At the 1929 Tri-State contest, broadcast on Amarillo's WDAG radio, twenty fiddlers competed before an audience of one thousand. Eck Robertson won that year, Milt Trout of Dimmitt took second place for the second year in a row, and Babe Helton of Canadian took third.[14] The 1930 contest featured thirty-seven fiddlers competing for the seventy-five-dollar first prize. (Perhaps the Depression accounted for the reduced prize money.) Major Franklin of Dosler won first place. George Cockrell of Mobeetie took second, and Zeke Welchel of Amarillo took third.[15] The rules apparently were changed to allow contestants under the age of forty. Henry Lester, for example, who placed fifth in the 1930 event, was twenty-one years old at the time.[16] This might explain the greater number of contestants in the later contests.

Contestant Henry Lester learned to play fiddle from his older brother, John, and by the time he was fourteen years old, he and his younger brother, Buster (Shorty), were performing for ranch dances.[17] A few years later, Henry and Buster played some ranch dances with guitar player

Johnny Britton, Bob Wills's cousin. Wills and Britton played ranch dances together until Wills left the panhandle in 1929.[18]

Lester related how he came to play in the 1930 Amarillo contest. Johnny Britton and a fiddler from the Memphis area were leaving to play in the contest, and they invited Lester along for the ride. During the trip the fiddler drank all of Britton's whiskey. Deeply offended, Britton exhorted Lester to borrow that fiddler's instrument and beat him in the contest.[19] Lester did precisely that, placing fifth in the open division (open to all ages) and winning $7.50 in prize money.[20]

In 1931, two contests were held in Amarillo. Sixty-one fiddlers pre-registered for the event held in February, including Mrs. Eva Deadwiley of Amarillo. Although women fiddlers were not unheard of, it was considered news in 1931 and drew this headline:

61 FIDDLERS TO PLAY HERE SATURDAY
LARGEST GROUP EVER TO BE IN TRI-STATE CONTEST;
WOMAN ENTERED

A. E. Rusk of Canyon won the fifty-dollar first prize, while Jess Morris and Eck Robertson took the second- and third-place honors.[21] Among the contestants was Bob Wills's father, John T. Wills, better known as Uncle John. John Wills fared better at the Tri-State contest held in April, placing third. Eck Robertson won this contest, and his family group performed. A promotional picture of Eck was used to advertise the event.[22] John Wills was one of the most respected dance and contest fiddlers in West Texas during this period. Charles Townsend, biographer of Bob Wills, related the following story about a contest in Munday, Texas, that pitted Eck Robertson against John Wills:

Eck went to the platform first and probably played "Beaumont Rag"—neither Bob nor Johnny Lee Wills could remember for sure; but Bob said "Beaumont Rag" was always Robertson's best. Whatever he played was good, and when he left the platform everyone knew he would be difficult to beat. John Wills, in his turn, probably played "Gone Indian," for that was one of his best. When John reached a certain place in the tune, he began hollering and held an elongated cry about an octave above his fiddle music so that his voice harmonized with the fiddle. His performance was a crowd and judge pleaser, and he won over his arch-rival. As Robertson left the scene of the contest, someone asked, "Eck, did John outfiddle you?" Eck answered, "Hell, no! He didn't outfiddle me. That damned old man Wills outhollered me."[23]

Recordings of Texas fiddle music of the 1920s—some of the earliest recordings of American country music—document the changes that had occurred in the music of the American Southeast transplanted to Texas. The recordings of such players as Eck Robertson and noted East Texas fiddler Ervin Soloman provide evidence that a distinct regional style had developed in Texas by the 1920s. While the fiddle music of their unrecorded contemporaries is lost, it seems likely that others played in similar styles. In 1922, Robertson traveled to Richmond, Virginia, to perform at the Old Confederate Soldiers Reunion. There he met Henry Gilliland, a former Justice of the Peace in Altus, Oklahoma, a Confederate veteran, and an accomplished fiddler. For no clear reason, this pair of fiddlers decided to travel to New York City to interest a recording company in their music.[24] Also unclear is why the Victor Recording Company decided to record the duo. The unannounced appearance of this pair in Victor's New York offices, dressed "in the garb of Western plainsmen," must have created a stir.[25] Indeed, Robertson said that people stopped and stared at them wherever they went.[26] The recordings made at this time were not released widely until the next year. Although obvious today, the idea that a market for rural music existed among rural audiences was a startling insight for record company officials in the 1920s.[27]

A total of ten selections were recorded during these two New York sessions. Recorded on June 30, 1922, were "Arkansas Traveler," "Turkey in the Straw," and two unreleased cuts, "Forked Deer" and "Apple Blossom," all featuring Robertson and Gilliland playing in a duet style. Robertson returned alone the next day to record "Sallie Gooden," "Ragtime Annie," "Sallie Johnson/Billy in the Lowground" (a medley), and "Done Gone." Two more selections, the first a medley of "General Logan Reel" and "Dominion Hornpipe," and the second a medley of "Brilliancy" and "Cheatum," were never released.[28] Of these, "Sallie Gooden" deserves special attention.

Robertson recorded "Sallie Gooden" on fiddle, unaccompanied. Unlike other tunes from these sessions, such as "Ragtime Annie," which consists of a basic melody statement and minor variations, "Sallie Gooden" is a fully developed piece featuring a two-part theme followed by thirteen distinct melodic variations. All modern Texas-style arrangements of this tune can be traced to Robertson's historic recording. Many consider it the best recorded version of the tune and a progenitor of the modern Texas fiddle style. In a tradition that nurtures change and innovation, Robertson's timeless rendition of "Sallie Gooden" remains the model for many Texas fiddlers.

Robertson recorded for Victor again in 1929, this time in Dallas. Accompanying him were his wife Nettie on guitar, son Dueron "Eck Junior" on banjo, daughter Daphne on guitar, and Dr. J. B. Cranfill on second fiddle. During two sessions held in August and October, sixteen selections were recorded, but only eight were released. These sessions marked the end of Robertson's early recording career.[29]

Robertson continued to perform in the 1930s and also began working as a piano tuner and instrument repairer, a career he continued until his late years. In 1937, he went to Hollywood to play in a hillbilly music group for the movies, but a conflict with his employer ended this venture. In 1940, Eck recorded one hundred musical selections for the Sellers

Transcription Studio in Dallas, but none of these recordings have been found.[30]

Although Robertson was well known in the Texas fiddling community throughout the 1940s and 1950s, his whereabouts were unknown to eastern folk music enthusiasts. The folk music world's search for country musicians who had recorded in the 1920s led to his rediscovery. Robertson's version of "Brilliancy Medley" from the 1929 Dallas sessions appeared on a popular Folkways anthology record released in 1951. As the folk music movement developed through the 1950s, more and more of the original musicians from early recordings were sought out and brought to folk festivals and college campuses in the northeastern United States, where they performed for enthusiastic audiences. The search for Eck Robertson may have been initiated by Ralph Rinzler of the Smithsonian Institution in Washington, D.C. Rinzler's initial inquiries resulted in an interview of Robertson conducted by students of folklore at the University of Texas under the direction of instructor Roger Abrahams. Printed copies of this interview circulated among members of the folk music community and came to the attention of John Cohen.

Cohen was then a member of the old-time music revivalist trio The New Lost City Ramblers, which also included well-known folk musicians Mike Seeger and Tracy Schwarz. Schwarz, Seeger, and Cohen visited Robertson at his Amarillo home in 1963, and Cohen wrote an article about Robertson for the major folk music publication of the day, SING OUT![31] As a result of all this publicity, Robertson, at the age of seventy-eight, made an appearance at the 1965 Newport Folk Festival, a premier showcase for folk talent at the time. Vanguard Records reportedly expressed interest in recording Eck's fiddling, but no recordings were made. During this period, he also appeared at the UCLA Folk Festival in California.

Robertson spent his last years in relative obscurity in Amarillo. In 1970, burglars took fifty dollars from his home in east Amarillo, "more money than I've spent on myself at any one time," Eck told a reporter. Soon after this episode, he moved to a nursing home in Borger, Texas, where he died in 1975 at the age of 88.[32]

The legacy of Eck Robertson is incalculable. Countless fiddlers have spent many hours learning the great music on his recordings. People who knew him remember a spry old man with a wonderfully confident, even brash, personality. Champion Texas fiddler Texas Shorty (aka Jim Chancellor) stopped at Robertson's home in the 1960s, and the pair would trade tunes all night. These sessions would often continue until daylight, when Robertson would cook breakfast for all at hand. Shorty remembers that while Eck appreciated the young fiddler's skill, he always offered to show Shorty the way the tune went "originally."[33]

Brother duo Dempson and Denmon Lewis made four recordings for the Victor Company in 1929 in El Paso.[34] The Lewis family was from Bandera County, Texas, and moved to Otero County, New Mexico, in 1902.[35] The patriarch, David Lewis, was a fiddler who taught each of his seven sons to play musical instruments. A year before the Victor recordings were made in El Paso, Dempson won a fiddle contest there and the first prize, a three-hundred-dollar saddle. Showing bravado typical of championship fiddlers, Dempson put the saddle on his car fender "and then had himself driven all over town, playing the fiddle while mounted on the saddle."[36]

The Victor recordings featured Dempson on fiddle accompanied by Denmon on guitar. Their sound and instrumentation were typical of the era's fiddle bands that played for house and ranch dances in Texas. The Lewis family music tradition continues today: nearly all of David Lewis's forty or so grandchildren play some kind of musical instrument.[37] Dempson's daughter, Norma Lewis Stringer of Dell City, Texas, is an accomplished fiddler and a featured performer at such events as the annual Lincoln County, New Mexico, Cowboy Symposium.[38]

The Cartwright Brothers were another West Texas fiddle and guitar band who made records in the 1920s. Bernard and Jack Cartwright grew up in Knox County, near Munday. Bernard learned to play fiddle from an older brother whom he soon surpassed in musical ability. Bernard's younger brother, Jack, born in 1901, learned to play the guitar to accompany his brother's fiddling. They played square dance tunes such as "Sally Goodin" and "Walk Along John" for house dances and later played for community dances held in dance halls. The brothers eventually moved to Munday, where their music was in demand.

A local druggist who sold phonograph records in his store told the Columbia Records salesman about the Cartwright brothers. After meeting with the brothers, the salesman arranged a recording session, which was held on December 2, 1927, in Dallas. Four instrumental selections were recorded at this session including "Sally Johnson" and "Kelley Waltz." A year later, on December 6, 1928, the Cartwrights recorded six more sides for Columbia including four vocal selections by Jack. The Cartwright Brothers' final sessions for Columbia were August 11 and October 16, 1929, in Dallas. Of the eight songs recorded at these sessions, only two were fiddle instrumentals. The remaining six selections were vocals by Jack including titles such as "The Dying Ranger," "Texas Ranger," "Pretty Little Doggies," and "The Wandering Cowboy." Jack Cartwright commented that the record company expected the brothers to sing.[39] This attitude may reflect the general trend in recording in the late 1920s and early 1930s away from instrumental country music toward singing "stars."

The brothers performed regularly on San Antonio radio stations WOAI and KTSA from 1935 to 1936, but they made no more records. Bernard retired from music in 1938 and served as postmaster in Boerne, Texas, until ill health forced his retirement in 1948. He died in 1955. Jack continued playing music with various groups until his retirement in 1954.[40]

Legendary country music entertainer Jimmie Rodgers performed in several West Texas towns in 1929, 1930, and 1931.[41] Originally from Meridian, Mississippi, and known throughout the American South as the "Singing Brakeman," Rodgers developed a unique "blue yodel," which served as a signature to his songs. His recordings for the Victor Talking Machine Company, beginning in 1927, quickly became popular throughout the South and places largely populated by former Southerners, such as Texas. Arguably the first country music star, Rodgers moved to Kerrville, Texas, in 1929.[42] Rodgers had been diagnosed with tuberculosis in 1924, and he moved to Texas to be close to a sanatorium.[43] In the spring of 1929, he appeared as a solo act at theaters in O'Donnell, Lubbock, and, reportedly, Big Spring.[44] The next year, traveling throughout the panhandle with Swain's Hollywood Follies, Rodgers performed in at least eight West Texas towns, including Quanah, Panhandle, and Canadian. In 1931, Rodgers appeared on the Will Rogers Red Cross Benefit Tour, which performed at San Angelo and Abilene.[45]

Rodgers died in 1933 at age thirty-five, only seven years after his first recordings.[46] Despite his brief career, he had a profound influence on generations of country music performers to come. Texans Gene Autry and Ernest Tubb are just two of the many who began their careers imitating Rodgers's unique style.

Traveling entertainment programs such as Swain's Hollywood Follies and numerous medicine shows flourished in the 1920s, and most of them featured music. These shows had considerable impact on the country music of West Texas. Fiddlers Eck Robertson, Bob Wills, and Matt Brown all worked in medicine shows at various times in their careers.[47] Western swing bandleader Cliff Bruner gained early experience as a performer with Doc Scott's medicine show. Like so many young men in the early 1930s, Bruner left home and drifted around, hopping trains and picking up odd jobs. The summer of 1933 found him picking cotton near Aspermont in West Texas. Doc Scott's Pierce Arrow automobile made a big impression on Bruner as the medicine show paraded through town. After the show, Bruner played his fiddle for Scott and was offered a job with the traveling show. He joined the show's band, which included Leo Raley and Cotton Thompson, both of whom would later work for Bruner in his Texas Wanderers band. Doc Scott sold a medicine called Liquidine. Bruner recalled fondly that they mixed it in the afternoon and sold it at night. While Doc pitched the medicine, salesmen passed through the crowd with bottles of Liquidine held in aprons they were wearing. Every so often a salesman shouted, "Sold out, Doc! Give me some more of that good old Liquidine!"[48]

Guitarist Brooke Kendrick was so taken with the show he saw that he started his own. Born in Dublin, Texas, in 1886, Kendrick and his brother performed music together in their early years at house dances and at schoolhouses in various communities. At ten cents a ticket, they would fill the school. After Brooke was married, he added his wife and later his children to the show.

Sometime around 1927, the JHG medicine show came to Cisco, Texas. The Kendrick family, as a popular local band, was asked to perform on the show, no doubt a common practice to help boost attendance at these shows.[49] Brooke's oldest son, Bob, eighteen years old, was hired to travel with the JHG show as a fiddle and mandolin player. That following summer the show traveled "up on the plains." They stayed for a week at a time in such towns as Floydada, Plainview, Ralls, Jayton, Roby, and Rotan. In the fall, Bob returned to Cisco to finish high school. Meanwhile, Brooke had decided to start his own medicine show. From around 1928 to 1932 it was the Kendrick family business. At this time, Brooke Kendrick adopted the name Doc. He soon developed a circuit of towns that reflected a keen business mind. The show "followed the money," playing the sheep country in the spring after shearing season, oil towns in the summer when work was plentiful, and cotton towns in the fall after harvest.

Promotion for the show consisted of the Kendrick boys driving up and down the residential sections of town with a megaphone yelling "Big show, free show tonight!" Bob Kendrick recalled how they could judge a town during the promotional ride:

> Do you know what they mean by "goosin'" anybody? . . . That's come out of the South, boys would goose each other. He'd slip up on him while he wasn't looking and touch him and then he hollers and laugh. That's the way you'd find out whether a town was gonna be good for a medicine show. If you drive down the street and the ol' boys was on the corner goosin' each other, it was a good show. But if they wouldn't pay no attention to you, you know it wasn't good.[50]

The shows were free; profits came from the sale of "medicine" at fifty cents a bottle and also from boxed candy. The medicine, purchased from the Gassaway Medicine Company of Fort Worth, was largely epsom salts in water. Bob Kendrick remembered that the local people looked forward to these shows and there were big crowds every night. A typical show would open with three or four musical numbers from the band, ending with a fast tune. Then a blackface comedy sketch would be presented and would end with a song. At this point, the Doc pitched the medicine and tried to make some sales. Another skit or specialty act such as magic tricks would follow. The final part of the program was a longer skit with slapstick comedy. The entire performance lasted about two hours. Because the show stayed a week in the same location, the performers had to vary the skits nightly. The skits were worked out only in a general way, and the performers ad-libbed much of the material.[51]

Traveling shows provided much-needed entertainment to an isolated population and invaluable training for a generation of rural musicians and stage performers, just as vaudeville did in urban areas. The performance skills learned in traveling shows and at ranch dances in the 1920s would serve West Texas musicians well in the next decade as radio became the primary source of musical entertainment.

3

HARD TIMES

AND

GOOD MUSIC

Whatever else the 1930s were to America, the decade was a great time for country music. Country music not only survived the thirties, it flourished; and nowhere was this truer than in Texas.[1] West Texas, especially the panhandle region, was hit hard by the Depression, drought, and dust of the 1930s. The dust storms were the result of an extended drought and farming practices that left the topsoil uncovered for much of the year. The hardest hit region of the Southwest, dubbed the Dust Bowl, included the Texas panhandle and extended into the southern regions of West Texas. Many people there gave up, pulled up stakes, and moved to the fabled "Green Pastures of Plenty" in California. One of these was folk music composer and singer Woodrow Wilson "Woody" Guthrie. In 1929, at age seventeen, Guthrie moved to Pampa, Texas, from Okemah, Oklahoma, to join his father, Charlie. Pampa was a boom town that developed rapidly with the discovery of oil in the Texas panhandle. Woody attended high school briefly in Pampa and worked variously as handy man, oil-field hand, fortune teller, healer, and sign painter. Shortly after his arrival in Texas, he learned to play the guitar from his uncle, Jeff Guthrie. Soon he was singing and playing at ranch dances in the region, sometimes earning as much as three dollars a night.[2] He performed with several local musicians and formed a group, the Corncob Trio. During the 1936 Centennial celebration of Texas independence, Guthrie performed with the Pampa Chamber of Commerce Band at the celebration in Dallas. Later the same year, he left Pampa for the "road" that became so much of his life.[3]

Although Guthrie lived only a few years in West Texas, his life there apparently had a big impact on him and his music. A number of Woody's songs, including "The Great Dust Storm" and "So Long, It's Been Good to Know You," were inspired by his experiences on the plains. Guthrie, in turn, influenced an entire generation of folk musicians in the 1950s and 1960s. American schoolchildren learn Guthrie's "This Land Is Your Land" at an early age, and it is so well known among the general population that it could serve as an unofficial national anthem.

Guthrie's prolific songwriting and landmark recordings have made him a folk music hero in America. Modern folk/rock musician Bob Dylan began his career closely patterning his image and songwriting after Guthrie's. Guthrie's son Arlo, a noted musician and singer/songwriter, observed with irony that Woody's greatest fame came after he was incapacitated in a New York hospital with Huntington's chorea, a degenerative disease of the nervous system that he inherited from his mother.[4] Woody Guthrie died in 1967, an American music legend.

Learning to play music was not always an easy task for a youngster growing up in isolated West Texas in the 1930s. Nessye Mae Roach of Fort Davis recalled:

When I was about twelve or fourteen years old, I finally had enough money saved [$7.98] to buy the cheap Silvertone guitar. . . . I saved what little money I got from the shearing of my pet rabbit and my dogie sheep to buy the guitar. When it came in on the mail, I immediately got in the back seat of our car, tuned it as I remembered my sister Leota tuning it when she had lived at home before she married, and learned to pick a tune before we got home.

I learned at home alone, all by ear, from listening to the records of Jimmie Rogers [sic], the Singing Brakeman; the Carter Family; Stamps Quartet; and others. But I actually learned more about where to place my fingers by watching the Mexican shearers who came twice a year to shear and tag the sheep. (Sheared in the spring; tagged in the fall.) They usually had some instruments with them, and often borrowed mine, too. I would watch them closely, and next day I'd try to play what they had. But my fondest memories of learning were from the ranch dances, where I'd get as close as possible to the band, and watch what they did. [5]

One of the groups Roach watched was Joe Teagarten's band at Barnhart, Texas. The band consisted of Teagarten with a fiddle and his brother Shorty playing guitar, a common combination for early West Texas dance bands.

Family music making was an important form of entertainment in the 1930s, and in some families it was an important source of income. The Stephenson family from McAdoo were cotton farmers who performed as the Stevenson String Band at picnics, old settlers' reunions, and house dances throughout the region. S. W. (Walter) Stevenson and his wife, Annie Garrett Stevenson, moved to West Texas from Arkansas around 1914, settling first in the Red Mud community near Spur and later buying some land at McAdoo in 1916. Walter, a prizewinning old-time fiddler, provided music for the first old settlers' reunion, held at Roaring Springs around 1917. A member of the Stevenson family has played music at every Roaring Springs reunion since its inception.

All of Walter and Annie's children were musical, and Nathan, born in 1913, and Robena, born in 1925, were particularly talented. These two were very successful at singing and fiddling contests. In the first contest she ever entered, a singing contest held in Dickens in 1934, Robena sang "That's Where My Money Goes" and won the first prize, five dollars—a heady sum for a nine-year-old in the 1930s.[6] A 1935 photograph shows Robena at age ten, playing a National brand guitar she had won at a contest and brother Nathan with a fiddle.

Between 1934 and 1939, Nathan and Robena competed in many amateur talent contests sponsored by the B. E. Needles Company, a Lubbock Brunswick tire dealership that also sold radios. The contests were held in towns across the south plains, including Brownfield, Lamesa, Littlefield, and Floydada during old settler's celebrations, county fairs, and other community events. The company had a sound truck nicknamed "Big Bertha" that served as a mobile stage for these contests. C. H. Hutto was a Needles salesperson and the organizer and announcer of the contests. To ensure a good contest, Hutto sent letters to talented performers throughout the area inviting them to participate in the contests.[7]

The motivation behind these contests was probably to cultivate customers for the Needles Company. A two-page form letter dated November 10, 1936, from "C. H. Hutto, Radio announcer for B. E. Needles" thanked the old settlers for their contributions to West Texas. Included in the letter was a poem by Mrs. Hutto entitled "The Settlers of the Old West" and a photograph of N. Y. Bicknell, president of the West Texas Old Settlers' Association, dancing to music provided by the B. E. Needles sound truck. The letter concluded with a sales pitch for the company and its products, including this unusual pitch to encourage radio sales: "Every home needs a radio, especially where there are young folks. You know 'Satan keeps school for neglected children'—if we don't furnish home entertainment for our youngsters, they make their own entertainment and sometimes innocent pleasure grows onto that which we would rather they wouldn't do. Then too, current news, market reports, etc., make the radio a business asset to anyone."[8]

Hutto was particularly impressed with the Stevenson String Band, especially Nathan and Robena, and encouraged them to attend as many of these events as possible. Hutto was so interested in Nathan and Robena attending the contests held at the Lamesa-Dawson County Fair October 15-17, 1936, that he offered the twosome a ride from Lubbock to the event in the sound truck and paid for their hotel expenses, a fact Hutto did not want the other contestants to know.[9] Robena was a favorite at these events, often winning first prize with her version of "Listen to the Mockingbird." During the performance of her specialty number, Robena played the melody while holding her fiddle behind her back, then by holding the bow between her knees and in other unusual positions. This entertaining novelty, combined with her young age and true fiddling talent, assured her of many first-place awards.[10] Hutto hired Nathan and Robena on numerous occasions in the late thirties to perform on concerts at Texas Tech University, KFYO radio programs, and other special events. The members of the Stevenson family continued to play music through the 1940s and 1950s. Nathan's son, Joe Nathan Stevenson, is a professional country fiddler and continues the family tradition.

Dutch LaRue grew up around Hamlin, Texas, and at age nineteen performed at the 1936 Texas centennial in Dallas. Around this same time, LaRue performed over his own radio station in Hamlin:

> You could broadcast with one watt in those days, and that would cover fifty miles. Well, I was sitting up in the window of the bank where I had my station, the Voice of Hamlin, which was all

handbuilt, when the Federal Communications Commission truck rolled up.

I knew it was them because of all the antennas and stuff all over it. Two guys came in and showed me all their credentials, and then asked me if I knew how much power I was broadcasting with. I said one watt and he said "No, 100,000 watts. They can't even give the stock report in New Orleans because you're blasting them off the air. You've got to shut down by midnight."[11]

LaRue soon moved to Sweetwater, where he formed the Lone Star Texas Playboys, a group that continued to perform in various forms until 1953. The group included Happy Daniels on fiddle, Jess Womack on banjo, Bob Neal on bass, Muggs Dennis on guitar, Chuck Rogers on guitar, and Dutch LaRue on steel guitar.[12] In 1940, as the Everlite Harvesters, the group performed a daily radio program for Harvest Queen Mill in Plainview. After completing an eighteen-month, seven-day-a-week contract, the band decided not to renew. Billed as the Lone Star Playboy Dance Band and Stage Show, the six-piece band performed throughout West Texas and eastern New Mexico, and, although playing music was never their sole source of income, the group was very active. LaRue considers the Playboys' performance at the 1949 U.S. Square Dance convention held in Big Spring (and touted as the largest square dance ever held) one of the highpoints of his career.[13]

Dance music was popular throughout America in the 1930s, and by mid-decade, the new "western swing" music, developed largely in Texas, was firmly established. Fort Worth can be called the birthplace of this new music, since so many of the early bands and individual musicians lived and worked there. Western swing, although it did not get this name until a decade later, was developed by a group of young musicians who admired the "Hot Dance," blues, and "race" recordings of the late 1920s and early 1930s. Much of the early repertoire of the first western swing bands came directly from the recordings of black musicians. Milton Brown's recordings, for example, are largely covers of earlier recordings by black artists. Brown went so far as to imitate the dialect of southern black speech on at least one recording.[14] While this dialect was presumably an attempt at racial humor, the musical performance on the recording reflects the greatest respect for black music. In an often-repeated pattern, white musicians copied the sound of their black counterparts and performed for new and larger audiences. Although there was undoubtedly some direct contact between black and white musicians in West Texas, it appears that radio and phonograph records played the larger role in introducing black music to whites. Western swing was defined and popularized predominantly by two Fort Worth-based bands: Milton Brown and his Musical Brownies and West Texan Bob Wills and the Texas Playboys. In the early 1930s, both Brown and Wills were members of the Light Crust Doughboys, sponsored by the Burris Flour Mill of Fort Worth. Brown left the Doughboys in 1932 and formed the Musical Brownies, whose blend of hot swing and dance music quickly became popular.[15] Brown's group became established at Crystal Springs, a club just outside Fort Worth, and drew large crowds. Wills, meanwhile, left the Doughboys in 1933 and established the Texas Playboys, who also gained rapid popularity.[16] Brown's untimely death in 1936, the result of an automobile accident, and Wills's recordings for Columbia the same year established Bob Wills and his Texas Playboys as the premier western swing organization.

Although not a native West Texan, Bob Wills is the musician most associated with the region, after 1950s rocker Buddy Holly. Born in Limestone County in 1905, Wills moved with his family in 1913 to Memphis, in the Texas panhandle. Wills's father, known as "Uncle John the fiddler," and many other members of the family were musicians. Young Bob soon began to play the mandolin, accompanying his father's fiddling at farm and ranch dances throughout the region. It was at one of these dances in 1915 that the younger Wills played fiddle in public for the first time. After John Wills failed to appear, Bob began to play the few tunes he knew for the impatient dancers.[17] Despite his limited repertoire, the dance was successful and launched a career that would change western music.

After leaving West Texas, Wills played around Fort Worth for several years in various groups including the Fort Worth Doughboys (later the Light Crust Doughboys) before forming his own band, Bob Wills and his Texas Playboys. The group eventually located in Tulsa, where they enjoyed phenomenal acclaim. With the success of the recording of "New San Antonio Rose" in 1940, Bob Wills became a national figure in American music.[18] Shortly after World War II, Wills was at a peak of popularity. Texas Playboys fiddler Johnny Gimble told the following story to illustrate: "It seems there was a young Texan who was working in a New York hotel as an elevator operator. One day when a man carrying a violin case entered the elevator, the Texan dutifully informed the man of the hotel policy that musicians were to ride the freight elevator. 'You don't know who I am!' replied the indignant musician. 'I am Rubinoff, the violinist!' The Texan replied, 'I don't care if you're Bob Wills, musicians ride in the freight elevator!'"[19]

Bob Wills left a huge personal legacy in West Texas. Many West Texans relate with pride their own Bob Wills stories. Some remember meeting him in person, while others recall attending his dances, perhaps with a sweetheart who became a lifelong companion. Although not always verifiable, many claim that they or a relative actually played music with Bob Wills. This story is told by so many that it is rare to meet a fiddler who claims he *never* played with Wills. West Texans express pride and affection for this legend, whom they consider one of their own.

Country vocalist Ray Price commented on Wills's importance, "People in the West would rather dance, more than they had to go to a concert. . . . If you play in the western part of the country, well you should be able to play a dance . . . you're gonna have to play some of Bob Wills music." Master guitarist Merle Travis summed it up this way: "Bob Wills put the beat into country music. He made it so you could dance to it."[20] For

Kentucky-born Travis this may have been the case, but West Texans had been dancing all along.

Although Bob Wills left West Texas in the late 1920s, he did not forget it completely. In 1936 he suggested to his cousin Son Lansford, who was playing the bass in Wills's band at the time, that a group similar to the Wills organization could work successfully in the Amarillo area. Later the same year, the Sons of the West, formed largely from Fort Worth-based musicians, arrived in Amarillo under Lansford's direction. Soon after their arrival in West Texas, the Sons began performing daily on radio station KGNC in Amarillo. The original members of the group were Son Lansford on fiddle, Jimmie Meek on bass and vocals, Freddie Dean on guitar, Cliff Wells on banjo, and Leonard Seago on fiddle. They became regulars at Amarillo's Rainbow Gardens dance hall. Within a short time, Lansford left the group to rejoin Bob Wills's band in Tulsa. Jimmie Meek, bass player and lead vocalist for the group, then became the leader.[21]

Jimmie Meek was born in Duncan, Oklahoma, in 1911. At age eight or nine, he built his first guitar from a cigar box. A few years later he built another guitar, this time a copy of an arch-top Gibson guitar. The family moved to Fort Worth in 1926 and soon Meek, age sixteen, and a friend were performing music regularly over KFJZ radio in Fort Worth. The duet eventually grew into a larger band and included some musicians who later played with the Hi-Flyers, an early western swing group based in Fort Worth. Meek's group received free room and board at the YMCA in exchange for a mention on the air during their radio program. Meek was hired to play bass for the Three Jacks, who were performing at the Majestic Theater in Fort Worth. He stayed with the group for a year or so and appeared in cities throughout the Southwest and Midwest, including Oklahoma City, Joplin, and Chicago. After leaving the Jacks, Meek returned to Fort Worth, where he was hired to sing and play bass with the Sons of the West.

Soon after they arrived in Amarillo, the band was working an average of five nights a week, appearing in Amarillo two nights at dance halls such as Rainbow Gardens and the Nat (short for *natatorium*), a club that featured a large dance floor built over a swimming pool, and performing in outlying areas the other three nights. Regional appearances included the Texas towns Borger, Turkey, Pampa, Lubbock, Clarendon, and Memphis, as well as towns in Oklahoma and New Mexico.

Despite the distances involved, the band had to be back in Amarillo by 7:00 each morning for the first of four daily radio programs. The other programs were at 10:00 a.m., 12:45 p.m., a remote broadcast from Cal Farley's tire store, and around 3:00 p.m., when school was getting out. Meek remembers that the band would sleep at the radio station between programs during this hectic period of their career.

In 1938, Dave Kapp of Decca Records arranged their first recording session on September 16 in San Antonio.[22] Ten selections were recorded on this date, including one original song, "Visions of the Past," written by Meek. The band then consisted of Jimmie Meek on bass and vocals,

Billy Briggs on steel guitar, Freddie Dean on guitar, Jess "Slick" Robertson on banjo, and Pat Trotter on fiddle. Briggs, who had come to the group from Fort Worth's Hi-Flyers, played amplified steel guitar in a style inspired by Milton Brown's steel player, Bob Dunn. The electric steel guitar was a new instrument in the 1930s; most players were self-taught, and many built their own instruments. Briggs is considered one of the early innovators of this now essential country music instrument.

The Sons of the West recorded twice more. In 1940, Dallas singer Bill Boyd used the Sons rather than his own band on a session in Dallas. Meek thinks the complexity of the material being recorded dictated this decision. By this time, the group lineup included former Light Crust Doughboy fiddler Buck Buchanan. Buchanan had formal musical training, and Meek credits him for the group's ability to play complex arrangements.[23]

While Decca was considering whether to renew their recording contract, the Sons were signed by Art Satherley of Columbia Records. This session took place in Dallas on March 19, 1941. On hand for the session were Jimmie Meek, bass and vocals; Billy Briggs, steel guitar; Buck Buchanan, fiddle; Loren Mitchell, piano; Slick Robertson, banjo; Pat Trotter, fiddle; and Jess Williams, guitar. All six songs recorded that day were originals by the band, including Briggs's "Panhandle Shuffle" and a delightful showcase for the entire band, Meek's "Sally's Got a Wooden Leg."[24]

At the outbreak of World War II, the group was broken up by the draft. After the war, Meek formed a new group for a brief time. Soon after that, he opened a violin and guitar shop that he still operated in the early 1990s.[25] Former Sons Billy Briggs, Jess Williams, and Pat Trotter regrouped after the war as the XIT Boys.

From the Stamford, Texas, area, J. R. Chatwell was a mainstay of Texas western swing groups throughout the late 1930s and 1940s. Performing on fiddle with such groups as the Hi-Flyers, the Modern Mountaineers, the Light Crust Doughboys, and on piano with Cliff Bruner's Texas Wanderers, Chatwell was an influence on later swing fiddlers such as Johnny Gimble.

It was Bruner who discovered young Chatwell. The year was 1936, and Bruner, himself only eighteen years old, was playing fiddle with Milton Brown's Musical Brownies. The group was performing a one-nighter in Stamford. The Brownies performed daily at noon on Fort Worth's WBAP and had to return, therefore, from their nightly engagements in time for these broadcasts. This particular night, Bruner noticed a red-headed youth in the audience who watched the band intensely throughout their performance. During an intermission, Bruner asked the boy if he was a musician. Chatwell replied that he was a fiddler, but that he was picking cotton for a living. Chatwell played for Bruner that night and soon thereafter, Bruner arranged a job for Chatwell with the staff band at KFJZ radio in Fort Worth for forty dollars a week, thereby launching Chatwell's professional music career.[26] Several years later, when Bruner left the Brownies to form his Texas Wanderers in Houston, he asked Chatwell to play piano in the group. Although he was a capable pianist, Chatwell initially refused, stating that he was a fiddler, not a piano player. Bruner countered by asking him, "Who got you out of the cottonfields?" Chatwell joined Bruner's group.[27]

Bob Skyles (Bob Kendrick) and his Skyrockets were from West Texas and made major label recordings in the 1930s. The group began as a family band that included Brooke "Doc" Kendrick and his sons, Bob, Sanford, and Clifford. After several years of running a traveling medicine show, the Kendricks took a job playing on KNEL radio in Brady, Texas. As a result of these performances they were invited in 1932 to play on KIUN in Pecos. They decided to give this offer a try, although they took their medicine show wagons along just in case the radio show did not work out. The radio program was a big success from the beginning, and the Kendricks never opened the medicine show again.

The Skyrockets performed three thirty-minute shows daily on KIUN. One program was with cowboy singer Slim Reinhardt, who later performed over Dr. Brinkley's XERF in Del Rio, Texas. In a pattern reminiscent of the Sons of the West, the Skyrockets "played out" two to four nights a week in a hundred-mile radius of Pecos. Performance sites included Van Horn, Marfa, Odessa, Monahans, and Eunice, New Mexico.[28]

The Skyrockets, and Bob Kendrick in particular, provide an interesting example of West Texas musicians of the 1930s. Whereas musicians such as Jimmie Meek and Henry Lester heard the pop sounds of the big bands and emulated them with fiddles and guitars, Kendrick learned to play saxophone and clarinet to duplicate the sound. Although a horn band, the Skyrockets started like many of their contemporaries who played western swing on stringed instruments. Bob's first memories of music are of playing with his father at house dances in and around their hometown of Cisco, Texas. His first musical instrument was the mandolin, and later he learned guitar and the fiddle.

Kendrick recalled that the music was changing in the late twenties and early thirties. The older tunes such as "Buffalo Gals" and "Redwing," more suited to the mandolin and fiddle, were not in as much demand as they previously had been. Dance audiences wanted to hear popular songs of the day, such as "Five Foot Two" and "Yes Sir, That's My Baby." Bob's father did not approve of the saxophone until Bob played it one night at a dance. After seeing how much the audience liked it, Bob's father encouraged him to include the saxophone in every show.

After a few years Bob left the band briefly. In late 1936 he recorded four sides with Jack Moser and his Oklahoma Cavaliers in San Antonio for RCA Records.[29] Kendrick worked with this group only briefly, but the session provided him an important contact: E. E. Oberstein of RCA. Bob soon rejoined the Skyrockets in Pecos and shortly thereafter contacted Oberstein, convincing him to record the Skyrockets. At Oberstein's suggestion, Bob used the last name Skyles, the better to fit with the group name. Bob Skyles and his Skyrockets recorded their first sides for RCA in San Antonio in 1937.[30]

In 1938 and 1939, the Skyrockets recorded approximately seventy selections for RCA's Bluebird label.[31] Some of this material has been rereleased on long-play album format, but most of it is unavailable except on the original 78-rpm records. These recordings feature a peppy, tight ensemble sound with an emphasis on novelty. The instrumentation includes several novelty instruments such as the saw, the ocarina, the swanee whistle, and the bazooka. Kendrick reported that the bazooka, "a slide deal with a funnel stuck on the end of it," was introduced by an Arkansas radio personality, Bob Burns. Kendrick played the bazooka with the Skyrockets on numerous recordings, including "The Arkansas Bazooka Swing," "The Bazooka Stomp," "My Arkansas Bazooka Gal," "Blue Bazooka Blues," and "Mr. Bazooka and Miss Clarinet."

From 1937 to 1940, the group played nightclubs and dance halls all over the region, notably in Pecos, El Paso, and Odessa. At different times during this period, the group included pianists Max Bennett and the legendary Moon Mullican. By this time, the group was playing mostly dance music and standards such as "Little Coquette" and "Sweet Georgia Brown." Their repertoire reflected the popularity of the big bands, and for a brief period the group used as many as seven pieces, including a female vocalist. In April 1940, the group recorded nine selections in Houston for the Decca label.[32]

Around this time, Bob Kendrick learned to tune pianos, motivated not by desire but necessity. The group did not carry a piano from place to place, and the pianos provided by the clubs were often out of tune and below standard pitch. Kendrick would have to tune the instrument to standard pitch, a time-consuming but unavoidable task. In later years Kendrick supported himself in part as a piano tuner. In the early 1990s, at eighty years old, Kendrick still tuned two pianos a day.

Kendrick met Bob Wills under unusual circumstances. The Skyrockets were playing a club in Oklahoma City that featured illegal gambling. Kendrick understood that the club owner had an "arrangement" with local authorities and was surprised, therefore, when the police shut the place down, and the Skyrockets found themselves out of work. Stranded in Oklahoma, Kendrick acted on the chance that a fellow musician would help them. Leaving the band in Oklahoma City, he drove ninety miles to Tulsa to see Bob Wills, who was performing regularly at Cain's Ballroom. During a break in the Playboys' performance, Kendrick introduced himself to Wills and explained his predicament. Wills took Kendrick to an office and introduced him to Millard Kelso, saying, "Here's an old friend of mine from Texas. He's got a little band and they are out of a job. See what you can find for them." Within thirty minutes, the Skyrockets were booked into the Longhorn Club in Tulsa.[33]

In 1940, the group moved to Bakersfield, California. They recorded for the last time in Los Angeles for Decca Records in October 1941. The eight selections recorded then reflect the more serious turn the band apparently took after 1940.[34] With the outbreak of World War II, the group disbanded. During the war, Kendrick worked several nights a week with Ray Wade's ten-piece, Bob Wills-style band and during the day at the shipyards along with several other members of that group.

After the war, Kendrick lived in California for a number of years before moving back to Texas, eventually settling in San Angelo. Shortly after this move, he was invited to attend a fiddle contest. He was skeptical at first: "In the old days, I wouldn't have crossed the street to hear a fiddle contest," Kendrick claimed. He was pleasantly surprised that the general level of musicianship among the fiddlers had improved so much since the 1930s. He began to learn the old fiddle tunes, mostly from recordings he purchased at fiddle contests, and soon amassed an impressive collection of contest trophies. [35]

Henry Lester was a fiddler who had a long and productive music career in West Texas. Henry and his brother Shorty moved to Amarillo from Memphis, Texas, around 1930 and joined the Amarillo Nighthawks, a six-piece dance group that played at the Rainbow Gardens dance hall. Other group members included Jack Short on piano; Slick Robertson, who later joined the Sons of the West, on banjo; and Johnny Britton on saxophone and guitar. The Nighthawks performed daily at 4:00 p.m. over Amarillo's KGRS radio. After a short time, however, the Lester brothers left the group and moved to Lubbock. [36]

One day, soon after their arrival in Lubbock, the brothers were playing in a downtown cafe for meals when the manager of the OS ranch at Post, Texas, hired them to play for a ranch dance. For playing from 5:00 or 6:00 p.m. until 3:00 or 4:00 a.m., with a break for midnight breakfast, Henry and Shorty received fifteen dollars each, a fortune to men who had been playing for food. [37] By 1931, Henry Lester and his brother had formed a larger group and were performing on Lubbock's KFYO radio. The first group was called the Kelly Kids, named for their sponsor, a Kelly Tire dealer. The band was busy performing four to five nights a week in a one hundred-mile radius of Lubbock until 1936, when the Lester brothers traveled to East Texas for about six months to visit their uncle. While in Tyler they met D. H. Williams of Mineola and Cloet Hamman, both members of the East Texas Serenaders, a fiddle band that had recorded for Brunswick Records in the late 1920s. [38] Henry and Shorty were asked to play on the Serenaders' recording session with Decca Records. They recorded six sides, and Henry remembered that the musicians' share was one percent royalty on two songs written by Williams. Ultimately, this translated into one check each for twenty-five dollars.

The sessions were held in a room of a downtown Dallas hotel. Shorty's banjo was too loud for the recording, so to get a good balance between the instruments, the recording engineer had Shorty sit in the bathroom on the toilet seat during the recording. Henry laughed to remember his brother leaning as far forward as possible on the seat, concerned that he would not be picked up by the microphone.

Back in Lubbock in 1937, Henry reformed his group as the Drug Store Cowboys, sponsored by Halsey Drug Store. Halsey's son Hop was a Texas state representative for two terms, and the Drug Store Cowboys were his campaign band. They would travel to a town and play fifteen to thirty minutes, Hop would give a brief speech, and then they would pack up and drive to the next town, usually thirty miles or so down the road, and repeat the performance. This was a profitable arrangement for the band, since their nights were free to play dances. Furthermore, their association with Halsey led the group to many interesting performances, including Governor O'Daniels's inaugural ball and Governor Stevenson's birthday ball, both held in Austin. Despite laws to the contrary, alcohol often was readily available at dances in the 1930s. Henry noted, "Bootleggers had to wear badges to keep from selling it to one another!" The first dances he played in Lubbock in the early 1930s paid about $2.50 per musician for a three-hour dance. Later he worked for half the door, which could result in twenty to thirty dollars a man. At Sled Allen's Arena in Lubbock, the admission was fifty cents per person. Attendance was so good that the band could make twenty to twenty-five dollars apiece. Eventually, promoters interested in higher profits offered the musicians a guarantee of about twenty dollars each.

Band personnel changed considerably over the years. Henry hired a four-piece band from Pampa, Texas, to be his new group after several of his players left at one time. The Pampa group had called themselves the Sons of the Saddle and included Duke Baker on fiddle, Pete Wilborn on guitar, Clyde Perkins on banjo, and Ken Bracher on bass fiddle. Baker and Perkins stayed with the group for nine years. The group was very busy with radio programs and dances throughout the 1940s and 1950s and even had a television program on Channel 13 in Lubbock as late as 1960. In the 1980s, Henry re-formed the Drug Store Cowboys and played weekly for eight years in Lubbock at a barbecue restaurant. Only when arthritis stopped his fiddling did Henry Lester retire from the music business.[39]

The O Bar O Cowboys' trip to Lubbock in 1933 might have been forgotten but for the fact that two members of this trio later joined with Bob Nolan to form the legendary Sons of the Pioneers. Tim Spencer, Leonard Slye, later known as Roy Rogers, and Slumber Nichols worked in Lubbock for about two months in 1933 performing on radio station KFYO. Spencer, who was born in Missouri and grew up in New Mexico and Oklahoma, moved to California in 1931 to try his luck in the music business. By answering a newspaper ad, he landed a job as the replacement for Bob Nolan in the Rocky Mountaineers, a western music group that included Slye and Nichols. After a brief tour as the International Cowboys, the trio became the O Bar O Cowboys and planned a trip to Texas.[40] The goal of this trip may have been to get a program on one of the big radio stations along the Texas border with Mexico, but the group never got that far.[41]

Velma Blanton was a high-school student in Lubbock at the time and recounted meeting Tim Spencer:

> This was when KFYO was just getting started up in the old Lubbock Hotel. . . . They [the O Bar O Cowboys] still were not

making too much money. They would go out to Brownfield and Littlefield and Silver Falls Lake and all these places around Lubbock to play in little theaters and to play dances and yet on the radio, they still had this audience of people who were very faithful to come up to the radio station, and I happened to go up with my girlfriend . . . and that's how it all started. They were still hungry, but they had a very wonderful technique. They would thank Mrs. Jones and Mrs. Brown, Mrs. Smith for the wonderful cakes, and pies and fried chicken that they had brought to the radio station. And sure enough, by the power of suggestion, the next day there would be all kind[s] of goodies for them to eat. I prevailed upon my Mom to bake her specialty, silk pecan pie, and took it up to the radio station. And that's how I met Tim Spencer, my husband-to-be.[42]

John Julian of Lubbock confirmed that the band was having a rough time of it. Julian was thirteen years old at the time and played mandolin with a friend who played guitar. The boys were invited to play on KFYO with the O Bar O Cowboys and later visited the band at the hotel where they were staying. Julian heard the band members joke about catching jackrabbits for food on the way from California. In a 1992 interview, Roy Rogers remembered those times and especially the jackrabbits.[43]

The trip to Texas was unsuccessful and might have been the undoing of the group. By late 1933, however, the group, now calling themselves the Pioneer Trio, landed a position on KFWB in Los Angeles. At that time, Texas fiddler Hugh Farr was added to the group lineup.[44]

Hugh and his brother Karl Farr grew up around Llano in central Texas. Hugh, the fiddler, was born in 1903. Beginning at age seven, he learned the traditional fiddle music his father and others played. In addition, he was influenced by the popular music he heard on radio at night. Karl, born in 1909, quickly became an accomplished guitarist under Hugh's tutelage. In the period from 1920 to 1925, Hugh and Karl with their brother Glen performed as the Three Farr Brothers. The boys also found music jobs on their own, such as Karl's job with the Chet Miller band in Big Springs at age thirteen.

The boys' father, Tom, was a builder who followed the construction work that accompanied the discovery of oil in the Southwest during the 1920s. The family gradually moved west, spending two years in Lamesa, Texas, and then moving to Artesia, New Mexico. In 1925, the family moved to southern California. Within a few years, Hugh and Karl were playing music full-time separately and occasionally together, with a variety of groups. In 1934, Hugh joined Len Slye, Tim Spencer, and Bob Nolan. With the addition of Karl in 1935, the original Sons of the Pioneers group was complete. Appearing in many motion pictures and on radio and recordings over the years, Hugh remained with the group until 1958, and Karl's career with the Pioneers ended only with his death in 1961.[45]

Ross Edwards was an early West Texas settler and fiddler, active in business. By the 1930s he had become a leading figure in Lubbock, and he was elected mayor in 1934 and 1936.[46] Edwards also had a musical group that played in the Lubbock area during this period. The Ross Edwards Orchestra consisted of Ruth Ford, Roy Bird, McDaniel Hub Hicks, Mrs. O. D. Burden, Nell Oldham, and Dee Brogden. A Mr. Sells was the soloist. The group played hotels and clubs such as the Trailers and the Westerners, and at Sled Allen's Arena in Lubbock, an establishment that booked wrestling matches and occasional dances featuring such groups as Bob Wills's Texas Playboys and Paul Whiteman's Orchestra. Edwards related, "After some twenty years of this fun, I happened to [sic] an accident with a table saw and reduced my finger count to eight, thus ending my fiddling to a marked degree . . . it shows what lengths a fellow will go to break himself of a bad habit."[47]

In 1929, J. E. (Eugene) Patterson, Charles Hunter, and Joe Ivan[s], all of Lynn County, located just south of Lubbock, formed the Arizona Wranglers.[48] Active on the West Coast in the early 1930s, the group was one of the earliest bands to feature western dress and song selection.[49] Other members of the group included Cal Short, Laverne Costello, Lynn Dossey, and Loyal Underwood. The group reportedly appeared in several western motion pictures and performed on Los Angeles radio station KNX.[50]

The Massey family of West Texas and New Mexico was a successful musical group through several decades. The family lived in Midland, Texas, after the turn of the century, and brother Curt was born there in 1910. By 1916, the Masseys had moved to Lincoln County, New Mexico. Henry Massey, the patriarch, was an old-time fiddler, and the entire family was musical. Their first group, called the Massey Five, consisted of the father, two sons, a son-in-law, and a daughter. Their first breaks were a radio program on KMBC in Kansas City and a two-year national Chautauqua tour. In 1933 the group became a regular featured act on "The National Barn Dance" on WLS in Chicago. In 1935, as Louise Massey and the Westerners, they moved to New York and performed on the NBC radio network. Perhaps their greatest fame came from Louise Massey's song "My Adobe Hacienda," written in 1941. It was a huge hit and was one of the nation's top songs of 1947. After the Westerners disbanded in the mid-1940s, Curt Massey continued with a career in radio and television. He was musical director and wrote the theme songs of two of the most popular television programs of the 1960s, "The Beverly Hillbillies," and "Petticoat Junction."[51]

The pattern of success for West Texas bands of the thirties is well defined: They all performed regularly on local radio. In the thirties it was relatively easy to get a radio program, and it was essential to the success of a musical group. It gave a group an opportunity to acquire and promote performances. A band could tour a regional area defined roughly by its radio station's listening area. Daily live radio broadcasts required that the performance engagements be within a few hundred miles of the station. Most of these groups were broken up by the draft at the outbreak of World War II, and, although some groups did resume after the war, most did not. Phonograph recording was not essential for the success of these groups. The Drug Store Cowboys never recorded commercially under their own name, and recording came relatively late in the careers of the Sons of the West and the Skyrockets. In the postwar years, phonograph recording would become increasingly important to the success or failure of a music group.

During those hard times, when so many people were leaving West Texas because of drought, dust, and the Depression, these musicians stayed and in many cases prospered. Bob Wills had left the area in the late twenties, but many imitators of the Wills sound performed throughout West Texas during the 1930s with success.

In *The Country Music Story*, the author related that in the 1930s a general store customer would approach the counter and say: "Let me have a pound of butter, a dozen eggs, and the latest Jimmie Rodgers record."[52] The idea that music is a staple of life during hard times gives insight into the success of music groups in West Texas during the 1930s. Music and dancing provided an important social diversion and emotional relief from the difficulties of daily life.

House and ranch dances were still popular in the thirties. Lubbock fiddler Cecil Caldwell remembered, "They'd take up a collection and we'd make sometimes 80 cents apiece. That was pretty good then, because at that time we chopped cotton ten hours for a dollar and I guarantee you playing beat the heck out of that."[53]

As evidenced by the pay these musicians received, people were willing to spend some of the little they had on entertainment. No one had to tell the musicians that picking the guitar beat picking cotton!

Dance party, circa 1920. The band includes bowed string bass, mandolin, and guitar. Courtesy Panhandle Plains Museum, Canyon, Texas.

Dance Party on a Panhandle ranch circa 1920. The dance platform was probably built for this occasion. Courtesy Panhandle Plains Museum, Canyon, Texas.

Earliest home, the dugout; early
Lubbock scenes circa 1891-1909.
Courtesy Southwest Collection, Texas Tech
University, Lubbock.

Jess Morris, Rita Blanca Photography Studio,
Dalhart, Texas, 1912. Courtesy Michael
Hunter.

An Eck Robertson publicity photo used to advertise a concert, AMARILLO NEWS, May 3, 1931. Courtesy Panhandle Plains Museum, Canyon, Texas.

Brooke "Doc" Kendrick's family medicine show, circa 1928 near Fort Worth (possibly Springtown.) The sign on the front of the stage reads: FREE SHOW, E. C. Gassaway Med. Co., Ft. Worth, Tex. Courtesy Bob Kendrick.

Eck Robertson in his fiddle shop, Amarillo, Texas, 1949; AMARILLO GLOBE NEWS. Courtesy Herb and Dorothy Mayfield.

Texas Shorty (Jim Chancellor) left, accompanying Uncle Eck Robertson, right, in fiddle contest at Quannah, Texas, May 22, 1964. The event was held in celebration of Pioneers Day and the arrival of a mule train from Spearman, Texas to Graham, Texas. Courtesy HALE CENTER AMERICAN.

Crowd at Hale Center Fiddle Contest held on July 4th, circa 1960s. This contest was held yearly beginning in 1946 until it was discontinued in 1990. Courtesy HALE CENTER AMERICAN.

Joe Teagarten Band, Barnhart, Texas, circa 1930; Shorty Teagarten on guitar and Joe Teagarten on fiddle. Courtesy Nessaye Mae Roach.

Fiddle contest, Wellington, Texas in the 1960s. Left to right: unidentified woman, piano; unidentified man (partially hidden by fiddler); Garland Gainer, fiddle; author Alan Munde, banjo; unidentified guitarist; Houston Chancellor, guitar; and unidentified fiddler. Photograph by Charles Gardner, author's collection.

Champion Texas Fiddler Benny Thomasson (left) with Robert Chancellor (right) on guitar at Hale Center, Texas, July 4th Fiddle contest, circa 1960s. Courtesy HALE CENTER AMERICAN.

Bob Swift's Joy Boys, Abilene, Texas, 1933. J. R. Chatwell is pictured with a fiddle, standing right of microphone. Mrs. J. R. Chatwell Collection. Courtesy Hank Harrison.

The Sons of the West at KGNC radio studio, Amarillo, mid 1930s. Left to right: Elza Harter, guitar; Pat Trotter, fiddle; Freddie Dean, guitar; Jimmie Meek, bass; Slick Robertson, banjo; and Billy Briggs, steel guitar. Courtesy Jimmie Meek.

Robena Stevenson, age 10, with the guitar she won in a contest, 1935, with her brother Nathan Stevenson on fiddle. Courtesy Robena Stevenson Watts.

The Skyrockets, Pecos, Texas, 1935. Left to right: Sanford Kendrick, trumpet; Bob Kendrick, saxophone; Clifford Kendrick, drums; and Brooke "Doc" Kendrick guitar. Courtesy Bob Kendrick.

The Westerners (The Massey Family), STANDBY! magazine, June 22, 1935, authors collection.

Panhandle dust storm, Perryton, Texas, 1935. The Perry Studio. Courtesy Southwest Collection, Texas Tech University, Lubbock.

The Girls of the Golden West, Dolly Goode on guitar and Millie Goode; STANDBY! magazine, December 5, 1936, author's collection.

Clif Bruner and his Boys, Beaumont, Texas, 1938. Left to right: Rip Ramsey, bass; Cone Scooler, steel guitar; Alton Buiden, banjo; Clif Bruner, fiddle; J. R. Chatwell, fiddle; E. W. Goodman, road manager; Morris Deason, guitar; and Max Bennett, piano. Mrs. J. R. Chatwell Collection. Courtesy Hank Harrison.

Nessaye Mae Roach at home on Crockett County ranch, 1940. Courtesy Nessaye Mae Roach.

The Sons of the Pioneers publicity photo, circa 1940s. Left to right: Hugh Farr, fiddle; Pat Brady, Bob Nolan; Karl Farr, Lloyd Perryman; Tim Spencer (seated on floor). Courtesy Hank Harrison.

Billy Briggs and his X.I.T. Boys, Avalon Club, Amarillo, Texas, late 1940s. Left to right: Billy Briggs, steel guitar; Pat Trotter, fiddle; Jess Williams, guitar; and Weldon Allard, bass. Courtesy Weldon Allard.

Square dance band, 1957. Left to right: Gibb Raglan, caller; Barney Watts, mandolin; Nathan Stevenson, fiddle; and Jearl Watts, guitar. Courtesy Robena Stevenson Watts.

Bob Wills on the set of his
KFJZ television program.
Fort Worth, early 1960s.
Authors collection.

Crowd at KSEL Western Jamboree, March
11, 1950, from KSEL Western Jamboree
program, July 15, 1950. Performers include
special guests Wayne Rainey (at
microphone), the Delmore Brothers, and
Lonnie Glosson; and regulars Dave Stone,
The Rhythm Wranglers, and Bill Myrick and
the Mayfield Brothers. Courtesy Pete Curtis.

KSEL's Big Western Jamboree

4

"IF YOU CAN'T DANCE TO IT, DON'T PLAY IT": WESTERN SWING AND ELECTRIC HONKY-TONK

The postwar years have been called the "Golden Age of Country Music"[1], and the music produced then is still the measure by which traditional country music is judged. Many modern features of the music, such as its instrumentation and lyric content, were introduced or became firmly established in the decade after 1945. It was the heyday for such country music legends as Hank Williams and Lefty Frizzell; female singers, following the lead of Kitty Wells, began making their first steps into this male-dominated field. Radio and later television became increasingly involved in the popularization of country music during these years.

World War II caused the breakup of many country music groups as band members left to join the armed services. After the war, many of these musicians did not return to professional music, thereby opening doors for a new generation of younger musicians. Young men returned with new-found interest in country music or with well-rooted country music ties strengthened by associations with other servicemen with similar musical tastes.

Lubbock native Tommy Hancock, for example, who went to war with little previous connection to country music, returned to his hometown and became the leader of one of the most prominent bands in the West Texas region. Edd Mayfield of Dimmit, in contrast, an accomplished singer and guitarist before the war, returned with an eye to a professional music career sparked by musical associations made while in the army. Several groups organized after the war became central figures in the West Texas country music scene during the 1950s: Tommy Hancock and the Roadside Playboys and the Maines Brothers band in Lubbock; Billy Briggs and the XIT Boys in Amarillo; Hoyle Nix and the West Texas Cowboys in Big Spring; Bill Myrick, Troy Jordan, and the Cross B Boys in the Midland-Odessa area; and the Miller Brothers in Wichita Falls.

In Texas, after the war, Bob Wills-style western swing was firmly established as a popular dance music. On a national scale, however, despite Wills's movie appearances and national hits such as "New San Antonio Rose," his prominence was limited to areas in which he had toured and performed on radio extensively: Oklahoma, Texas, and California. As a result, Wills had very little contact with the eastern country music community. Many of his innovations were too modern for that country music establishment. Possibly because Wills's music was closer to jazz than were the Grand Ole Opry offerings, his style was seen as renegade. Band leader Tommy Hancock said, "Bob Wills, Adolph Hofner, and a few other big, good western swing bands were the

IF
YOU
CAN'T
DANCE
TO
IT...

61

counterculture, and Nashville was the straight culture."[2] He added that western swing "was always an outcast in the music game."

That Wills's music was not embraced by Nashville is supported by the often-told story of Wills's first appearance on the Grand Ole Opry on December 30, 1944. Texas Playboy drummer Monte Mountjoy remembered that the band was setting up as usual when an Opry official told them they could not use drums on the program. After some discussion, a compromise was struck whereby the drums would be used but concealed by a curtain. When Wills arrived, however, he stated flatly that the Playboys would perform normally, with drums, or they would leave. This occasion marked the first appearance of a full drum set on the Opry stage.[3] Indeed, it was not until the 1960s that a lone snare drum was permanently added to the Opry stage band. According to Opry comedienne Minnie Pearl, on the night of Wills's performance Roy Acuff declared that Wills's electrified fiddles would ruin the Opry forever.[4]

Despite the resistance of traditionalists, many of Wills's musical innovations were soon incorporated into the mainstream in a new type of country music. The changing face of country music audiences after World War II and the popularity of dance halls, roadhouses, clubs, and honky-tonks after the war led to the development of a music form uniquely suited to these environments: honky-tonk music.

Honky-tonk music, an offspring of western swing, was born in the early 1940s and came into its own by the early 1950s. It shared with western swing the use of twin fiddles, electric lead instruments such as the steel guitar, and a beat made for dancing. The heavy beat of honky-tonk music eventually replaced the lighter "swing" beat of western swing, so that by the late 1950s even Bob Wills used the heavier honky-tonk beat on his recordings. Honky-tonk bands were typically smaller than western swing groups. During the heyday of western swing in the early 1940s, groups often featured as many as fourteen or more musicians. Postwar country music groups might feature only five to seven pieces. In Texas, honky-tonk music was an evolution of the strong dance tradition that has shaped the sound of country music from frontier times to the present.

Texas singer and Grand Ole Opry member Ernest Tubb was a major contributor to the development of electric honky-tonk music. Certainly Tubb's membership in the Grand Ole Opry helped to legitimize the use of the electric guitar in country groups as early as 1941.[5] Bob Wills, too, had been using electric instruments and drums in his orchestra since its formation in 1935.

Honky-tonk music was shaped in part by the needs of a machine—the jukebox. By the end of the war, jukeboxes were a fixture of honky-tonks and roadhouses throughout the southern United States.[6] Those environments called for louder music with a solid dance rhythm, and country artists responded by adding electric instruments, pianos, and drums. It is not surprising, then, that the records of Bob Wills were popular on jukeboxes, for his band featured all those elements. In 1948, Texas

Playboy Johnny Gimble saw a jukebox in a San Angelo cafe that had twenty records, twelve of them by Bob Wills.[7]

By the 1950s, West Texas was booming with establishments that provided live country music for the steadily growing population of workers in the oil fields, on ranches and farms, and in related services. Variously referred to as clubs, nightclubs, honky-tonks, or roadhouses, these places were attractive because they provided an inexpensive evening's entertainment and a place for social interaction. Whereas in previous decades dances were often held in homes, barns, or school-houses, clubs became the new dance place of the 1950s.[8] Honky-tonk music flourished in these environs. The Cotton Club, the Glassarama, and the Bamboo Club in Lubbock; the Nat, the Clover, and the Avalon Club in Amarillo; the Stampede in Big Spring; the Silver Saddle Club in Odessa; and countless others throughout West Texas regularly featured honky-tonk music.

Country music took an incongruent turn in this era: It was a music born in the family, where the "folk" played guitars, mandolins, and fiddles and sang to entertain themselves and others at community socials and churches. Thus the music was an advocate for the moral values of the family, and its rural neighborhood and a connection with the past. But eventually it became a music for dancing, drinking, and carousing in the rough honky-tonk atmosphere. Such places served as a proving ground for the rising talents of Buddy Holly, Sonny Curtis, Weldon Myrick, Roy Orbison, Waylon Jennings, Charline Arthur, Slim Willet, and many others whose lives and careers stayed centered in West Texas.

For many musicians, the smaller venues frequented by the working class were the least desirable places to play. The clientele was often a hard-drinking group, and playing music for them could be difficult and occasionally dangerous. Ironically, these jobs were often the easiest to get and, in some areas, the only country music jobs to be had. Characterized by many musicians as the kind of place a person wanted to phone before going to, in order to make sure that all the blood had been mopped up before one went, such establishments were an unavoidable feature of the West Texas country music scene for many postwar musicians.

Sonny Curtis and Tommy Hancock, veterans of the West Texas club scene, remembered such places as the home of orchestrated fistfights—fights being so common and predictable as to seem planned. Hancock, Curtis, and many other West Texas musicians who played the clubs in the twenty-year period following the war were greatly relieved when they were able to escape that scene.

The lyrics of country songs began to reflect the new honky-tonk atmosphere. Floyd Tillman's 1949 hit "Slippin' Around," perhaps his greatest success, ushered in the "cheating song," a genre tailor made for the honky-tonk clientele. Floyd Tillman was an influential singer and songwriter in the 1940s who spent his teenage years in Post, Texas. His songs include classics such as "It Makes No Difference Now," recorded by Cliff Bruner's Texas Wanderers in 1938 and later by Gene Autry and Bill Monroe. During World War II, Tillman had hits of his own with

"They Took the Stars Out of Heaven" and "G. I. Blues." After the war, with Columbia Records he wrote and recorded "I Love You So Much It Hurts," and "This Cold War with You." Tillman's own version of "Slippin' Around" reached as high as number five on the country charts, while the embarrassing pop version by Margaret Whiting and Jimmy Wakley reached number one on both the country and pop charts.[9]

Dance continued to be popular in West Texas even after it waned in other parts of the country, a phenomenon central to both the short-term and long-term success of the musicians whose careers passed through the region.[10] Until the emergence of the singer/songwriters Jimmy Dale Gilmore, Butch Hancock, Terry Allen, and Joe Ely in the 1970s, dance venues were the only reliable work for musicians in West Texas. From the end of the war through the 1960s, despite the onslaught of rock and roll, musicians who worked steadily in country music in West Texas played for dance. Western swing master Tommy Allsup located in Odessa in the 1950s because, as he put it, "people really dance good in West Texas." So successful was Allsup's Odessa-based swing band that he was able to attract boogie-woogie pianist and King recording artist Moon Mullican to join the group.[11]

As honky-tonk music emerged, western swing continued to be popular with West Texas musicians and fans alike. For a time in the mid-1950s, Bob Wills lived and performed in Amarillo, appeared on a daily noontime radio program, and was a regular Friday night feature at the Cotton Club in Lubbock.[12] West Texas was also the retreat for many of Bob Wills's former musicians who found a home with Hoyle Nix's group in Big Spring. Despite the decline of western swing music in other parts of the West during the 1950s, Nix experienced great success.

Hoyle Nix is second only to Bob Wills in West Texas western swing.[13] Unlike many musicians of West Texas, Nix had a successful music career without leaving the region. For nearly forty years, from the formation of his West Texas Cowboys in 1946 until his death in 1985, Nix entertained West Texas audiences with his own brand of Wills-inspired western swing dance music and kept the tradition alive. During the late 1950s and early 1960s, while the country music industry was reeling from the effects of the rock and roll invasion, Nix's group was at its zenith. Traveling in a bus, they worked steadily, made recordings, and attracted a number of Wills's alumni to the band. This impressive record is without equal in the region.

Born in Azle, Texas, on March 22, 1918, Nix moved with his family one year later to a farm near Big Spring, Texas, where he lived the rest of his life. Coming from a long line of fiddlers, Hoyle learned to play from his father, Jonah. Music was an avocation at this time; cotton farming provided most of the family income. During the 1930s, Hoyle along with brother Ben on guitar formed the Centerpoint Serenaders. In 1946, Hoyle formed the West Texas Cowboys, a Bob Wills-style dance band that included Hoyle, brother Ben Nix, Loran Warren, Low Wheeler, and Charles Smith.[14] Nix soon found his band in big demand throughout the region. In 1949, he recorded for the first time his composition "Big

Ball's in Cowtown" for the Dallas-based Talent label. This song became a western swing standard and the song most associated with Nix. In 1954, Hoyle built a country music club in Big Spring called the Stampede, which served as a home to the West Texas Cowboys throughout the rest of Hoyle's career.

In 1960, Nix added his eight-year-old son Jody, born June 25, 1952, to his band as the drummer. The band lineup included several former Texas Playboys, including Eldon Shamblin and Louis and Mancel Tierney. Jody, who began learning to play drums at age four, remembered this period fondly: "I was playing with the 'big boys' now. I really had to get it. . . . We played Tuesday at Brownfield, Wednesday at Lamesa, Thursday at Abilene, and Big Spring at the Stampede on Saturday."[15] Despite this schedule of five late nights a week, Jody was expected to attend school regularly.

In 1972, Hoyle and Jody Nix recorded the landmark United Artists album, *For the Last Time: Bob Wills and his Texas Playboys* along with Merle Haggard and a who's-who of former Texas Playboys. Although never a member of Wills's group, Hoyle Nix was asked to play fiddle and sing on the recording in a capacity similar to Wills's. Nix's own "Big Ball's in Cowtown" was recorded on this session, as well as "Crippled Turkey," one of Nix's favorite fiddle tunes. Jody, age twenty-one years old, sang several songs on the album. This album is often credited for starting the western swing music revival of the 1970s.

After Hoyle's death in 1985, Jody continued performing with the band. Having played drums with the band since childhood, he was well prepared to carry on in his father's tradition. Jody started fiddling at age eleven but actively worked on it only after his father's death. He was named for Bob Wills's jazzy left-handed fiddler, Joe Holley, whom Wills often called "Jody" in on-record introductions. Hoyle was said to have wished for a left-handed boy fiddler and, strangely enough, got just that. Jody is left-handed and plays the fiddle on the right shoulder without reversing the string order, just as his namesake did.[16]

Today, Jody and his band, the Texas Cowboys, play throughout the year at rodeo dances, VFW halls, and dance halls, just as his father did. In 1988, Jody played in Washington, D.C. during the inauguration of President Bush at the request of Texas state representative Charles Stenholm of Stamford. This event generated media coverage and increased interest in Jody's group. The Stampede, Hoyle Nix's club in Big Spring, now is owned and operated by Ben Nix.

Billy Briggs and his various groups in the Amarillo area had success similar to that of Hoyle Nix during the late 1940s and through the 1950s. Briggs came to Amarillo in 1938 to join the Sons of the West band. After the war, Briggs formed his own group, the XIT Boys.[17] Formed in January 1947, the band consisted of Billy Briggs on steel guitar, Weldon Allard on bass, Pat Trotter on fiddle, and Jess Williams on guitar. Briggs, Trotter, and Williams had played together in the Sons of the West. The XIT Boys worked five nights a week at the Avalon club in Amarillo and performed several times daily over local radio stations KGNC and KAMQ. Pianist

George Turley later replaced Trotter, who found the schedule of five nights of music a week plus a full-time bricklaying job too demanding.

In 1951, the group recorded a Briggs original, "Chew Tobacco Rag," which became a hit on the Imperial label. As a result, the act changed its name to Billy Briggs and his Chew Tobacco Rag Boys and used the song to sign on and off their radio shows. In 1956, Briggs left the band to open another nightclub and formed a new group. Allard and Williams stayed at the Avalon and renamed the group the Cavaliers, which continued to play there until 1959.[18] Briggs eventually left Amarillo and retired in California.[19]

The Miller Brothers Band was a touring western dance band based in Wichita Falls, Texas, from the late 1940s to the mid-1960s. The group saw many personnel changes in its history. One lineup in the early 1950s included Bill Jourdan, Smiley Weaver, Jim McGraw, Leon Gibbs, Dutch Engram, Troy Jordan, Madge Bowlan Sutter, and Lee Cochran. For seventeen years, the group performed throughout the United States, touring in specially made vehicles and recording for the California-based 4-Star Records.

The group originated shortly after the war as the Gibbs Brothers. Nat and Sam, who were twins, and younger brother Leon were working for the newspaper in Wichita Falls and performing on radio station KWFT. Their boss at the newspaper insisted that the brothers quit the radio show, since both businesses were involved in advertising. The Gibbs Brothers wanted to keep both jobs and, at the suggestion of a radio station official, they changed the group name to the Miller Brothers and continued working.

By the late 1940s, the brothers owned the M B Corral nightclub, broadcast six radio shows a week, ran their own booking agency, and still worked dances in and around Wichita Falls. The booking agency was called Sam Gibbs's Orchestra Service, which Sam operated. Leon Gibbs, who went by Leon Miller at this time, remembered that since he had a different last name, Sam Gibbs could wholeheartedly recommend the Miller Brothers to promoters, who would not know Sam was talking about his own brothers.

When the group was on tour, other acts were booked into the Corral, including Bob Wills, Hank Thompson, and Ernest Tubb. In the summer, when the heat slowed down attendance at the club, the group traveled throughout the United States and Canada. In 1955, the group was ranked number three in the nation by *Cashbox* magazine. During this period they recorded fifty-two sides for 4-Star Records of Pasadena. The Miller Brothers band name was sold to Bobby Rhodes of San Jon, New Mexico, in 1965.[20]

Sam Gibbs continued to operate his booking agency throughout the late 1950s and early 1960s. From the late 1950s until Bob Wills retired, Gibbs was Wills's manager.[21] During this time Wills played in Las Vegas and Lake Tahoe with a band and then began touring as a solo act, usually bringing one singer with him and playing with the house band. The fact that Gibbs booked both the Miller Brothers Band and the Bob Wills group resulted in a stroke of fortune for Miller Brothers fiddler Frankie McWhorter.

McWhorter was born in 1931 in Memphis only a few miles from Turkey, the home of Bob Wills. Frankie learned ranch work at an early age and specialized in breaking horses. After returning from military service in the early 1950s, Frankie worked as a fiddler for various bands around Texas; by 1960, he was fiddling with the Miller Brothers Band. Bob Wills heard Frankie fiddling at the Golden Nugget nightclub in Las Vegas and invited him to join the Texas Playboys. McWhorter took the job and worked with Wills until 1962, when he returned to Memphis, Texas, to break horses.[22]

Tommy Hancock led an important band in the 1950s that played in the Lubbock area. Tommy pointed out that bands had distinct territories in those days. Hancock's Roadside Playboys did not go to Amarillo because groups like Billy Briggs's XIT Boys and the Panhandle Playboys were so popular there, while to the south, Hoyle Nix was the big draw. Those groups did not play often in Lubbock, to avoid conflict with Hancock.

Hancock's career is an interesting example of a West Texas country musician's life. Born in Lubbock on March 25, 1929, Hancock grew up with little exposure to country music. Encouraged by his grandmother to take up the violin, he played in the junior high school orchestra. At the age of sixteen he joined the Merchant Marine just as World War II was ending, and by the time he was seventeen he was serving in the army in the Pacific. "That's where I really learned to play the fiddle," said Hancock. Being a Texan with a violin, everyone assumed he was a fiddler, although he had never heard any country fiddle music. Urged by a sergeant, Hancock learned tunes and fiddle songs from guitar players in his company, who would hum the melodies to him. Through this oral process, Hancock learned his first country fiddle music.

During his stay in postwar Japan, Hancock studied with a Japanese violin master: "My fiddle playing really came along while I was in the army, because I was learning ad-lib fiddle, the tunes and fiddle songs from the guys I was with, at the same time learning more technical expertise from my teacher, plus I had plenty of time to practice." After his discharge from the army, the eighteen-year-old Hancock returned to Lubbock and located a job playing the fiddle at a club on East Broadway called Danceland. For the first evening he earned the princely sum of five dollars: "I realized I was in on myself a career right there, if they're going to pay me five bucks for playing the fiddle when I've been playing it all along for nothing. Boy, I thought that was great." The Danceland gig began at midnight on weekdays and 1:00 a.m. on Saturdays and usually ran until 4:00 a.m., or "until some fight wiped the place completely out, which was a common occurrence in those days," Hancock recalled. Alcohol sales were prohibited throughout a large part of West Texas, and to enter a private club, patrons had to buy memberships, bring their own liquor, and pay for a setup (a glass, ice, and water or soda). "It was a dangerous place run by hoodlums and had all the things about it you don't like in clubs, including bad music," Tommy stated. He added, "Then, only people on the wild side of life went to the clubs, and we had that following because we played on the wild side of life."

Tommy described the music of the 1940s as "real simple country music . . . something that could be played on relatively few instruments with almost no amplification." The band was called Squeaky Rhodes and the Roadside Playboys. Squeaky was a steel player from the small community of Shallowater, located a few miles northwest of Lubbock. In addition to their club performances, the band played for such events as weddings, rodeos, and openings of drive-in restaurants. Hancock remembered this early band as "having the town sewed up pretty early as far as a popular band is concerned."

The band continued until Squeaky was called back into the service for a time. On his return, family concerns kept him from rejoining the band. "I was kind of the natural one to take over the band," said Tommy, "and we done real well almost from the word *go*."

Part of the formula for the band's long success was their ability to copy convincingly the music of popular artists. In that respect, the music and material played by Tommy Hancock and the Roadside Playboys was not much different from that of other bands in the region. "We tended to play the hits no matter what category they were in. As much as [was] feasible with the instruments and vocalists we had, we were a copy band," Hancock related. Although the Roadside Playboys played hits of many styles, Lefty Frizzell and Hank Williams were the most popular artists, followed by long-time Texas favorite Bob Wills and others, including western swing pioneer Adolph Hofner. Hancock's winning personality, his ability to select the right songs, and the high quality of musicians all contributed to the band's success.

To his skills as a bandleader, Hancock added business acumen in identifying and creating opportunities to work. He would book a dance, for instance, for a Saturday night at a VFW hall in Plainview, sixty miles north of Lubbock. He hired what he referred to as a "couple of hustlers" who would go weeks in advance to a town between Plainview and Lubbock to sell the downtown merchants a promotion for the afternoon of the same Saturday. On that Saturday afternoon, Tommy Hancock and the Roadside Playboys, en route to Plainview, would set up and play on the town square, pulling in the Saturday afternoon crowd and advertising the businesses that had paid their fee. At a time when television had not yet come to dominate the entertainment and advertising scenes and shopping malls had not replaced the downtown merchants, "we could do that in any direction out of Lubbock," Hancock stated.

Tommy Hancock and the Roadside Playboys proved to be one of the most popular and enduring dance bands for Lubbock and environs, providing work for many of the better players in the area. Among the Roadside Playboys at one time or another were fiddlers Curley Lawler and Homer Logan, brother of bluegrass fiddler Tex Logan; steel guitarists Bob Stuffelbean and Bill Manley; and guitarist Sonny Curtis, a performer of special note. Tommy remembered Sonny as one who was going to make it in the music business because "he'd be playing the guitar before we left, in the band van he'd be playing, and [he would] play all the way to the job. He'd play at the intermissions. On the way back, he'd play that guitar all the time." Hancock, in an effort to recognize the musician's lot in life, had membership cards printed for his "Under Appreciated Musicians Club" and made Sonny the first member.[23]

As an owner and operator of the New Cotton Club in Lubbock, Tommy Hancock saw the music business from another point of view. The original Cotton Club was opened in the 1940s and, according to Hancock, was established to appeal to the high society of Lubbock. The club featured groups like the orchestras of Harry James, Benny Goodman, and Guy Lombardo. Hancock speculated, "There ain't enough classy people in town to support a fourteen-hundred seating capacity club, so they started booking other things, and as they did, the class element stopped [attending] and it started a slow degeneration that really increased along about the fifties." Finally the club succumbed to a common ailment of clubs during this era: it burned. "If a club didn't have any business," he explained, "the owner would burn it [to collect insurance]. If it did have business, your competitor would burn it."[24]

Hancock opened a club in the early 1960s and asked the former owner of the Cotton Club for permission to use its name. He began operations as the New Cotton Club in a new building located between Lubbock and Slaton on the Slaton highway. His run in the club business took a similar course to the original Cotton Club. He began by trying to book in top-name country acts but soon resorted to lesser known acts that attracted a rougher crowd. Among the acts that played the New Cotton Club during Hancock's stewardship was Willie Nelson, at a time when Nelson was known primarily as a songwriter and had only a few records. Hancock remembers that Nelson's then drummer Johnny Bush, who had a string of popular recordings, became the bigger draw of the two at the New Cotton Club. During a run of bad luck that plagued the club, a performance by the emerging star Merle Haggard was canceled by mutual agreement in response to the Kennedy assassination. Hancock continued to operate the New Cotton Club until 1980.

Tommy pointed out that clubs during the fifties engaged in the practice of advertising artists who were not in fact contracted to appear. This business tactic arose from the unreliability of a few artists in their promises to show and perform. Hancock booked both Stonewall Jackson and Freddie Hart, moderately popular country artists, neither of whom showed for the contracted date. Realizing that on such occasions the customers remained at the club, had a good time, and spent money, some unscrupulous club owners began to advertise artists not contracted to appear. Tommy explained:

> The star's ability to draw a crowd was the most important thing. It wasn't his performance, especially in the old Cotton Club. The sound was real out of proportion to the volume [capacity] of the building. When the club managers found out you could advertise

a star and draw a crowd and then not have to pay the star, that really worked out good, 'cause there wouldn't be ten people [that would] ask for their money back. They'd have a good time waiting all night for the star. . . . I had never done that because I detested the whole idea.[25]

Radio grew in importance and became an essential element in the success of the music and its performers during this period. Lubbock boasted the nation's first all-country-format radio station, "Pappy" Dave Stone's KDAV. Other stations featured country music in segments or live stage shows, such as the "Western Jamboree" on Lubbock's KSEL, Abilene's "Big State Jamboree" on KBRC, the XIT Boys' noon shows on KGNC in Amarillo, and live broadcasts from the Stampede in Big Spring featuring Hoyle Nix and his band. Radio also served as a springboard for such notables as singer and radio personality Bill Mack, comedian-singer Don Bowman, record producer Snuff Garrett, and country singer Waylon Jennings.

Dave Stone was a major figure in West Texas country format radio and music promotion from the late 1940s to 1960s.[26] His contribution to the development of local country music in West Texas was great. The country music played on his stations was loved by his audience and studied by the musicians. His promotion of national country music acts in West Texas offered fans and musicians opportunities to see and hear their favorite performers in person. By using local talent on his live radio programs and concerts, he encouraged the growth and development of West Texas musicians, many of whom in later years found careers in the music business.

Born David Pinkston on November 11, 1913 in Post, Texas, Stone grew up loving country music through the phonograph records of his parents, friends, and relatives. Stone listened to country music records on the Edison label: "They were the big old thick records. I would go down there [to a friend's house] and play people like Vernon Dalhart and Carson Robison."[27] Although he never felt an urge to become a performer, he nonetheless developed a lifelong love of country music.

While David was still very young, the Pinkston family moved to Slaton, fifteen miles from Lubbock. After graduating from Slaton High School, David spent time as a journalism major at Texas Tech in Lubbock. Not finding journalism to his liking, David attended Draughon's Business College in Brownfield, Texas, and, after graduating, went to work as an accountant and office manager for the Arizona Chemical Company in Brownfield. He continued this employment during the war.

After the war, David found that two new radio stations, KSEL and KCBC, were going on the air in Lubbock. He had always been interested in radio and country music and so applied as a bookkeeper for both stations. Each station offered him a job, and because KSEL went on the air first, he took that position and began work November 1, 1946. A KSEL deejay's dislike of country music paved the way for David's career in radio broadcasting:

I was very interested in country music, and we had a boy there who was running the Western Roundup show on KSEL from 3:00 to 3:30, and he made some sarcastic remarks about some of the artists, especially Ernest Tubb and his "Rainbow at Midnight." He was getting mail all right, but it was letting him have it pretty good and he walked out of the studio one day and he said, "Dave, I happen to know you got a lot of country records and you like country music and you can take that program." I said, "Man, I don't know a thing in the world about being on the air." But the next thing I knew he was talking to the program director [and] then the manager of the station and I heard the manager say, "Okay, Dave, take the Western Roundup."

The response from the listening audience was so great from this change that the program was expanded from thirty minutes to a full hour. His popularity on the Western Roundup earned Dave offers from two stations just beginning operations, one in nearby Levelland as station manager and another from Brownfield. To keep him at KSEL, he was offered the position of station manager. David, now using the name Dave Stone, became station manager at KSEL in late 1948 and soon after expanded the time allotted to country music and installed a live Saturday night broadcast called the Western Jamboree.

The idea for the live broadcast came about quite by accident in 1949. Dave recalled:

We had a Saturday night record program, and we got to cutting up, and we'd act like we had Hank Snow and Ernest Tubb all there at the studio. And actually, of course, we announced it was re-corded, but we acted like it was live. Well, a couple of guys came in one night and it was Earl [Montgomery] and Scottie [James Scott], and said they'd moved from Shreveport to Lubbock and they had been on the Louisiana Hayride and they wanted to entertain in person. [In Lubbock, Scott performed as Scottie and his Rhythm Wranglers and Montgomery performed with the Rambling Cowboys.] So we said, well, okay, . . . we'll put you on. And they went over real good, and we added some other live talent, and first thing we knew there was no way in the world for people [those who dropped by KSEL expecting a live show] to get into the studio.

Stone ran the program as a live talent show broadcast from the KSEL studio. Response to the program was overwhelming, and the studios were so crowded with performers and visitors that Pappy Dave moved the show into the carpenters' union hall in Lubbock. The first broadcast from Carpenter's Hall was on January 21, 1950.[28] Stone remembered, "We had five hundred people inside and about five thousand people outside wanting to get in."[29] Seeing the need for an even larger venue, he moved the show to a local wrestling arena at 606 Texas Avenue, operated by promoter Sled Allen.

The first performance at Sled Allen's Arena was held January 28, 1950.[30] Stone sold tickets at the door until the eleven hundred-seat arena was full, closed the doors, and started the show. Later the station located an old hangar building near the Lubbock airport that had been part of the military base during the war. Christened "Jamboree Hall," from 1950 to 1953 the venue featured national acts such as Hank Locklin, Little Jimmy Dickens, the Delmore Brothers, and the Maddox Brothers and Rose. Stone also gave local talent a chance to perform before the large studio audience. Noteworthy West Texas musicians who appeared on the Western Jamboree were Bill Myrick and the Mayfield Brothers, Billy Walker, Ben Hall, Tommy Hancock, Buddy Holly, Weldon Myrick, and Sonny Curtis.

In 1953, Stone left KSEL to begin a new Lubbock radio station along with partner Leroy Elmore. KDAV went on the air on September 19, 1953. The station made history as the first station in the world to broadcast, as Stone boasted, "one hundred percent country music." He related Elmore's shocked response to the proposed all-country format: "You mean every time the people tune in, they hear geetar pickin'?" "That's fine with me," said Stone and applied to the FCC for a license. At that time it was normal for radio to follow a block programming format featuring many different types of music and programs scheduled throughout the day, usually in fifteen- and thirty-minute segments. Country music was typically aired as only a part of the broadcast, sharing the day with big band, classical, and Hispanic music, along with soap operas, news, and talk shows. "The FCC wasn't quite as lenient as they are now in permitting stations to specialize in one kind of music," Stone said, "but we were about the fourth or fifth station in Lubbock." The FCC, perhaps thinking the market was large enough for specialized radio programming, granted the license to Stone and Elmore.

The success of the KSEL Western Jamboree and country music programming in general led Stone, now part owner and general manager of KDAV, to believe the new format would work. Local merchants apparently agreed, as all the available on-air commercial time was sold before the station began broadcasting. KDAV's immediate success was aided by a number of former KSEL employees including well-known on-the-air staff and sales personnel whom Stone had convinced to follow him to the new station.

The station's grand opening featured a country music concert staged in the parking lot of the KDAV building. Broadcast live, the show featured Nashville recording artists Ferlin Huskey and Jean Shepherd and area artists Billy Walker from Clovis, New Mexico, and Slim Willet from Abilene.

From November 1954 through June 1957, Stone and Elmore repeated the success of the all-country format at sister stations KCBT in San Angelo, KGIT in Amarillo, and KPIK in Colorado Springs, Colorado. Each station had the first all-country format in its market. As Stone recalled, "All of these stations, listenerwise, were tremendously successful. We didn't get rich, by any means, but we managed to keep our head above water." In addition to the radio business, Stone promoted many country music concerts in Lubbock, San Angelo, Amarillo, and Colorado Springs using his stations to help advertise the events: "We had all the big stars, Johnny Cash, Ernest Tubb, Jim Reeves. . . . Just about anybody you could name, we brought them in for a personal appearance. The last booking I had was Buck Owens, and I started with them [Owens and band] in San Angelo, Lubbock, Amarillo, and on up to Colorado Springs."

Radio provided the first step into the music business for many country musicians, such as Slim Willet. Born Winston Moore in 1919 at Victor in Erath County, Texas, Willet was a 1949 graduate of Abilene's Hardin-Simmons University. Willet became station manager of the college radio station during his senior year. In 1950 his "Pinball Millionaire" was recorded by Hank Locklin for 4-Star Records and by Jene O'Quin for Capitol Records. That same year Willet hosted a radio program on Abilene's KRBC radio.[31]

Willet had several hit songs in the 1950s, including "Tool Pusher from Snyder" and the well-known "Don't Let the Stars Get in Your Eyes." From 1950 to 1954 he hosted a weekly country music concert in Abilene called the Big State Jamboree. Willet later became the owner of KCAD radio in Abilene and continued there until his death in 1965 at age forty-six.[32] The Big State Jamboree featured local talent and national figures such as Elvis Presley, Pat Boone, and Marty Robbins. According to John Turner, a radio technician for the live radio broadcast of the Jamboree on KRBC, the 1,120-seat auditorium was nearly full every Saturday night. After the introduction of television in Abilene, however, the crowds dwindled. The Jamboree was produced briefly as a television program but was soon dropped from the air.[33]

The Big Spring Jamboree was another weekly country music concert held in West Texas in the early 1950s. Promoted by country singer "Bozo" Darnell and hosted by radio personality Keith Ward, the Jamboree featured artists such as fiddler "Big Red" Hayes, Troy Jordan and the Cross B Boys, the Callahan Brothers, George Jones, and Jimmie Seals, later of the pop music duo Seals and Crofts. The Jamboree was held on Saturday nights during 1954.[34]

Steel guitarist Wally Moyers, Sr. performed with nearly all the Lubbock-based country bands in the 1950s and 1960s. Wally was born in Childress in 1934, and in 1938 the Moyers family moved to Lubbock. Shortly after the war, Wally began to take steel guitar lessons from a door to door teacher/salesperson: "He [the salesperson] would give you a talent test, and if you passed you were offered lessons for $1.50 per lesson. Of course, everyone passed, and so did I. Mom and Dad bought me a student course for my birthday. I used to ride my bike to take my lesson with my steel hanging from my handle bars every week."[35] Soon Wally began to perform on KSEL's Saturday morning program "Future Stars of Lubbock," which featured talented youngsters Charlene Condray and James Solley, among others. Around 1949, Wally became a member of the Melody Five, a group organized by Jimmy Johnson which included, at various times, Wayne Hill, James Solley, Wayne Maines, Lester York, Freddy Maxey, Mark Webb, Homer Taylor, and Jimmy Hamer. This group performed for dances throughout the area until Jimmy Johnson left Lubbock and the band broke up.

After performing briefly with Jimmy Comer on the KSEL Western Jamboree, Wally was asked by Hi Pockets Duncan to form a house band for the Jamboree. Wally called several friends from the Melody Five and formed a group that was eventually called Hi Pockets Duncan and the Texas Hotshots. In addition to a daily radio program on KSEL, the Hotshots played six nights a week at the Cotton Club. Moyers recalled, "I was 17 at the time, and [I] was making sixty dollars a week. That was twice what I could make on any day job that I could get." Wally left the Hotshots to get married, but soon he was playing music again. Around 1951, he started to work with Jimmy Comer again, played briefly with Slim Whitman on a Texas tour, worked on Jack Huddle's Circle 13 Roundup on KDUB TV in Lubbock, and eventually rejoined Hi Pockets and the Texas Hotshots.

During the next two decades, Moyers worked with many Lubbock musicians and entertainers, including Wilburn Roach, Bill Mack, Waylon Jennings, Sky Corbin, and Tommy Hancock, as well as leading several of his own bands.[36] Around 1970, Wally gave his steel, amplifier, and his job playing with Tommy Hancock's band to his son, Wally Moyers, Jr. The younger Moyers had never played a steel guitar but went to work with Tommy Hancock's group only a few days after he started learning the instrument. Despite his apparent retirement from music, Wally Sr. continued to play periodically in Lubbock until his death in 1991.[37] Wally Moyers, Jr., is a major musician in the Lubbock music scene today.

Hank Harral was a radio personality, country musician, and record company owner in West Texas from the late 1940s through the 1950s. Harral's music reflects the changing sound of country music during this period, from the western swing of the late 1940s to the honky-tonk sound of the early 1950s to the rockabilly beat of the late 1950s. To collectors of rockabilly music throughout the world, Harral's *Tank Town Boogie* is a highly prized collectible.

Harral was born in 1913 in Pushmataha County, Oklahoma, and moved with his family to Amarillo in 1926. Harral began a career in radio early in his life. As the "Happy Yodeler," he performed over Amarillo stations KGRS and KDAG in 1928. Later he had his own show on KGRS and performed with the Air Sweet Boys. By 1933 Hank was working with the Texas Wranglers over KICA in Clovis, New Mexico. It was here that Harral began his career as a radio announcer. Harral received twelve dollars a week when he started. He later became known as "Hank the Cowhand," so named because of the cowboy music he performed on his program.[38]

Harral relocated to Lubbock in 1947 and began working at KSEL radio.[39] He formed his first group, Hank Harral and the Plains Riders, which consisted of Hank on vocal and guitar, Clyde Perkins on lead guitar, Lee Searsy on rhythm guitar and vocals, Sam Baker on fiddle, and Tollie Stephenson on bass. This group recorded six sides in 1947, but only one selection was released.[40] Harral also recorded during this period with Merle Lindsay's Oklahoma Nightriders.

In 1948, Harral formed a new group, the Palomino Cowhands. This group included Harral on lead guitar and vocals, Ace Ball (Balch) on rhythm guitar, Cecil Hadaway on fiddle, Sam Baker on piano, Harvey Wilson on steel guitar, and Curley Thomas on bass. The group recorded four songs at Lubbock's KSEL radio station in 1949 or 1950; by 1949, Harral was chief announcer and program director at KSEL.[41] In 1950 and 1951 the group recorded again. Harral had contacted the Star Talent record company in Dallas, and several songs from this session were released on that label. Four songs from these KSEL sessions along with "Dilly Dally Doodle" from the 1947 session appear on the Dutch White Label recording *Boppin' Hillbilly, Volume 14*.

Working as a radio personality during these years, Harral had joined KHEM radio in Big Spring by 1957. At this time, he formed Caprock Records to record and publish his original music. He also recorded and released records of other regional artists before closing the company in 1960. Harral released four records under his own name during this period. These were recorded at Ben Hall's recording studio in Big Spring. Included on these sessions, recorded between 1957 and 1959, were Weldon Myrick on lead and steel guitars, Dina Hall (Ben's wife) on bass, and Red Stone on rhythm guitar.

After 1960, Harral continued to work as a radio announcer throughout the West Texas and eastern New Mexico region. In 1984, he was working on radio in Roswell, New Mexico. Hank Harral died December 28, 1985.[42]

Although Harral had formed Caprock to record his own compositions, being in an area with few record labels, he was approached by numerous regional artists who wanted to record.[43] The first of these was Dixie Rogers from Snyder, Texas, a high school senior who wrote her own material. Rogers recorded a total of six songs, backed by the house band at Ben Hall's studio, which included Weldon Myrick, Dina Hall, and Red Stone.

Hoyle Nix recorded six sides for Caprock. Nix had previously recorded with Star Talent in Dallas and the Queen label in Snyder. "Summit Ridge Drive" from these sessions shows off Nix's band for the sophisticated western swing unit it was. Although this group had a smaller sound than that of the big 1940s groups, the guitar work of former Texas Playboy Eldon Shamblin and Red Hayes's electric mandolin solos put this recording up with the best of the Bob Wills recordings.

Other artists who recorded on Caprock included Durwood Haddock, who recorded as Durwood Daily, Roy New and the Trans-Pecos Melody Boys, about whom very little is known, and Ace Ball (Balch), who had played rhythm guitar on Hank Harral's Star Talent material and worked with him in Big Spring on KHEM. Caprock artist Durwood Haddock was a radio announcer and country musician who lived and worked in West

Texas during the 1950s. Raised near Denison in north central Texas, Haddock learned to play several instruments by the time he was in high school. By the early fifties he was playing fiddle in honky-tonks throughout north central Texas and southern Oklahoma. In 1954 he was playing with Tiny Colbert's band, and he moved to Odessa that year with the group. Haddock recalled, "We landed a job at Danceland club there. It was actually the first professional job I ever had. I made $65 a week which was pretty good money in 1954. The gig lasted three months."[44] In Odessa Haddock met Eddie Miller, who had played with the Colbert band before Haddock joined and who had written "Release Me," a big country hit for several artists. Miller rejoined the group and, after losing the Danceland job, they went to work at Weaver's Inn in Kermit. The band during this time included Tiny Colbert, Eddie Miller, Larry Eudy (drums), and Durwood Haddock on fiddle. Haddock reported, "In the fall of 1954, we went to Lamesa, Texas where we did a 30-minute show on KPET radio. Eddie [Miller] was then recording for 4-Star Records and so we became known as the 4-Star Caravan. A fellow by the name of Joe Treadway booked us all over Texas."[45] Haddock and Miller wrote a number of songs together, many of which were later recorded by Lefty Frizzell. "There She Goes" was written during this period. Haddock recorded two of his compositions in October 1954 under the stage name "Durwood Dailey." "There She Goes" and "I Don't Wanna" were recorded at radio station KECK in Odessa. "There She Goes" was recorded by Carl Smith in 1955 and became a major hit of that year. "I Don't Wanna" was later recorded by Patsy Cline.

In the late fifties, Haddock worked as a disc jockey at radio stations around West Texas, including KSFT in Fort Stockton, KECK in Odessa, KVKM in Monahans, and KERB in Kermit. In 1957, he recorded "That's the Way It Goes" for Hank Harral's Big Springs-based Caprock Records. He also recorded for Big D Records and performed several times on the Big D Jamboree in Dallas. In 1962, Haddock had his first national hit with "Big Night at My House," which was leased to United Artists records. He left West Texas in the sixties and eventually relocated to Nashville, where he worked with several music companies as a songwriter, promoter, and distributor.[46]

Television came to West Texas in the early 1950s, and country music quickly became a part of that new medium. KDUB-TV, Channel 13 in Lubbock, was the first television station in West Texas, signing on the air November 13, 1952.[47] Jack Huddle, who hosted KDUB's daily "Children's Theater," also was the host of the one of the first live music broadcasts from the station. "The Circle 13 Dude Ranch" aired for a hour, Saturday nights at 11:00. Featured were Huddle and Clyde Hankins on guitar, Wally Moyers on steel guitar, Harold Giese on bass, Harold's sister Jackie Giese on accordion, and Homer Logan on fiddle.[48] The band performed throughout the region for supermarket openings, oil company functions, civic clubs and special events. To Wally Moyers, the money was good at these events.[49] By KDUB's first anniversary, the "Dude Ranch" had been moved to 7:30 on Thursday nights.[50] A Who's Who of

Lubbock area musicians performed with the band at various times. A 1954 lineup included Clyde Perkins on steel guitar, Harold Giese on bass, Homer Logan on fiddle, Jody Pilliod on guitar, and vocalist Charlene Condray, who later married Lubbock musician Tommy Hancock.

Before the war, the role of women in country music had been very limited. In the late 1940s and through the 1950s, however, women increasingly became involved in country music performance. Perhaps encouraged by the success of national country music performers such as Kitty Wells, West Texas women began to appear as musicians and vocalists throughout the region. Because of their extraordinary love of the music, women performers of the postwar decades overcame the many obstacles to success and made a place for themselves in a business that is still male dominated. In the process, they blazed a trail for the many female country music performers who would follow in the years to come. West Texas women who performed with country groups during the 1950s and early 1960s include Madge Bowlan, pianist with the Miller Brothers in Wichita Falls; Jewett James on piano with Hoyle Nix and many others; Edna Lee, Hope Griffith, Ralna English, and Terry Sue Newman, all vocalists in Lubbock; Jackie Giese on accordion with the Circle 13 Dude Ranchers in Lubbock; and Charlene Condray with the Dude Ranchers and later Tommy Hancock's Roadside Playboys in Lubbock.

Charlene Condray was born in Morton. Both her parents were musical, and Charlene sang with her family at church singings from an early age. In addition to religious material, Charlene's mother and father sang popular country favorites such as Patsy Montana's "I Want to be a Cowboy's Sweetheart" and the songs of Jimmie Rodgers.

When Charlene was eight, the family moved to Lubbock after living in Ohio for several years. Charlene sang in talent contests held at movie theaters on Saturday mornings before the movies were shown. She won prize money, perhaps a handful of dimes or quarters. Through one of these contests she came to the attention of Pop Echols and the Melody Boys quartet. Soon she was performing with this group in and around the Lubbock area at high school auditoriums and theaters on package shows that also featured Bill Myrick and the Mayfield Brothers.

Around 1952, KDUB's Jack Huddle heard Charlene and invited her to guest on the "Circle 13 Dude Ranch" program. In response to the positive letters from viewers, Charlene, at age fourteen, was added to the Dude Rancher band; she continued to perform on the show for several years. Impressed with her singing, Tommy Hancock asked Charlene to join the Roadside Playboys. Hancock's female vocalist, Betty Olive, had left the group, and Hancock was looking for a new singer to perform pop material.

Charlene was singing popular songs by such current artists as Patti Page and Jo Stafford. Country music of the early 1950s was predominantly sung by males, so Charlene had few models in country music on which to base her singing. Charlene's pop style gave the Playboys an added dimension, helping the band to appeal to a larger audience.

Charlene joined the Roadside Playboys and with her mother as chaperone began performing with the group at all their performances, except for club dates. Charlene's mother would not allow her daughter to perform at these venues at so young an age. After several years, Charlene and Tommy started dating and they were eventually married.

Charlene remembered that the rigid standards of behavior expected from all women in the 1950s applied doubly to her as a stage performer. At a time when all young women were encouraged to be careful not to give an impression of impropriety through a word, gesture, or even a glance, just being on stage was a bit daring. Charlene's mother instructed her on proper behavior, reminding her that all eyes were on her when she was on stage and all her actions were important. When performing for high school prom dances, Charlene would dress in the same kind of popular strapless gown worn by the women attending the dance. On one occasion, however, Charlene was asked by a school official to wear a jacket to cover her bare shoulders during her performance on stage. While perfectly acceptable to officials on the dance floor, the dress became too daring or suggestive on stage. Charlene also recalled that in later years when performing at private parties she could not sing some of the honky-tonk material she sang in clubs.

Charlene continued her music career through the 1960s, although the demands of raising children kept her performances to a minimum. In the early 1970s, Charlene and Tommy formed the Supernatural Family Band, a group that included their children. Since the late 1980s, Charlene has performed with her daughters as the Texana Dames.[51]

One of the few women to make a national career in the male-dominated country music scene during the late forties through the fifties was Charline Arthur. Born Charline Highsmith in Henrietta, Texas, on December 2, 1929, she began her career in the East Texas town of Paris, where she learned to play the guitar and sing gospel songs from her mother. Charline bought her first guitar with money earned by refunding soft drink bottles she had picked up from the roadside. After learning a few basic guitar chords, she teamed with her sister Dottie and performed at various family and community functions.

In 1945, Charline performed regularly on a Paris radio station. That same year she won a talent contest sponsored by a traveling medicine show. Not yet sixteen, she joined the medicine show, with her father's permission, and toured throughout Texas. During this tour, she met and eventually married Jack Arthur.

After leaving the medicine show, Charline performed in the regular venues of country performers of the day: clubs and honky-tonks. In 1950, while in Dallas, she made her first record, "I've Got the Boogie Blues" and "Love is a Gamble" for the Nashville-based Bullet label. That year, Arthur relocated to the West Texas town of Kermit, where she formed her own band and performed as a singer and disc jockey on radio station KERB six days a week. Among the talent featured on her program was the Wink Westerners, which included future rock and roll star Roy Orbison.[52]

While singing on the radio in Kermit, Arthur came to the attention of Colonel Tom Parker, later to achieve fame for his discovery and promotion of the young Elvis Presley. Parker was traveling through the area with country performer Eddy Arnold. Impressed with her singing and songwriting, Parker helped Arthur secure a recording contract with RCA Records. Beginning in 1953, Arthur participated in thirteen recording sessions for RCA and for the next few years enjoyed her greatest success as a touring artist. She appeared several times on the Big D Jamboree, the Louisiana Hayride, Red Foley's Ozark Jamboree, and once on the Grand Ole Opry, where parts of the somewhat racy lyrics to "Kiss the Baby Goodnight" had to be left out at the request of the Opry management.

With her increased recording and touring schedule, Arthur left West Texas and by 1957 had moved to Dallas. Although Charline Arthur's career lasted into the 1970s, her impact was not great after the 1950s. What she did offer, along with West coast singer Rose Maddox, was an alternative female role model to the gingham-dressed female singers from the east. Arthur dressed in slacks suits and sang songs with a "bold, brassy and slightly blues-flavored country vocal style," in the words of music historian Bob Allen. He further asserted, "As both singer and a personality, her unique presence was indeed a far cry from the prim and proper image and style that the conservative music industry routinely demanded of female country singers in that era."[53] Arthur herself commented, "I was the first to break out of the Kitty Wells stereotype and boogie woogie. I was shakin' that thing on stage long before Elvis even thought about it."[54] Arthur helped pave the way for such artists as Brenda Lee, Wanda Jackson, and Patsy Cline.

Contest-style fiddling was still popular in the postwar decades. With contests scattered across the region, West Texas fiddlers continued to hone their skills for competition. One of the greatest, Bryant Houston, never recorded commercially and was unknown to the general public, but he won more than 450 first-place finishes in fiddle contests throughout the state and was highly regarded by his fiddle-playing peers. Champion fiddler Texas Shorty, for example, considers Houston one of the greatest Texas-style fiddlers, and Houston was a big influence on Shorty's music.[55] Houston is particularly remembered for his excellent rendition of "Limerock," arguably the most difficult piece in the Texas tradition.

Born William Bryant Houston in Abilene in 1911, he was the son of Captain Poe Houston, a noted fiddler who, according to Bryant, wrote the Texas fiddle standard "Chuck in the Bush."[56] The Houston family formed a band in 1925 and played for the next few years in theaters throughout West Texas, Oklahoma, Arkansas, and Kansas. In the late twenties, the family moved to California where they lived for several years before returning to Texas in the mid-1930s. Back in Texas, the family band played in Winters, Ballinger, and Brownwood. In 1938, "Cap" Houston won the fiddle contest held at Stamford during the Stamford

Stampede celebration.[57] Bryant Houston spent his last years in a nursing home in Rising Star.[58]

In the two decades following World War II, the modern form of West Texas country music took shape. Clubs, honky-tonks, and other drinking and dancing establishments are still important venues for live country music, and modern country bands play the same dance beats (i.e., two-step, waltz, schottische) that groups played in the 1940s. Classic songs from this period, such as Bob Wills's "Faded Love," are on the song lists of nearly every successful West Texas dance band, and the modern country band instrumentation of bass, drums, piano, fiddle, guitar, and steel guitar was firmly established in those years. With only a few changes, such as the inclusion of some rock and roll, West Texas country musicians today continue to play the same type of music fans danced to forty years ago.

Ace Balch (Ball) with his first guitar (Montgomery Ward) in front of the house in which he was born, New Home, Texas, circa 1934. Courtesy Ace Balch.

Miller Brothers Band, late 1940s. Left to right: Bill Jourdan, steel guitar; Smiley Weaver, guitar; Jim McGraw, Leon Gibbs (Miller), fiddle; Dutch Ingram, drums; Troy Jordan, fiddle; Pascal Williams, bass; Madge Bowlan Sutter, piano; and Lee Cochran (Miller), trumpet. Courtesy Keith Ward.

Floyd Tillman publicity photo, 1948. Mrs. J. R. Chatwell Collection. Courtesy Hank Harrison.

Bob Wills and his Texas Playboys, Amarillo, Texas, 1949. Left to right (on stage): Eldon Shamblin, Bob White, Tiny Moore, Luke Wills, Keith Coleman, Bob Wills, Billy Jack Wills, Jack Lloyd, Johnny Gimble, Herb Remington, and Mancel Tierney. Standing on floor: unidentified woman and (shaking hands with Bob Wills) X.I.T Boy, Pat Trotter. Photo by Souvenier Studio, Courtesy Weldon Allard.

Billy Briggs and his X.I.T. Boys promotional postcard, late 1940s. Left to right: Jess Williams, guitar; Billy Briggs, steel guitar; and Weldon Allard, bass. Courtesy Weldon Allard.

Billy Briggs and his X.I.T. Boys remote radio broadcast, late 1940s or early 1950s. Band left to right: Briggs, Williams, and Allard. AMARILLO TIMES photo, Ray Monroe. Courtesy Weldon Allard.

RCA recording artist Charline
Arthur, publicity photo, mid
1950s. Courtesy Keith Ward.

KDUB-TV Circle 13 Dude Ranchers Band, circa 1950. Left to right: Jack Huddle, guitar; Charlene Condray (Hancock) vocals;
Homer Logan fiddle; Clyde Perkins, steel guitar; Jody Pilliod, bass; and Clyde Hankins, guitar. Courtesy Homer Logan.

Hank Harral, KSEL Western Jamboree Program, June 3, 1950. Courtesy Pete Curtis.

Ace Balch (Ball) performs at the Midtown Jamboree, Amarillo, 1955. Bozo Darnell on fiddle and Ace Ball on guitar. Courtesy Ace Balch.

Musician/promoter "Bozo" Darnell publicity photo, 1950s. Courtesy Keith Ward.

KSEL Western Jamboree Program, May 13, 1950. Courtesy Pete Curtis.

Slim Willet in the KRBC-TV studio with the Hired Hands (band) and the Starlight Sisters, 1953. Courtesy Hank Harrison.

Slim Willet (Winston Moore)
publicity shot, 1953. KRBC-TV,
Abilene, Texas. Courtesy Hank
Harrison.

The Rambling Cowboys, KSEL Western
Jamboree program, July 1, 1950. Courtesy
Pete Curtis.

WESTERN JAMBOREE PROGRAM

JIM EVANS, Publisher

Allen's Arena — 606 Texas Ave. — Saturday, July 1,

THE RAMBLING COWBOYS—Miss June, David Dodge with
Sandy, Les Willard and Earl Montgomery

rs open at 6—Show starts at 7—On the air from 7:45 until

"Pappy" Dave Stone, founder of KDAV,
Lubbock's first all country music format
radio station. From KSEL Western
Jamboree program, July 22, 1950.
Courtesy Pete Curtis.

Charlene Condray, vocals; Homer Logan, fiddle; and Jack Huddle, guitar. KDUB-TV March of Dimes Telethon, Lubbock, Texas, 1954. Courtesy Dub Rogers Collection, South Plains College, Levelland, Texas.

The Hired Hands on stage at the Big State Jamboree, Abilene, Texas, 1953. Left to right: Mac Fletcher, J. L. Jones, James Wood, Rex Jones, and Smokey Donaldson. Courtesy Smokey Donaldson.

Shorty Underwood and the Brushcutters, 1953. Left to right: standing: Jean Standsburg, guitar; Shorty Underwood, fiddle; and Georgia Underwood, bass. Seated left to right: Vaughn O'Shields, guitar, steel; Price Self, piano; and Earl Montgomery, guitar, bass. KRBC photo. Courtesy Hank Harrison.

Bill Mack performs at Womble Oldsmobile dealership promotion, Lubbock, Texas, 1959. Mack is a noted singer/radio personality who worked in Lubbock in the late 1950s. The band includes Wally Moyers Sr. on steel guitar. Courtesy Dub Rogers Collections, South Plains College, Levelland, Texas.

The four Wills brothers in the 1950s. All four were musicians and bandleaders in their own right. Left to right: Luke, Johnny Lee, Bob, and Billy Jack. Courtesy Billy Joe Foster.

The Roadside Playboys with guest vocalist Tommy Duncan at the Glassarama Club, Lubbock, Texas, 1959. Left to right: Louis Martinez, guitar; Guy "Tex" Brooks, drums; guest Tommy Duncan (at microphone); Homer Logan, fiddle; and bandleader Tommy Hancock, fiddle. Courtesy Homer Logan.

The Silver Saddle Club, Odessa, Texas, 1960. Left to right: Dale Burkett, piano; Tommy Allen, bass; Bill Myrick, guitar; Clint Bagwell, drums; Freddie Frank, fiddle; Merle David, fiddle; and Jimmy Latham, steel guitar (not pictured). Courtesy Bill Myrick.

Jody Nix fiddles with Bob Wills at Musick's Night Club, Midland, Texas, 1966 or '67. Left to right: Jody Nix, fiddle; Hoyle Nix, drums; Bob Wills, fiddle; and Joe Andrews, vocal. Courtesy Southwest Collection, Texas Tech University, Lubbock.

Hoyle Nix and the West Texas Cowboys at the Stampede Club in Big Spring. Left to right: Hoyle Nix, fiddle; Ben Nix, rhythm guitar, vocal; Tommy Harvel, lead guitar; Larry Nix, bass, vocals; Jody Nix, drums, vocals; and Dusty Stewart, steel guitar. Courtesy Southwest Collection, Texas Tech University, Lubbock.

First place winner William Bryant Houston, age 62, performing at the Texas Cowboy Reunion Old Fiddler's Contest, Stamford, Texas, July 5, 1973. Courtesy ABILENE REPORTER NEWS.

Homer Logan publicity photo, circa 1985. Logan was a popular Western Swing fiddler in Texas and brother of Bluegrass fiddler, Tex Logan. Courtesy Homer Logan.

Frankie McWhorter on fiddle and author Carr on guitar perform at South Plains College in Levelland, Texas, 1986. Courtesy South Plains College.

Jody Nix publicity photo, 1992.
Courtesy Jody Nix.

5

MOUNTAIN

MUSIC

ON THE

PRAIRIE

In the mid-1940s an exciting new music developed on the stage of the Grand Ole Opry in Nashville, with Kentucky-born musician Bill Monroe as its fountainhead. Many miles away, in West Texas, this new bluegrass music captured the attention of a small but influential group of musicians, including Edd Mayfield and Benjamin "Tex" Logan, who both later became legendary bluegrass music figures. As West Texans, Mayfield and Logan brought a unique approach to this eastern mountain music style called bluegrass.

Bluegrass music made its way onto the plains of West Texas and into the homes of the people who lived there just as it did in the eastern mountain states: through the dazzling performances of Bill Monroe and the Bluegrass Boys on the national radio broadcasts of the WSM Grand Ole Opry from Nashville. Although not the first or only nationally broadcast program of country music, the Grand Ole Opry became the longest lived and most influential of such programs, broadcasting live country music performances every weekend beginning November 28, 1925.[1] Starting with humble broadcasts from a Nashville hotel room studio featuring local rural folk artists, the Opry grew to national prominence after World War II with nationwide network hook-ups, developing into a major force in the promotion of the country music industry emerging in Nashville.

Bluegrass music surfaced as a new musical genre under the direction of Grand Ole Opry member Bill Monroe. Hailing from Kentucky, the bluegrass state, Monroe called his act Bill Monroe and the Bluegrass Boys. The name *bluegrass* was eventually taken up by fans, promoters, and record retailers in an effort to identify this music, which they perceived as different from the other forms of country music.[2]

Bluegrass music is a modern expression and outgrowth of the rural stringband music of the Southeast during the 1920s and 1930s. Such bands as Gid Tanner and the Skillet Lickers, Charlie Poole and the North Carolina Ramblers, and the Carter Family were the popular radio and recording artists of their day for rural audiences. Out of this stringband tradition came Bill Monroe of Rosine, Kentucky.

First in a band with his brothers Charlie and Birch and later teaming only with Charlie, mandolinist Bill Monroe had a successful career in country music during the mid-1930s. Bill and Charlie ultimately split; in 1939, Bill formed his backup band, the Bluegrass Boys, and auditioned for and became a member of the Grand Ole Opry in the fall of that year. His unit was not much different from other country music bands in its instrumentation and repertoire. What was to make Monroe's music unique was his vision and single-mindedness. According to Monroe, bluegrass music began with his arrangement in 1939 of "The New Muleskinner Blues." This reworking of a Jimmie Rodgers blue yodel song was propelled at the rapid tempo of a fiddle breakdown by Monroe's guitar rhythm. Usually a mandolin player, Monroe was unable to get the feel and rhythm he envisioned for the music from his guitar player, so he played the guitar part himself. This driving rhythm was to become the power and force behind the new emerging bluegrass sound.

By the mid-1940s, Bill Monroe, with the Bluegrass Boys, had become an established, commercially successful act: they had a spot on the Opry's weekly broadcasts, a recording contract, a regular touring schedule, and a following among the upcoming young musicians in the South. The unit that was to define the bluegrass sound came together in Monroe's band when singer/guitarist Lester Flatt from Sparta, Tennessee, banjo picker Earl Scruggs from Shelby, North Carolina, and fiddler Chubby Wise from Lake City, Florida, joined forces. The hallmark sound of this unit was the polished, blazing, rippling three-fingered picking style of Earl Scruggs on the five-string banjo, the smooth and mellow tones of Lester Flatt's lead vocals, and the blues fiddling of Chubby Wise, combined with the visionary drive and feel on the mandolin of their leader Bill Monroe. This band was together until 1948, when Flatt and Scruggs left Monroe and formed their group, the Foggy Mountain Boys.

After Monroe's initial period of commercial success with this seminal band in the late forties, mass-appeal country music centering around "the Nashville sound" and, later, rock and roll, would push his music into relative obscurity. Added to this trend was Monroe's unwillingness to change his music to suit that changing market. Indeed, Monroe's refusal to regularly use drums and electric instruments on his recordings may have been responsible for his limited popularity in West Texas. To many West Texans accustomed to the dance-oriented music of Bob Wills and Ernest Tubb, Bill Monroe's music seemed foreign and undanceable.

Diminished popularity and the resulting decreased income during the fifties and into the sixties made it difficult for Monroe to keep a well-rehearsed band intact, as he had with the Flatt, Scruggs and Wise unit. Despite the fluidity in band membership during this time, he managed to record some of the most powerful and meaningful music of his career, such as "Panhandle Country," "Rawhide," "Uncle Pen," and "Memories of Mother and Dad." As the founder of the music, a member of the prestigious Grand Ole Opry, and a Decca Records artist with an unbreakable will and personal charisma, Monroe managed to attract many young players and singers to his music. Membership in his band did not necessarily lead to fame and fortune, but it was a promising path into the business and a chance to play and learn from the master of the bluegrass sound. Two West Texans who played an important role in the Monroe story beginning in the 1950s were singer/guitarist Edd Mayfield of Dimmitt and fiddler/songwriter Benjamin "Tex" Logan of Big Spring.

Born and raised on the Green Valley Ranch near Dawn in 1926, Thomas Edward "Edd" Mayfield and his brothers Herb and Smokey were among the first musicians on the plains of West Texas to embrace this basically eastern mountain-born bluegrass music. Like many others in the region, they gained a heightened awareness of the outside world with the introduction of the radio. On these remote plains, the first radios, which were battery powered, came through the mail from catalog stores such as Sears, Roebuck and Company.

Edd Mayfield's elementary school classmate Alvie Ivey of Pep remembered driving the family's Model A Ford up to a house window and hooking the car battery to the radio to catch the broadcast of the Grand Ole Opry. Despite the great distances involved, West Texans could receive WSM's clear channel signal directly from Nashville, and from time to time, thirty-minute segments of the Opry were broadcast on the nearby stations in Amarillo and Lubbock. Ivey related that it was not unusual to run the car battery down with this Saturday evening entertainment and later have to join his brothers in push-starting the car to get it back to the barn.[3]

Edd Mayfield and his brothers were involved in family music-making before the introduction of the radio into the household. Both parents, William Fletcher Mayfield and Penelope Ruth Drake Mayfield, were musicians. William played the fiddle, while Penelope accompanied him on the piano or guitar. The couple met at a community dance and later performed at house parties and dances through their courting days, playing such staple fiddle tunes as "Durang's Hornpipe," "Wednesday Night Waltz," "Red Wing," and one of William's favorites, "Forked Deer."[4] William and Penelope were soon married, and in 1916 they moved to West Texas from Clay County, in north-central Texas.

William and Penelope Mayfield taught all their children, six sons and two daughters, to play musical instruments and sing. The mandolin, because of its small size and the ease of fretting the strings to form chords, was the first instrument each child learned to play. Later the boys each learned to play the guitar to accompany their father's fiddling. The sisters would join in to sing old songs like "The Jeweling Pond" and "Life's Railway to Heaven." Arnold Geiger, a Santa Fe Railroad worker, taught the boys to play "runs" on their guitars to fill in between the chord changes and rhythm strums. Herb Mayfield remembered that he and his brothers were so interested in music that they would often race in to the house after doing the ranch chores in order to have time to practice. Eventually, Smokey chose the fiddle as his instrument. Too small to hold the full-sized instrument correctly, young Smokey propped the fiddle between his chest and the wall of the barn in order to hold it in position to play. He continued to play in that position, with the fiddle on his chest rather than under his chin, into adulthood.

In addition to radio, the phonograph also brought the sounds of distant musicians to West Texans in the late 1920s and the early 1930s. In the mid-1920s, the recording industry found an audience for "hillbilly" or "mountain music" records in the homes of the rural folk of the Southeast. Increasingly popular, those recordings made their way out to the country music fans of West Texas. The Mayfields would travel thirty miles to a small music store in Hereford to find recordings of the music they liked. Record stores often provided a booth equipped with a record player for a trial listen before the purchase.

Searching for the string music they enjoyed, Herb, Smokey, and Edd came across a recording of Gid Tanner and the Skillet Lickers. This stringband group from northern Georgia recorded during the late 1920s and featured the blind guitarist Riley Puckett. Behind the fiddling of Gid Tanner and Clayton McMichen, Puckett displayed a dazzling array of guitar runs that raised the level of guitar accompaniment to a status almost equal to that of the soloist. This guitar style appealed to the Mayfields, who quickly bought and ordered more Skillet Licker recordings. Each brother tried his hand at deciphering the style of Riley Puckett, and his guitar runs soon became part of their music. Those Puckett-style runs would later serve Edd well during his tenure as a guitarist with Bill Monroe's band. Monroe was one of the Mayfields' favorite country performers, and they bought the records of the Monroe Brothers and later those of Bill Monroe and the Bluegrass Boys.

The Mayfield family moved off the ranch to Dimmitt in 1932 but continued their ranching and farming activity. Besides leading the rugged life of a cowhand, Edd was active in athletics, playing on the first Dimmitt High School team to go to the state championship. An athletic bent also was apparent in the boys' love of rodeo competition. Specializing in calf roping and wild cow milking, the brothers won several events. Later, when Edd was living in Indiana, he would use his rodeo skills during visits to Dimmitt to raise money for his family's return trip.

Edd seems to have been the most performance-oriented of the brothers. Alvie Ivey recalled that Edd brought his guitar to school and, using the covered entry to the basement boiler room as a stage, entertained the other students during recess.[5]

After military service in World War II, the brothers returned to Dimmitt to resume their farming and ranching life, and they continued to play music together for their own entertainment. They chose their instruments to achieve a band sound: Edd concentrated on the guitar; Smokey, the fiddle; and Herb, the mandolin, the better to imitate the sound of the Monroe band with Flatt, Scruggs, and Wise. Although the Mayfield Brothers never featured a banjo, often considered the hallmark of the bluegrass sound, they nonetheless thought of themselves as disciples of the Monroe bluegrass style.

An army buddy of Edd's sparked increased activity for the Mayfield brothers. Bill Myrick, from Monroe, Louisiana, had worked for Bill Monroe as a driver and singer and had promoted some Monroe appearances in Louisiana and elsewhere in the South shortly after the war. Myrick and Edd had kept in touch, and with Edd's encouragement, in March of 1950 Myrick moved to West Texas to join the Mayfield Brothers as guitarist and singer. The group performed as Bill Myrick and the Mayfield Brothers.[6]

Throughout 1950, Myrick and the Mayfields appeared as regulars on the weekly KSEL Jamboree in Lubbock. Their fifteen-minute segment of bluegrass music opened many of the Saturday night broadcasts. Sonny Curtis, in grade school at the time, remembered hearing the Mayfields on the Jamboree, and he saw them as the stars of the show: "They had a lot of charisma and really played good back in those days. Edd could just hang in there with the best of them, I thought." Promoter Dave Stone recalled that Bill Myrick and the Mayfield Brothers would just "disrupt the show when they would come in and walk down the arena. Whoever was on stage was practically not heard because they would get such a hand, walking down the aisle."[7]

In late 1950 Bill Myrick promoted concerts by Bill Monroe and the Bluegrass Boys in Amarillo, Plainview, Big Spring, and Lubbock, with Bill Myrick and the Mayfield Brothers as the opening act. Also on the Plainview date were the West coast-based Maddox Brothers and Rose, a popular country group who performed in West Texas many times during their career. Although the shows were not well attended, it was an exhilarating few days for the Mayfields. Herb recalled being amazed that Monroe and his musicians played so well, with breath-taking tempos, outstanding harmonies, and flawless instrumental skill. It was no wonder that Herb, Smokey, and Edd were thrilled with the music, for it featured, in addition to Monroe on mandolin and vocals, Jimmy Martin on lead vocals and guitar, Rudy Lyle on banjo, and Red Taylor on fiddle—one of Monroe's great bands. It was a heady time for the three brothers. This was Monroe's first meeting with the Mayfields, and he was impressed with their performances, commenting to Herb that he especially liked their version of the Browns Ferry Four's "Keep on the Firing Line."

Myrick also arranged for the group to have a guest spot on the Louisiana Hayride in Shreveport. Bill Myrick and the Mayfield Brothers appeared on the Hayride in April 1951 and were such a hit that they were included in a feature article about the radio program in *Shreveport Magazine*. The novelty of "FOUR COWPUNCHERS from Dimmitt, Texas" playing hillbilly music appealed to the management, audience, and media.[8] The band was so well received that regular Hayride member Webb Pierce gave up his fifteen-minute spot so that they could perform again. Later that same night, as a result of the audience response and their obvious talents, Myrick and the Mayfields were offered a regular spot on the Hayride that would begin in two weeks.

Upon his return to the hotel that night, Edd received a message to call Bill Monroe. Monroe, remembering Edd's singing and playing skills, had called to offer him a job in his band. It was a terrible dilemma for the group, but after some discussion they decided that Edd should not pass up this opportunity.[9] This was to be the first of three stints for Edd under Monroe's tutelage. Myrick tried working the Hayride with another group but eventually moved back to Odessa in West Texas, where he worked variously as a police officer, country disc jockey, bandleader, and concert promoter. Herb and Smokey returned to West Texas and continued their careers in ranching and farming, performing only periodically.

Edd's West Texas background made a big impression on his fellow Bluegrass Boys. Many of Monroe's sidemen who worked with Edd shared the same observation: "He was a real cowboy, you know." Edd always kept a rope with him and would keep in practice by roping his fellow band members. Banjo player Larry Richardson fondly remembered Edd demonstrating his roping skill by having Larry run as fast as he could, and then Edd would rope and pull him to the ground.[10]

Bobby Hicks, fiddler on many of Monroe's classic recordings, noted Edd's physical strength, which was required of the rhythm guitarists in the early days of country music, when sound-reproduction technology was primitive and guitars unamplified. Edd, said Hicks, could "chord a guitar all day long and not get tired."[11] In addition to his endurance and power, Edd's rhythm guitar playing was musically as strong and solid as that of any who had performed with Monroe. Monroe banjoist Joe Drumright said of Edd, "You couldn't get him out of time, and he played some of the best backing notes you ever heard in your life. Edd was way ahead of his time. There wasn't anyone even close to him back then."[12] Eventually, Edd would record one of the rare guitar solos to appear on a Monroe recording with his bass string rendition on "Panhandle Country."

Vocally, Edd was a perfect match to Monroe's singing, according to John Hartford, banjo player, fiddler, writer, and composer of "Gentle on My Mind." Hartford was backstage at the Grand Ole Opry in the late 1950s and heard what he identified as Monroe's powerful, stylized singing coming from one of the dressing rooms. On searching out the Monroe sound, he was surprised to find it was Mayfield.[13]

On October 28, 1951, during his first stint with Monroe, Edd recorded "The First Whippoorwill" and "Christmas Time's A-Coming," both destined to become bluegrass standards.[14] Edd stayed with Monroe from 1951 until early 1952 and then returned to Texas. Monroe was having difficulty getting show dates, and as a result he could not pay enough to attract and keep musicians. Brother Herb recalled that Edd could not make enough to support his family by playing with Monroe. At the end of one of his stints as a Bluegrass Boy, Edd was so broke that Herb and Smokey had to drive to Bean Blossom, Indiana, where Edd was living, and provide the transportation and money to get him back to Texas.[15]

Back in Texas, Edd worked as a cowboy and again played with his brothers, who were appearing as the Green Valley Boys on a daily show on radio station KGNC in Amarillo. The brothers drove to Amarillo on Saturdays and recorded a whole week of programs, which were sponsored by a Ford dealership and a lumber yard. During the week they enjoyed listening to their own music on the radio each afternoon.

In early 1953 Edd once again moved east, this time to work with Bill Monroe's brother Birch, who managed Bill's country music show, the Brown County Jamboree, in Bean Blossom, Indiana. Operating out of an old barn, Birch ran the weekend shows that Bill booked, featuring some local musicians and headlined by Bill's fellow Grand Ole Opry acts. Edd, Birch, and banjoist Larry Richardson performed as the house band and opening act or accompanied the featured solo artist if need be. While in

Bean Blossom, Edd and his family and Larry Richardson made a trip back to Dimmitt for a two-week visit. Richardson, from North Carolina, was one of the earliest banjo players performing in the three-fingered picking style popularized by Earl Scruggs just a few years before. During the visit, Richardson played frequently in the area with Herb, Smokey, and Edd. Larry was the first banjo player of this style that Herb Mayfield had ever played with, and he believes that Larry was the first such player that many of his musician friends on the plains had ever seen.[16] After his return to Bean Blossom, Edd got a call from Bill Monroe to rejoin the band, replacing Jimmy Martin. On June 26, 1954, Edd recorded some more classic Monroe material, including "Close By," "My Little Georgia Rose," and "Put My Little Shoes Away," all vocal solos by Monroe. In September of that year Edd participated in a new recording of an earlier Monroe hit, "Blue Moon of Kentucky." Few of the recordings of this period featured Edd as Monroe's singing partner, as most cuts were vocal solos by Monroe.[17]

Again the pay was not enough to support a wife and growing family, and Edd returned to Dimmitt. This time he went to work for rodeo producer Morris Stevens of Silverton, Texas. Edd handled the Stevens livestock that was used in the major rodeos in the Texas panhandle, New Mexico, and Oklahoma. He also entered a number of these rodeos as a contestant. But the Texas ranch life was not enough for Edd. He had a vision of a music career of his own, or perhaps with his brothers. At Norman Petty's studio in Clovis, New Mexico, Herb, Smokey, and Edd recorded "Poison Love" and had about ten demo copies pressed, as Herb said, "with the hope of trying to get a record contract in Nashville." This was mostly Edd's idea, as Herb doubted that he would or could have made the move if they had gotten a record deal, due to family and work obligations.[18]

After Edd's final return to Nashville in early 1958, he recorded a number of songs with Monroe, later released on the gospel album *I Saw the Light*. Edd sang lead and some tenor in the quartets and played guitar on two instrumentals, "Panhandle Country," and "Scotland."[19] This was Edd's last recording session as a Bluegrass Boy. While on tour with Monroe, he succumbed to leukemia in a hospital in Bluefield, West Virginia, in July 1958.[20]

In all, Edd Mayfield's recorded output includes only the twenty songs he made as a member of Bill Monroe's Bluegrass Boys, the Mayfield Brothers' demo, and one live recording sought by collectors. The studio recordings make up some of Monroe's most powerful and fertile music and reveal Edd as one of the finest guitarists and singers in the long line of outstanding musicians who have contributed to Monroe's bluegrass sound. This relatively small library of recorded material, coupled with Edd's early death, has led Doug Green, country music historian and former Bluegrass Boy, to label Edd Mayfield "the mystery man" of bluegrass.[21]

Many of the talented young performers of bluegrass emerging during the 1960s looked to Edd Mayfield as a source of power in the music.

Peter Rowan, a guiding figure in the urban youth involvement in blue-grass music and a pivotal member of Monroe's band from 1965 through 1967, sang a song he learned from a rare, noncommercial tape recording of a Monroe show featuring Edd Mayfield. On this tape Edd sang "I'm Knocking on Your Door" and a Red Taylor composition, "I'm Not Broke But I'm Badly Bent." Rowan recorded "I'm Knocking on Your Door" on the album *Old and in the Way* and titled one of his own albums *The First Whippoorwill*, the first song Edd recorded with Monroe. Mandolinist David Grisman also heard that tape and recorded the Red Taylor song, using Ricky Skaggs as the vocalist.[22]

In addition to Edd's influence in bluegrass, the Mayfield Brothers' radio performances and their personal appearances in the West Texas region are important early memories of many of the musical greats to come from West Texas. Sonny Curtis, Waylon Jennings, and Buddy Holly all heard and were inspired by the music of the Mayfield Brothers.[23]

After the band's active period of performance in the 1950s, Herb, a welder in Dimmitt, continued to sing and play in area bluegrass jam sessions, and Smokey, foreman of the Turkey Track Ranch near Spearman, played only occasionally at family get-togethers. On May 6, 1989, a tribute to the Mayfield Brothers was held at South Plains College in Levelland with a concert performed to a full house by Herb, Smokey, Edd's son Freddy, and Smokey's son Clint.

Another native West Texan has had a long and influential career in bluegrass music. Benjamin "Tex" Logan was born in 1927 in Coahoma, ten miles east of Big Spring. His father, Benjamin F. Logan, Sr., known as Frank, was a respected old-time fiddler and fiddle collector who moved to West Texas from Centerville, Alabama, shortly after the turn of the century. As an old-time breakdown fiddler, he spent many social evenings involved in "fiddlings." On these occasions, people would gather at the home of a fiddler or fiddle enthusiast to socialize to the sounds of breakdowns, waltzes, schottisches, polkas, and popular melodies performed by the community fiddlers. These gatherings were often held in the Logan home. One of Frank's fiddling friends in Howard County was Jonah Nix, father of Hoyle Nix and grandfather of Jody Nix, the western swing performers from Big Spring.

Growing up in this atmosphere, Tex, not surprisingly, aspired to be a fiddler like his father and took violin lessons. Finding that the lessons did not include the breakdowns that his father played, he became discouraged at the chore of practice, and soon his heart was not in the fiddle. His love of music, however, drew him to the school band, for which he played trumpet from grade school through high school.

One day during his last year in high school, Tex experienced what might be called a supernatural happening:

> It suddenly hit me one day, I remember it very plainly. Going home from school, suddenly I had a feeling in my arm. The big thing is the bow. You've got to have that rhythm in the bow or know what to do with the bow. I could feel it, and I went in the

bedroom, shut myself in there, got my fiddle out. I hadn't played in a long time, and kind of played, kept sawing around until I could kind of play "Arkansas Traveler." That's how I got going pretty good.[24]

Around this time Tex bought a few used records from juke box supplier Oscar Glick in Big Spring.[25] Among these records was a Bill Monroe recording of "Katy Hill" featuring supercharged fiddler Tommy Magness. Tex's excitement over this recording led his younger brother Homer to use this recording to wake Tex in the mornings for school. Radio broadcasts of the Grand Ole Opry were popular in the Logan home, and young Tex heard many fiddlers, including those in Monroe's band, who were among the finest. From this early exposure to what Tex calls "mountain fiddling" and his proximity to his father's eastern style, he developed an affinity for mountain-style fiddling rather than the western swing and Texas contest-style of fiddling that attracted most other Texas-born fiddlers.

Tex played the fiddle around the house, with his brother Russell on guitar and Homer on the mandolin. Tex also became friends with a transplanted East Texas fiddler, H. M. Hubbard. Although Hubbard was much older than Tex, the two shared a mutual interest in the fiddle and traveled to fiddle socials together. Tex later recorded "Jordan Am a Hard Road to Travel," which he learned from Hubbard, who called the tune "The Old Grey Goose."

Despite the call of the fiddle, Tex let the "feeling in my arm" lie partially dormant to pursue an electrical engineering degree at Texas Tech University in Lubbock. His college studies allowed him little time to play until his senior year, when he performed on a few occasions around campus or when H. M. Hubbard visited for fiddle socializing. When time permitted, he visited the Halsey Drugstore to hear the Drug Store Cowboys, who played through the noon hour for the lunch crowd at the drugstore food counter.

Upon graduation from Texas Tech, Tex was accepted as a research assistant at the Massachusetts Institute of Technology in Cambridge, Massachusetts. Before heading east, he worked with Hoyle Nix's western swing band in Big Spring the summer of 1946. Tex met several fine musicians working with Nix, including fiddler Red Hayes, composer of the hit song "Satisfied Mind." Hoyle and Tex both loved fiddle breakdowns, and the two played twin fiddle renditions of their favorite tunes at every dance show. Tex continued to play with the Hoyle Nix group every time he was home.

Tex had a fine send-off to Boston and MIT. He had sent in a request to Big Howdy Forrester and Georgia Slim, fiddlers featured on live broadcasts from KRLD in Dallas, to play "Listen to the Mockingbird" and "Black Mountain Blues" for his farewell, which they did.

Tex left to attend MIT in the fall of 1946 with his fiddle in hand and music in his head. By this time he admitted he "really had the fiddle bug." Many times during his college days he let his classes and research duties slide and went off to play music. Living in the Boston area, Tex looked for any opportunity to play. Square dancing was popular among the college students and, although Tex had never been to a square dance, let alone played for one in his native Texas, he volunteered to provide the fiddle music at these dances, accompanied on twelve-string guitar by fellow college student Dick Best.

Spurred by the thrill of performing, Tex and Dick searched for another venue and appeared on a local Boston radio station, WMEX, where they were heard by Jerry Howorth and Sky Snow, a popular country music act in the Boston area. Impressed with Tex's fiddling, they hired him in the spring of 1947 to perform full-time with their band. Jerry and Sky and the Melody Men worked all over New England and into Nova Scotia, promoting themselves through their radio show on WHDH in Boston. Jerry and Sky hung the exotic-sounding name of "Tex" on Logan to appeal to their eastern audience. Included in the band with Tex was Ralph Jones, playing dobro and mandolin, and Allen "Bud" Arthur on string bass. Tex described the style of the band as "old-time mountain like the Blue Sky Boys, Whitey and Hogan, mixed in with [the yodeling style of] Montana Slim."[26]

The pressure of traveling all over New England to perform with Jerry and Sky led Tex in 1947 to request a reduction in his course studies and to resign his research assistantship to work full-time in music. Many times Tex would not get back to town until the morning hours, dragging into school and his research duties at three or four in the afternoon. His graduate school adviser would not grant the reduction, commenting that only foreign students were allowed a reduced load in order to work. Tex suggested that Texas was foreign enough, but the adviser denied the request. His more sympathetic department head, H. L. Hazen, suggested that he quit school and try music but extended an invitation to return if the music career didn't work out. Tex decided to give up his assistantship in favor of the music business. The dilemma for Tex throughout his career was how to balance music with, first, school, and then later, family and work.

Jerry and Sky's success was cut short by a bit of bad advice offered by the group's manager. The manager felt that the "grass was greener" in the area of Albany, New York, and in the spring of 1948 the band made the move there, giving up their radio show and their audience. Shut out by the musicians' union in Albany and unable to get on the radio, the band soon dissolved. In the summer of 1948 Tex returned to West Texas to work in the oil fields around Midland and again played with Hoyle Nix in Big Spring.

It did not take much encouragement to get Tex out of the oil field business and back into music. Ralph Jones, who played with Tex in the Jerry and Sky unit, had moved on to work with Wilma Lee and Stoney Cooper and the Clinch Mountain Clan on the WWVA Jamboree in Wheeling, West Virginia. Ralph invited Tex to move to Wheeling and try the music business there. Wheeling's Jamboree was comparable to Nashville's Grand Ole Opry but with an audience mostly in the Northeast.

Tex was hired to work with Red Belcher and the Kentucky Ridge Runners. The Ridge Runners were Tex and Everett and Bea Lilly, a mandolin, guitar, and vocal duet from West Virginia. They worked the early morning radio show hosted by Belcher in addition to performing on the Jamboree. In 1948, while in Wheeling, Tex recorded two songs with the Red Belcher group: "Kentucky Is Only a Dream," and "The Old Grey Goose," the piece Tex learned from H. M. Hubbard.[27]

Later, Tex signed on with Hawkshaw Hawkins and Big Slim, "the Lone Cowboy," who had teamed up to perform together on the Jamboree. Hawkins would gain additional notoriety in losing his life in the plane crash that killed the legendary country singer Patsy Cline.

Tex felt guilty about leaving MIT and the education his parents had sacrificed for and also discovered that the music business was not as lucrative as he had hoped. In February of 1949, he returned to MIT as a research assistant.

Back in school, Tex continued to play, working around the Boston area with Frank and Pete Lane, known as the Lane Brothers. During the summers of 1949, 1950, and 1951, he traveled to Wheeling and worked with Wilma Lee and Stoney Cooper and the Clinch Mountain Clan, telling the school officials that he was returning to Texas to help with his father's mail route. During these summers off from school Tex recorded with Wilma Lee and Stoney Cooper "Ain't Gonna Work Tomorrow," "Legend of the Dogwood Tree," and "White Rose" in New York City and "Sunny Side of the Mountain" and "Stoney, Are You Mad at Your Gal?" in Nashville. In all, Tex recorded fifteen sides with Wilma Lee and Stoney Cooper between 1950 and 1952, playing fiddle, harmonica, and piano.[28]

Despite his heavy playing and touring schedule, Tex completed his studies and received a bachelor's degree from MIT in 1951. With draft into the military imminent, he spent the summer playing with Wilma Lee and Stoney Cooper. The last show he worked with them before returning to Texas and the draft was a coliseum show in Baltimore in October 1951. The bill also included Flatt and Scruggs, Wayne Raney, Cowboy Copas, and Bill Monroe and the Bluegrass Boys. Tex, an admirer of Monroe's music, now had the chance to meet Monroe. While working with the Lilly Brothers, Tex had written a Christmas song, "Christmas Time's A-Comin'" with Monroe in mind. Backstage at this show, Tex and dobroist Buck Graves (also known as "Uncle Josh") sang the song for Monroe, who liked it immediately and agreed to record it. Tex, on his way to Texas, met with Monroe in Nashville and taught him the song. Logan was to return to Nashville in a week or two to fiddle on Monroe's recording of the song. Tex had worked out the fiddle part using an odd tuning that Monroe liked. Unfortunately, Tex and his brother Russell had car trouble on the drive to Nashville and Tex was unable to make the date. Coincidentally, West Texan Edd Mayfield shared the vocal chores with Monroe, thus ensuring a Texas contribution on the recording. After the recording date, Monroe called Tex and played the cut over the phone to get Tex's approval, which he gave.

Tex received a deferment from the draft in 1951 to become a member of the research staff at MIT doing work on missile guidance systems. He attended school and played music through the winter of 1951 with Frank and Pete Lane. Billing themselves as the Lane Brothers and Logan, they landed a spot on the Hayloft Jamboree on WCOP in Boston hosted by Nelson Bragg, the Merry Mayor of Milo, Maine. This radio show, performed before a live audience, was a big success, bringing in well-known performers to the area. The first big-time performer on the show was Tex's old boss Hawkshaw Hawkins, who scored a big hit with his rendition of "Rattlesnake Daddy."

Guitarist Frank Lane was drafted into the service, and in search of a replacement, Pete and Tex traveled south, eventually to Raleigh, North Carolina, where they visited with bluegrass performers Flatt and Scruggs and inquired about their former mandolin player and singer Curly Seckler. Mandolinist Everett Lilly, who was working with Flatt and Scruggs, told Tex confidentially that he was hoping to leave the band and rejoin his brother Bea. Everett explained he would be willing to leave Flatt and Scruggs if Tex could use them both. Tex felt there might be a possibility of using both brothers but first wanted to locate Curly Seckler to offer him the job. Unable to locate Seckler, Tex and Pete returned to Boston. Tex recalled, "Shortly after we got back to Boston Everett called and said they were coming up. . . . Everett and Bea show[ed] up in Boston, along with a young banjo picker, Don Stover, . . . and then we form[ed] the first bluegrass band in Boston, the Confederate Mountaineers."[29]

The Lilly Brothers with Pete Lane and Tex Logan performed as much as seven nights a week at clubs like the Hillbilly Ranch and on the radio program Hayloft Jamboree. Performing with the Lilly Brothers, Tex was heard by a new generation of New England area players who went on to have influential careers in bluegrass, including guitarist and singer Peter Rowan, singer and record producer Jim Rooney, banjoist Bill Keith, and mandolinist Joe Val.

Tex again found himself neglecting his studies. He quit performing with the band full-time but continued to appear occasionally as the need would arise. The Lilly Brothers and Don Stover continued playing and spent many years in Boston at the Hillbilly Ranch.

In 1956, with a master's degree in electrical engineering, Tex took a job at Bell Laboratories in northern New Jersey and began work on a Ph.D. at Columbia University in New York City. Job, a wife and child, and school kept him busy, but in the summer of 1959, after abstaining from music for several years, Tex traveled to Sunset Park in West Grove, Pennsylvania, to see his former employers and friends, Wilma Lee and Stoney Cooper. Sunset Park, in the southeastern corner of the state near the Maryland line, was one of the northernmost outdoor parks that featured country music on weekends during the summer. Because of its relative proximity to the heavily populated northeast, it attracted the young urbanites who were becoming interested in bluegrass music as part of the folk revival. At the park, Tex was invited onstage to perform with Wilma Lee and Stoney. The tune he played was, as Tex described it, "a crazy number that I put a strange tuning to, called 'Natchez Under the Hill.'" He continued, "A guy came up to me after that and introduced himself as Mike Seeger and wanted me to play on an album he was doing of various people and wanted that tune on the record."[30] Seeger was a member of the influential folk revival group the New Lost City Ramblers and the producer of the album *Mountain Music Bluegrass Style*. Later in 1959, Tex participated in the recording of this historic album. Accompanying Tex on his recording of "Natchez under the Hill" and "Katy Hill" were John Cohen on guitar and Mike Seeger on five-string banjo. In addition to the fine music, the album package was important in that it included, in a twelve-page booklet by Seeger, the first written information about bluegrass music, and it was possibly the first album of that music to be recorded in the North for a northern urban audience.[31]

As a result of the attention he received from this recording, Tex was invited to appear at the prestigious Newport Folk Festival in 1963. Vanguard Records later released a recording made at the festival of Tex, backed by the New Lost City Ramblers, performing the song, "Jordan Am a Hard Road To Travel (The Old Grey Goose)." In 1964 Tex recorded with the Boston-based bluegrass group the Charles River Valley Boys. He also performed at the 1965 Newport Folk Festival with the Lilly Brothers and Don Stover, and their "Black Mountain Rag" was released on a Vanguard recording of that year's festival.

Logan's professional music career again lay dormant for three years as work and family took priority. "Then along came bluegrass festivals," Tex explained. The first bluegrass festival was held in 1965 near Roanoke, Virginia, and was promoted by Carlton Haney.[32] Soon these weekend outdoor music festivals mushroomed throughout the South, providing a new venue for bluegrass artists and a focal point for the fans' intense feelings about the music. The festival circuit was a godsend for struggling professional bluegrass artists, for it provided the possibility of employment from early May through October. Although Tex was by then working at Bell Laboratories and did not depend on the festivals for his income, he did welcome the increased opportunity to perform and to be among his musician friends.

In 1968, Tex attended a Haney festival in Berryville, Virginia. He enjoyed the event and soon began performing regularly at bluegrass festivals with Don Stover and the Lilly Brothers. Sparked by his renewed interest, the enthusiasm of the bluegrass fans, and his friendship with Bill Monroe, Tex, with the help of his wife Peggy and daughters "Bitsy" and Jody, began hosting annual parties at his New Jersey home featuring all-night music-making and a barbecue. In addition to the guests of honor, Bill Monroe and the Bluegrass Boys, many professional bluegrass musicians and fans attended.

Tex's enthusiasm for the music and the festival scene led him to perform at Bill Monroe's Bean Blossom, Indiana, festival as a "floater," as he termed it, playing with whatever band he could pick up. This job, done mostly out of his friendship for Bill Monroe, proved to be a hard and demanding position. About 1977, Peter Rowan, former lead singer and guitarist with the Bluegrass Boys, played the Bean Blossom festival in a similar capacity, showing up to perform without a band. Tex had met Rowan when he auditioned for Monroe at a show in Boston. Peter asked Tex to play fiddle on his portion of the Bean Blossom festival show, and Tex remembered, "It was pretty rough, nothing rehearsed, just feelings." The audience must have enjoyed those feelings, because they were called back for several encores. Tex related, "I would hate to have to hear it [now], but it was fun and I guess they [the audience] really knew it. After the show we would go out there and play to the moon."[33]

As a consequence of this chance meeting and the empathy each felt for the other's music, Peter and Tex began performing together in 1978 as Pete Rowan, Tex Logan, and the Green Grass Gringos. The band featured former Monroe banjoist Lamar Grier, bassists Roger Mason and Rich Campbell, and mandolinist Barry Mitterhoff. The group recorded a few songs that appeared on an album under Pete Rowan's name and toured occasionally in the northeast. Tex, Pete, and various others made several trips to Europe to perform. On one trip to Europe, Tex, Pete, and guitarist Greg Douglass recorded the album *Revelry* on the English Waterfront label.

In 1983 Tex realized he could not "hack these two jobs, working at Bell Labs and fiddling all over the country and Europe—playing a bluegrass festival, driving a thousand miles through the night, staying up all day, going to work on Monday, crazy things like that," so he and Pete Rowan split up. Tex went on to organize the Northeast Seaborn Band, featuring guitarist and vocalist Danny Weiss, mandolinist Barry Mitterhoff, guitarist John Carlini, and bassist Larry Cohen. Danny, Barry, and Larry left to form another group, and Tex joined with multi-instrumentalist Jimmy Arnold from North Carolina and recorded an album that has never been released. Since his last participation in a band in 1985, Tex has forsaken the fiddle to write a book on what he called "a bunch of math stuff I've developed."

Tex's influence on bluegrass music through his unique fiddling and songwriting has been substantial. A West Texan, Logan helped introduce bluegrass music, born in Kentucky and Tennessee, to a new generation of fans and musicians, many of whom lived in the northern states. He stands as an important contributor to the sound of bluegrass music during its early period of development.

Since its birth in the 1940s, bluegrass music has had a slow but steady increase in popularity throughout the nation. In West Texas, as elsewhere, a growing group of fans and musicians discovered bluegrass and became active participants in the music.

Although bluegrass was in part spawned by the commercialization of country music developing around Nashville in the mid-1940s, since the early 1970s it has reverted in part to a folk music. Whereas it was at first performed only by professional musicians like those in the Bill Monroe band, the music now has a large element of part-time players who find bluegrass music a creative pastime. In West Texas, bluegrass music has come to be identified not only as a musical style but as a catchword for wholesomeness and family atmosphere. Many of the Saturday night community musicals in West Texas use the word *bluegrass* in their publicity, even though bluegrass music may not be featured. It is used to announce good, clean, family entertainment and no trouble.

Music historian Roger Mason has observed the decline of active participation in rural entertainment since the early part of this century. Rural and small-town families once gathered often in their homes and in community groups to make music and entertain one another, but the trend of this century has been toward more passive forms of entertainment. The phonograph, radio, television, and live concerts and shows have all served to take entertainment away from the people and to place it in the hands of the "experts." Community singing and homemade music have become anachronisms.[34] The bluegrass music subculture bucks this trend and offers an opportunity to become involved in music making.

In response to a grassroots interest in bluegrass music, fans and amateur musicians now come together periodically for picking sessions or organized shows featuring club bands. The most successful of these clubs in West Texas is the Panhandle Bluegrass and Old-Tyme Music Association in Amarillo. The club features monthly meetings and pickings, midwinter weekend jam sessions, and a summer festival at Mobeetie. None of these events use paid professional bluegrass musicians, featuring instead club bands and bands from nearby regions. On occasion, usually with a burst of enthusiasm of some hardy member, the club will promote a show with a professional band. The club has sponsored a show with Grand Ole Opry stars the Osborne Brothers and other concerts by Country Gazette and Larry Sparks.

Bluegrass festivals, the focal point of bluegrass activity in other areas of the country, have been few and far between in West Texas. Buffalo Gap, near Abilene, was the site for an annual festival during the 1970s, and in recent years there have been periodic attempts at promoting a festival near Andrews featuring professional bands. These have been artistic successes, with enthusiastic but small crowds, but financially unsuccessful.

Surprisingly, West Texas is home to the world's only college degree program in bluegrass music. South Plains College in Levelland established this unique program in 1975 and has attracted students from throughout the United States, Canada, and several other foreign countries. In addition to the student bluegrass ensembles that perform throughout the region as part of their training, the school is a focal point for regional bluegrass activity. The student recitals at the end of each semester, billed as Bluegrass Fairs, are open to the public, and they attract large crowds from all over West Texas. Many professional bluegrass groups and musicians have performed and presented workshops at the college and members of the faculty tour throughout the United States as performers and clinicians.

Bluegrass music appeals to a select group of fans and musicians in West Texas. Despite its limited commercial success, bluegrass continues to garner a cultish support in the West Texas music community because of its traditional country and folk roots.

While the Mayfield Brothers, Tex Logan, and others were playing bluegrass music in the early 1950s, another new music was brewing in the South that would soon explode across the nation and change American music, including that of West Texas, forever—rock and roll.

Bill Myrick and the Mayfield Brothers in Shrevesport, Louisiana on the occasion of their performance at the Louisiana Hayride, April, 1951. Left to right: Edd, Herb and Smokey Mayfield and Bill Myrick. Courtesy Bill Myrick.

Bill Myrick and the Mayfield Brothers with guest vocalist Anne Jones at the KSEL Western Jamboree in 1949 or 1950. Left to right: Bill Myrick, Anne Jones, Smokey Mayfield, and Edd Mayfield. Courtesy Bill Myrick.

·}KSEL{·

WESTERN JAMBOREE PROGRAM

JIM EVANS, Publisher

Sled Allen's Arena—606 Texas Ave.—Saturday, May 27, 1950

Bill Myrick and the Mayfield Brothers, KSEL Western Jamboree program, Lubbock, Texas, May 27, 1950. Courtesy Pete Curtis.

BILL MYRICK and the MAYFIELD BROTHERS

EDD, SMOKY and HERB MAYFIELD standing, BILL MYRICK center

Doors open at 6—Show starts at 7—On the air from 7:45 until 11

Backstage concert photo, 1950s. Left to right standing: Charlie Cline, Edd Mayfield, Bill Monroe and Larry Richardson (all of Bill Monroe's Bluegrass Boys) and kneeling: Chet Atkins and Joe Clark. Courtesy Larry Richardson.

B. F. Logan, Sr. (1878-1971), 1950s. Mr. Logan is shown here with part of his large fiddle collection. Courtesy Homer Logan.

Tex Logan publicity photo, circa 1970.
Courtesy Homer Logan.

TEX LOGAN
BLUE GRASS FIDDLER

Buddy Spicher's fiddle jam, Franklin,
Tennessee, 1978. Left to right: Tex
Logan, Homer Logan, Buddy Spicher.
Courtesy Homer Logan.

South Plains College Bluegrass Band during Community College Week at state capitol grounds, Austin, Texas, 1989. Left to right standing: instructor Alan Munde and students: Nathan Dennis, banjo; Chris Vandertuin, guitar; Shane Bowerbank, bass; Dawn Watson, mandolin; and kneeling, Jason Jones, fiddle. Courtesy South Plains College.

6

COUNTRY BOY

ROCK

AND ROLL

COUNTRY
BOY
ROCK
AND
ROLL

119

Rock and roll music was not born in West Texas, but it was rapidly and enthusiastically accepted by young West Texas fans and musicians. Beginning as imitators, West Texans soon put their own stamp on the music and became leading innovators of the style. Perhaps surprisingly, rock and roll found a home in the land of western swing and honky-tonk music.

The postwar country music scene did not offer developing artists a great deal of money or the high esteem of the popular media, yet it did provide those with stamina and ambition a friendly, nurturing environment. Some of the most beautifully performed, influential, and enduring rock and roll music emerged from West Texas.[1]

In the postwar decade, the artists and adult-oriented lyrics of country music—with its emerging themes of honky-tonking, boozing, carousing, and cheating—had little to offer the teenage population; neither did much of the smooth, horn-band sound of pop music. Few artists directly addressed the themes that reflected teenage lives at this time.[2] Also adult-oriented was country music's rhythm: well disciplined, well defined, sometimes plodding, and rather predictable. The basic 2/4 rhythm was generated by the acoustic bass playing on the downbeat and a guitar playing "sock" rhythm, supplying the offbeat or upbeat.[3] This pattern, so popular with the dancers of West Texas, seldom changed, and there was no indication that it would ever need to.

A few performers made rhythmically exciting music that set them apart from this conservative approach: the exhilarating tempos and fluid rhythms of bluegrass musicians; the exuberant pre-rockabilly sound of the Maddox Brothers and Rose, with their slap bass and electric guitar solos; the mischievous antics of Little Jimmy Dickens; the boogie-woogie blues music of East Texas pianist Moon Mullican; and the somewhat racy, rowdy music of West Texan Charline Arthur. Despite these exceptions, the basic form and beat of West Texas country music might never have changed, if not for the music of a catalyst from outside the region.

Country music's metamorphosis into rock and roll in West Texas began with a young singer from Memphis, Tennessee: Elvis Presley. Presley's music and act dramatically changed the lives and musical direction of an entire generation of West Texas musicians. An impressive group of these young musicians became rock and roll legends: Buddy Holly, Roy Orbison, Buddy Knox, Jimmy Bowen, Sonny Curtis, Jerry Allison, and Joe B. Mauldin. There were rock and roll artists before Presley, but none was to have the impact on young West Texas musicians that Presley had following his recording debut in July 1954.[4]

Before Elvis, most young West Texas musicians played country music. Rockabilly, as the rock and roll music of Elvis and his Memphis contemporaries was called, blended country music, especially honky-tonk and boogie-woogie, with rhythm and blues. West Texas musicians found it relatively easy to add the rhythms of rock and roll to their already polished country music skills.

The mainstays of country music during the postwar decade included Roy Acuff, Hank Williams, Hank Snow, Webb Pierce, Carl Smith, Kitty Wells, Bill Monroe, Lester Flatt and Earl Scruggs, Ernest Tubb, Lefty Frizzell, Eddy Arnold, Faron Young, Tex Ritter, Slim Whitman, and other, mostly eastern-based artists. A notable California-based country act was the Maddox Brothers and Rose. Many of these performers appeared as regulars on weekly radio shows such as the Louisiana Hayride from Shreveport and the Grand Ole Opry from Nashville, Tennessee, both of which were heard by the fans in West Texas.

Country music radio programming grew ever more popular throughout the region in the 1950s, and live country music programs were very successful. Lubbock, Midland-Odessa, Wichita Falls, Abilene, and Amarillo were tour stops for national artists who performed at the larger arenas and the important night spots. Other venues for country music included movie theaters that featured music during intermissions, live radio shows, and dances at VFW and American Legion halls and schoolhouses. Country artists found work in clubs and honky-tonks that ranged from the desirable to the dangerous.

Many regional musicians recall the support of family and friends in pursuing careers in music. Buddy Holly's older brother, Larry Holley, not only provided rides for Buddy and his musician friends but also employed them in his tile-setting business between music jobs.[5] Sonny Curtis likewise reported that "anytime a ride was needed to go play music they [Sonny's parents] would provide it."[6] Local radio stations were always in need of musicians for live broadcasts and encouraged the young players, providing them opportunities to increase their visibility and gain valuable performance experience. Perhaps the parents and older family members and friends of these young musicians saw a country music career, with its glamour, prestige, and seemingly easy money, as a viable way to rise above the sometimes rough economic conditions that the Depression had brought upon their elders. Many also believed that music was a wonderful, noble endeavor. Few people were blessed with the talent to make music and bring pleasure, and, whether for vocation or avocation, the musicians were encouraged. A talent was not to be squandered.

Sonny Curtis was one of those talented young musicians in the 1950s, and he became one of the most successful West Texas-born country songwriters and performers. Born in a dugout May 9, 1937, near the small agricultural community of Meadow, Sonny first was exposed to music within the family circle: his Aunt Lorena was the sister of Herb, Edd and Smokey Mayfield. Sonny's first memories of music around the Curtis house are of the Mayfield family visiting and playing "Listen to the

Mockingbird." The Curtis and Mayfield families visited often with the purpose of music-making. Sonny recalled, "I didn't know what music was until I heard them play. It really blew me away. We idolized the Mayfield Brothers and would drive up to Dimmitt on the weekends to play."

Sonny's father bought a couple of inexpensive used acoustic guitars for Sonny and his older brothers, Pete and Dean. The guitars, which were not quality instruments to begin with, were made even worse when Sonny left them out in the rain a time or two. Eventually, Pete bought a nice Gibson acoustic guitar, and "that put us in the guitar [playing] business," remembered Sonny.

Aunt Lorena Mayfield became Sonny's first music teacher, showing him the guitar chords to "Little Brown Jug." His hands were so small at that early age that he played only on the first four strings, learning the G, C, and D7 positions. Pete also found an old broken fiddle and glued it together, and soon both Dean and Sonny learned to play it. Later, some of Sonny's earliest professional music jobs were as a fiddle player.

Influenced by the Mayfields, the Curtis brothers played and listened to bluegrass music. "If it had electric instruments, we thought it was sissy," Sonny recalled. "We were bluegrass fans, and that was it." They listened to the Grand Ole Opry for the new bluegrass sounds of Bill Monroe and the Bluegrass Boys and Flatt and Scruggs. At U. V. Blake's or Adair's Music in Lubbock, they bought 78-rpm records of these and other bluegrass artists, such as Mac Wiseman or Reno and Smiley. Sonny struggled out of bed at 5:45 each morning to hear Mac Wiseman's bluegrass music show on Shreveport's KWKH. "It would kill me," he said, "but I would get up and go out and sit in the car and listen."

Locally, noontime radio programs aimed at the rural audience. Sonny and Pete listened to fiddler Wiley Walker and guitarist Gene Sullivan on KFYO in Lubbock. As Wiley and Gene, the duo had their greatest success as the writers of "When My Blue Moon Turns to Gold Again," "Live and Let Live," and the Maddox Brothers and Rose radio theme song "Live and Love." Sonny and Pete also were present at the 1950 Bill Monroe and Mayfield Brothers concert at the Jamboree Hall in Lubbock, a rare West Texas appearance by a known, touring bluegrass unit. "We were totally knocked out. All we ever talked about was that show," Sonny recalled.

Sonny pursued his musical bent all the way through school. Performing at age eight on a local country music show, he sang "You're Just a Speckled Pup." In high school he won a talent contest sponsored by the Future Farmers of America, and at the national competition in Kansas City he met President Truman. Sonny recalled, "We would play at the drop of a hat or a quarter—a quarter is all we were worth." All through school he continued to listen to music on the radio and records and do the time-honored musician pastime, "learn the licks."

While in high school, Sonny expanded his musical horizons beyond bluegrass. He began to study the music of guitarist Chet Atkins. Sonny heard Atkins and his popular guitar style on KFYO in Lubbock, which

COUNTRY
BOY
ROCK
AND
ROLL

121

carried the Prince Albert Tobacco-sponsored portion of the syndicated Grand Old Opry broadcast. Sonny bought Chet Atkins records but was perplexed as to how Atkins was getting his unique sound. "It sounded like there were two people playing," Curtis recalled. Atkins had popularized a guitar-playing style employing the thumb to play bass notes and an accompanying chord in rhythm on the lower strings while the fingers picked out the melody on the upper strings. Sonny Stewart, a camera operator for a Lubbock television station and an amateur guitarist, invited Curtis to his home and demonstrated how it was done. "Once I got that down, that's all I did. I sat around playing Chet Atkins style. I probably owe as much to Chet Atkins as anybody," Curtis added.

When Sonny was a senior in high school, he met jazz guitarist Clyde Hankins, a salesperson and guitar teacher at Adair's Music Store in Lubbock who had played with Jack Huddle on the KDUB "Dude Ranch" in the early 1950s. Hankins, an accomplished guitarist, had been the band arranger for the Stan Kenton orchestra and had performed as accompanist for the Andrews Sisters and other professional acts. Hankins started the youngster on his musical education. He taught Sonny the inner game of guitar playing, including music theory, ultimately hiring him to teach guitar at the store. "That was a good period for me," Sonny noted. "I got to hang out with Clyde Hankins everyday, all day long. I absorbed the music from him like a sponge." In those high school years Sonny met and performed with another young musician named Buddy Holly.

Rock and roll legend Charles Hardin "Buddy" Holley was born in Lubbock, Texas, on September 7, 1937.[7] Although his two older brothers played guitar and sang, none of the Holley family members had performed professionally. They did provide encouragement when Buddy showed a penchant for singing and playing the guitar. According to an oft-repeated story, the older brothers took five-year-old Buddy along to a local talent contest and let him appear with them, singing and playing the fiddle. They had greased the fiddle bow so that no sound could be made. And, of course, the Holleys won mostly because Buddy was so cute sawing away on the silent fiddle.[8]

Buddy Holly historian Bill Griggs has reported that by the age of thirteen Buddy was able to hear a song on the radio and then sing it and play the guitar part. An early home recording bears this out: thirteen-year-old Holly sings a popular Hank Snow tune and accompanies himself skillfully on the guitar, including a surprisingly sophisticated guitar introduction.[9]

Duing his grade school days Buddy teamed up with fellow music enthusiast Bob Montgomery. Billing themselves as Buddy and Bob, they played together throughout their high school years, performing at every opportunity: remote broadcasts, openings of car lots, and grocery store promotions. Early in their duet days, Bob sang lead and played the guitar and Buddy sang tenor and played the tenor banjo or guitar.[10] With this instrumentation they tried to copy the bluegrass music they heard locally from the Mayfield Brothers and the recordings of well-known national bluegrass groups, in addition to the more electric country music heard on the radio. Sonny Curtis remarked, "Buddy and Bob were big bluegrass fans, but before they could develop as [bluegrass] pickers, they got involved in more commercial country music."

The banjo may have contributed to the development of Holly's unique electric guitar style. Fiddle and guitar were the standard folk instruments of West Texas, while the five-string banjo was rare and, in fact, nearly extinct in popular music nationwide. Country music fans, even those from the eastern mountains, easily identified the hallmark sound of bluegrass as the banjo. It was tricky, however, to know, without seeing the instrument, that it was the *five-string* banjo picked with the thumb, index, and middle fingers of the right hand, not the four-string tenor banjo played with a flat pick. When Curtis first met Holly, Buddy "played banjo, a four-string with a flat pick trying to get that three-finger bluegrass style. He got those songs sounding kind of like bluegrass, we thought." With no local players of the five-string banjo to serve as a guide, Holly had invented his own approach to his instrument, a four-string model.

Holly would have been aware of the bluegrass mandolin style of Bill Monroe. The mandolin is tuned similarly to the tenor banjo, is played with a flat pick, and can match the energy and rhythmic output of the bluegrass banjo with rapid up-and-down strums of the pick. And certainly tenor and plectrum banjo players were visible on many of the television variety shows of the late forties and early fifties. The "Ed Sullivan Show" and various Walt Disney programs, for example, featured the four-string tenor banjo played frantically with a flat pick, for both musical and visual effect. Perhaps it was the high-energy sound of the five-string bluegrass banjo coupled with the flat pick technique of the mandolin and tenor banjo that Buddy played on his banjo to approximate the bluegrass style. Ben Hall, a Lubbock disc jockey and country music performer, believed that Buddy developed the rhythm style by accompanying the fast bluegrass breakdown fiddling of Sonny Curtis. According to Hall, "Buddy would start double stripping the guitar [strumming both down and up with the flat pick] . . . and that's where I believe he picked up his lead style that he used on his records."[11] Hall believes this technique and rhythmic energy resurfaced in Holly's electric guitar playing.

Watchful for peers with interest in music, Buddy and Bob spotted Sonny Curtis playing a guest spot on the "Bernie Howell Show" on Lubbock television station KCBD. A local organist, Howell had heard Curtis performing at a country club in Brownfield. Buddy and Bob contacted Sonny through a mutual friend, Olan Finley. When Sonny found that they played bluegrass, he made a date to meet Bob after school at Bob's father's Gin Cafe in Lubbock. From there, Olan drove them to Buddy's house. "There was not one minute of small talk before we got to picking," Sonny noted. Sonny added the fiddle to the group as well as his guitar skills, which now included the Chet Atkins style. Joining Buddy, Bob, and Sonny was bass player Larry Welborn, a friend of Buddy and Bob from high school.

COUNTRY
BOY
ROCK
AND
ROLL

123

Buddy, Bob, Larry, and Sonny, still high school students, performed at every opportunity, with any one of them serving as the leader. "At this time it was all homogenized," Sonny reported. "If Buddy got a job, he would call and get the other players; if I got a job, I would call. We played a lot of places that we were not old enough to be in. Anytime, anywhere anyone wanted music, we were ready and willing to provide it."

It was not long before the boys played on local radio. Radio stations greatly influenced popular music and culture in West Texas, as elsewhere in the country. Not only did the stations spread state-of-the-art country music by playing major-label records, but they offered a focal point for the local music scene. Many country and blues artists of the late 1940s, 1950s, and the 1960s were employed at some point in their careers as radio disc jockeys.

The local country radio station was the place to be, the place where something was happening or might happen. In addition to in-studio programming, the stations used local artists to help with advertising promotions, such as grand opening celebrations or live remote broadcasts from an advertiser's business site. There was always the chance of being given time on a live show to perform. Musicians often spent time at a radio station hoping to meet somebody there or talk about the music business with a disc jockey, station owner, manager, sales agent, or engineer during a break.[12] The radio station was one of the few places where a player or singer had a chance to meet a recording artist or a promoter dropping in to promote a new record or a local appearance. There might be an opportunity to pitch a song or ask for a job in the band or get a free pass to a show that evening.

By 1955 Sonny, Larry, Buddy, and Bob, through their willingness to play "anytime, anywhere," came to the attention of KDAV radio owner "Pappy" Dave Stone and station manager Hi Pockets Duncan. They hired "Buddy and Bob" for small, informal promotions, such as the grand opening of a grocery store, which featured Buddy, Bob, Larry, and Sonny performing all afternoon for fifteen dollars while KDAV broadcast the event live.[13]

Later, the Buddy and Bob group performed live on the "Sunday Party" on KDAV, a show designed to give local performers a chance to play on the radio. Sonny Curtis performed as a soloist and then played with other performers, including Holly, who needed fiddle or guitar accompaniment. Weldon Myrick, from Jayton, Texas, who today is one of Nashville's leading session steel guitar players, also played in these informal backup groups on the "Sunday Party." Sonny described it as a "real serious music scene."

In addition to bluegrass and commercial country music, the boys became increasingly aware of rhythm and blues music. Sonny would often spend the night at Buddy's, and the two would stay up late and listen to music on the radio in the car. After the country music of the Grand Ole Opry, the Louisiana Hayride, the Ozark Jubilee, or the Big D Jamboree, they listened to the black artists on a late-night show broadcast on KWKH from Shreveport. Here they heard the spirited records of such artists as Lonnie Johnson, Bo Diddley, Little Richard, Chuck Berry, Ray Charles, and Fats Domino. The boys soon learned rhythm and blues material and incorporated black styles of musical performance into their playing and singing, just as Elvis would and as Jimmie Rodgers, Hank Williams, and many other white artists had.

Lubbock did not have a large black community, but Sonny, Buddy, and other musical friends took advantage of the few entertainment venues for local blacks and touring acts that did exist. Locally, the Hi-Hat Club featured Tony Ford, Jr., and his Jive Jump, All-Colored Orchestra every Saturday night, and the Cotton Club from time to time brought in black artists.[14] KSEL featured black artists on a thirty-minute program called "Sepia Parade," broadcast daily at 4:00 p.m. Sonny Curtis once was the only white person at a Cotton Club appearance by black artist Charles Brown.[15] Little Richard also played the Cotton Club, drawing a racially mixed audience. Accompanying Sonny and Buddy to these events was another schoolmate, drummer Jerry Allison. Curtis feels that Jerry Allison's influential drum style on the early Holly records originated there, especially in the "Ancient Rhythms," as a Lubbock newspaper headline described rock and roll. Curtis was especially impressed by Little Richard's drummers and "their great eighth-note feel."

In 1953 some black rock and roll was featured on the radio in Lubbock on programs like "Sepia Parade," and by late 1954, Elvis was a force in the music of the South and Southwest through his recordings and his appearances on the Louisiana Hayride. During live performances on the "Sunday Party," Buddy included his own renditions of rhythm and blues songs he and Sonny had heard on those late-night broadcasts from Shreveport. They also received requests to perform some of Elvis's material, and in time these young performers attracted a crowd for the radio show. Teenagers came to the radio station parking lot and listened on their car radios while watching their classmates through the studio windows.[16] Buddy and his friends could never have guessed that their lives would change forever with the first appearances of Elvis Presley in West Texas.

Other country artists added a distinctive twist to country music, but none put it together like Elvis Presley, "The King of Western Bop." Numerous white artists had successfully incorporated black musical styles into their music, such as Jimmie Rodgers, Bob Wills, and Bill Monroe, but Elvis was far and away the most blatant in his use of black singing and performance styles and would prove to be the most popular. Sam Phillips, head of Sun Records, had reportedly commented, "If I could find a white boy who could sing like a nigger, I could make a million dollars."[17] In Elvis he found his man.

Elvis Presley hit the music scene in mid-1954 with a string of hit records coming from the Sun Studio, run by Sam Phillips in Memphis, Tennessee. Elvis played guitar and sang, accompanied by a backup group composed of Scotty Moore on the electric guitar and Bill Black on the stand-up acoustic bass. The music they played was an energized amalgam of the popular country music of the rural South, typified by the

COUNTRY
BOY
ROCK
AND
ROLL

125

Grand Ole Opry performers and the black rhythm and blues of such artists as Bo Diddley, Chuck Berry, and Little Richard.

Through his black-styled dress, his seemingly motorized gyrations, and black-influenced singing, Elvis opened the eyes and ears of a generation of teenagers and young adults ready to break away from the pedestrian country and pop music of their parents. The first time Sonny Curtis saw Elvis, he was wearing a "red jacket, orange pants, and white buck shoes. He looked like a motorcycle headlight coming at you."

Part of the uproar from fans and detractors of Elvis alike was about his body movements during performances. There were country artists before Elvis who used body movement in their performances. Hank Williams performed with bent knees to reinforce a soulful moan, and Little Jimmy Dickens swayed his body and swung his guitar back and forth in time with the music in a playful, mischievous way and with a wink in his eye as he sang, "I got my education out behind the barn," the country version of coming of age sexually. None, however, were overtly as sexual and sensuous as Elvis's movements. He actually stepped out from behind his guitar and the microphone and walked to the front of the stage so that no movement was hidden. There was no misreading the wink of Elvis's eye or the movement of his hips.[18] One female observer commented that country and bluegrass music made her tap her toes, but the rock and roll of Elvis Presley made her move her hips.[19]

Elvis had a staggering effect on the budding young country musicians of his day. The day after Elvis appeared in Lubbock, Buddy Holly borrowed Sonny Curtis's acoustic guitar for performances because that was the kind of guitar Elvis played. After witnessing an Elvis concert in Kilgore, Texas, future Grand Ole Opry performer Bob Luman resolved never again to sing like Webb Pierce or Lefty Frizzell.[20] Everyone had a "first-time-I-saw-Elvis" story: for these and many other aspiring musicians, Elvis was a life-changing experience.

One medium for Elvis's invasion of West Texas was the Louisiana Hayride, the weekly radio show from Shreveport, Louisiana. Presley, along with Scotty Moore and Bill Black, had already appeared on the Grand Ole Opry on September 25, 1954. Elvis's act was not well received by the show's conservative hierarchy or its regular audience. Justin Tubb, son of long-time Opry performer Ernest Tubb, said that "the audience was polite to him, no booing or anything like that, but I think he came expecting to set them on their ears and it didn't happen." Opry manager Jim Denny is reported to have told Elvis to go back to truck driving.[21]

Rejected at the Opry, Elvis went next to the Louisiana Hayride, where he became a regular member. He appeared for the first time on October 16, 1954, and toured in the station's listening region.[22] Broadcast live every Saturday evening over fifty-thousand-watt station KWKH, the Hayride reached into Arkansas to the north and as far as New Mexico to the west. For a time, Lubbock station KFYO carried a thirty-minute segment of the Hayride, followed by thirty minutes of the Big D Jamboree from Dallas. The power and attraction of the Hayride was such that, despite the fact that Shreveport was six hundred miles from the West

Texas town of Meadow, it was not too far for a senior class trip by the Meadow High School class of 1949. Pete Curtis remembered the thrill of going to the Hayride on that trip and hearing Hank Williams dedicate his current hit, "Love Sick Blues," to the students.[23]

It is not surprising that Elvis found a spot on the Hayride. Throughout its history, the Hayride had a more liberal and open-minded management than the Opry, allowing artists to use drums on the program some time before the Opry did. It also featured full-fledged rockabilly artists such as Jimmy Lee, while the Opry was trying to pass off boogie-woogie piano as rock and roll in a poor attempt to accommodate that market.[24] It was on the Hayride that Hank Williams began his career and to it that he returned when he was booted off the Opry for drinking. The Hayride introduced such artists as Slim Whitman, Faron Young, Webb Pierce, Lefty Frizzell, Carl Belew, and Johnny Horton. It was also at the Hayride that Elvis picked up his first drummer, D. J. Fontana. Because the more successful Hayride artists moved to the Opry as their popularity increased, the Shreveport program was often called the "Cradle of the Stars."

The music industry clearly identified Presley's early recordings as hillbilly, as country music was called then. He was billed as "the Hillbilly Cat," or the "Folk Music Fireball," and his music was labeled "Western Bop."[25] Dave Stone of KDAV, who promoted several of his appearances in Lubbock, considered Elvis, Carl Perkins, Johnny Cash, and Jerry Lee Lewis country artists with a rock beat, but country nonetheless. Stone played their records and promoted their shows to his country audience, drawing large crowds. Despite the country music tag, however, Elvis attracted an audience of more than just traditional country music fans: he reached a younger crowd with much more interest in Elvis-the-phenomenon than Elvis-the-country-music-singer. Presley did draw big crowds both at concerts and appearances on the Louisiana Hayride, but it was a following that had little interest in the other country entertainers on the show. At the Hayride, the auditorium filled with young fans who wanted Elvis but had little patience for the smooth, easy singing style of Slim Whitman and Jim Reeves. One possible reason artists left the Hayride for the Grand Ole Opry during this period may have been to avoid the competition of Presley.[26]

Stories abound of Elvis's first appearance on concerts with country artists who felt that they were the bigger celebrity and that they, rather than Elvis, should close the show. The result was that in each instance, Elvis stole the show and was later repositioned to be the closing act. Webb Pierce related to Sonny Curtis his experience of following Elvis on stage: "It was over; when I got on nobody was interested." Dave Stone remembered, "Hank Snow was at that time a bigger star, or so he thought, than Elvis, so he insisted on going on last. Elvis came on ahead of Hank. When Elvis got through, most of the people had come to see him, and about half the crowd got up and left. Hank Snow said, 'Never again am I going to work another show with that guy.'"[27] The crowds were there to see and hear Elvis, and other stars were eclipsed.

COUNTRY
BOY
ROCK
AND
ROLL

127

Although Presley was billed as a country artist, he brought on a change in musical taste that devastated the country music industry. Attendance at the bastion of country music, the Grand Ole Opry, fell drastically during the first wave of rock and roll artists led by Bill Haley and kicked into high gear by Elvis. "From 1953—when rock and roll began—to 1960 the Grand Ole Opry ticket buyers had fallen off by nearly forty-four percent," reported Grand Ole Opry historian Chet Hagan.[28]

Elvis first appeared in Lubbock sometime during the early part of January 1955, performing in an auditorium as part of a country music concert promoted by Pappy Dave Stone.[29] Sonny Curtis performed on the program as a backup musician for the headliner Billy Walker and the duet of Jimmy and Johnny. Curtis described Elvis's performance that night: "[He] had everybody laying in the aisles. They [the promoters] had anticipated what the deal was and had taken cotton bales and lined them up all around the stage and had cops all over the place. They [the audience] were trying to get on stage with him. It was madness. I had never seen anything like it." After that performance Sonny, who had not been paid, heard that the performers had gone to the old Cotton Club at Fiftieth Street and Railroad Avenue. He followed the crowd to the club and found Billy Walker, who gave Sonny five dollars for his contribution to the show. Elvis performed at the club that night, although it is unclear whether he was booked to perform or just did an impromptu guest set.[30]

Only a month before this Presley appearance, Tex Ritter and Red Foley had headlined a country music show at the Lubbock Fair Park Coliseum. A Lubbock newspaper reviewer viewed the "folk music" show as "relaxed and informal . . . as comfortable as an old shoe."[31] After Elvis, it would become more difficult to sell this kind of music, and the record industry would have to make extraordinary adjustments to realign itself with the soon-to-explode rock and roll market.

The greatest impact of that January 1955 Elvis concert may have been on Buddy Holly and the other young musicians who now witnessed the phenomenon of Elvis Presley first hand. It may not have been for Buddy Holly as it was for John Lennon, "Before Elvis there was nothing,"[32] but it was a life-altering experience. As Sonny Curtis related, "When Elvis came through Lubbock, we were still in high school and Buddy really got hung up on Elvis. We started the next day after he left town doing his songs. I had a Martin D-28 and Buddy had a Stratocaster and we traded because the Martin was the kind of guitar Elvis played and Buddy wanted to be like Elvis. The next day after Elvis left town, we had all his stuff together." Larry Holley confirmed that it was not long after hearing Elvis that Buddy was performing Presley's material.[33] Buddy had been using drummer Jerry Allison in his group, but seeing that Elvis did not have a drummer, Buddy dropped the drums. When Elvis later added drums, Buddy brought Allison back into the group.[34]

Why was it so easy for these young players and singers to be basically country musicians and the very next day become rock and rollers? Certainly the motivation was there. For Sonny Curtis, girls first told him about Elvis, saying, "Boy, you've gotta hear this guy." He did and was not particularly impressed: "Something in his voice aggravated me." But many young men were interested in what their female acquaintances liked. Another teenage rock and roll idol, Ricky Nelson, began his musical career after witnessing the interest shown by his date in Elvis. In an effort to impress her, Nelson offered that he, too, was going to make a record.[35] The reaction was much the same for future rock and roll recording artists Buddy Knox of Happy and Jimmy Bowen of Dumas when they saw Elvis in Amarillo. Bowen found that "he wrecked the place. The girls were tearing at his clothing and we thought, 'This is for us!'" Knox and Bowen, both students at West Texas State College in Canyon, recognized immediately that "we had been playing the same type of music anyway."[36] While students at the college, Knox and Bowen performed as the "Rhythm Orchids" and went to the Norman Petty Studio in Clovis, New Mexico, to record "Party Doll," which became a national hit for the group.[37]

COUNTRY
BOY
ROCK
AND
ROLL

129

The transition from country to Elvis's style of music also was an easy one for Buddy Holly and his friends. The music they were playing in Lubbock in 1955 was already very close to what Elvis was doing: country music with an energized rhythm and vocal style. Elvis and his group had shown that there was interest in and a market for this musical synthesis. Even on first hearing, Elvis must have struck a very familiar chord with these young players. Elvis and his group, as others had done before, created a model based upon older, recognizable forms of American music, played with the same musical chords and progressions on the instruments of country music. Bill Monroe had synthesized fast-paced fiddle music and the black-influenced lyrics and vocal inflections of Jimmie Rodgers's "blue yodel" number "Mule Skinner Blues" in 1940 to create bluegrass music.[38] Following this pattern of amalgamation of styles, Presley helped develop rock and roll in 1954, reworking the Bill Monroe country waltz "Blue Moon of Kentucky" into an electrically energized, fast 4/4 beat, and restyling the Arthur "Big Boy" Crudup song "That's All Right, Mama." Certainly Sonny Curtis easily recognized the guitar style of Elvis's lead guitar player Scotty Moore as "pretty much a Chet [Atkins] lick."

Elvis's impact was so great at that first concert that Dave Stone brought him back to Lubbock a few weeks later, on February 13, 1955, to headline a show at the Fair Park Coliseum. The newspaper ad read, "By Popular Demand, Elvis Presley, the Be-Bop Western Star of the LA. Hayride Returns to Lubbock." Also appearing on the program were Opry star "The Duke of Paducah" (Whitey Ford); West Texan Charline Arthur; Jimmie Rodgers Snow, son of Hank Snow; Ace Ball; Bill Myrick and the Rainbow Riders from Odessa; and last on the billing, Buddy and Bob.[39] Promoters Dave Stone and Hi Pockets Duncan had placed the duo on the show.

Buddy Holly, Sonny Curtis, Larry Welborn, and other young country musicians and singers had the opportunity to see and hear Elvis on quite a few occasions during the year. Elvis made many appearances in West Texas during 1955, at least six in Lubbock alone. In addition to the Fair

Park Coliseum package shows of early January and February, Elvis also appeared at the Cotton Club on April 29, 1955. On June 3, 1955, he appeared on a show that featured Ferlin Huskey; earlier that day Elvis was at the Johnson-Connelley Pontiac dealership, where he performed a short show in the service area and moved to the showroom to sign autographs. On October 15, 1955, Presley headlined yet another show at the Fair Park Coliseum and appeared the next day at Hub City Motors.[40]

Buddy, Sonny, and the others were able to get close to Elvis during these early days, before his career became tightly controlled by manager Colonel Tom Parker. On several occasions Buddy visited with Elvis before and after the gigs. Buddy, Bob, and Larry even made an ill-planned trip to Shreveport at the invitation of Elvis to be on the Hayride as his guest. When the three arrived, they found that Presley was on tour that weekend and the management would not allow them in the building, let alone perform.[41]

On October 14, 1955, "Lubbock's Own Buddy, Bob and Larry," as the newspaper announced, appeared on a concert produced by Dave Stone and headlined by Bill Haley and the Comets.[42] Stone had placed Holly on the show so he could be seen and heard by Nashville music scout Eddie Crandall, who was in the audience that night. Crandall was impressed with Buddy, and, after a few more hearings, he convinced Jim Denny, former Opry manager and then head of his own promotion company, to seek a recording contract for Holly. Stone sent a demo tape of Holly, and Denny secured a record deal with Decca Records through Paul Cohen. Nashville record labels were looking for an artist to compete with Elvis and the Memphis Sun label's roster of rock and roll artists. They hoped Buddy Holly would be that artist.

On three different occasions within the year, beginning January 26, 1956, Buddy Holly and Sonny Curtis traveled to Nashville to record, but by all accounts, the music from those sessions was less than satisfying. Buddy was uncomfortable working within the confines of the recording format in place there: although Buddy chose the songs, the producer Owen Bradley picked the backup musicians and the arrangements. Buddy wanted more control, but the record people in Nashville felt they had more music and business savvy than these naive teenagers from Lubbock.[43]

After the first record was released in April 1956, Sonny thought they had it made: "[We] thought we were going straight up hill. Needless to say, we were wrong. We came back to Lubbock and starved to death."[44] They did work some: Jim Denny arranged a tour featuring Faron Young and Sonny James, and Buddy's group opened the show with "Blue Days, Black Nights" and "Love Me," the two sides of their first release, then played as the backup band for singers Tommy Collins and Sonny James.[45] They worked as Buddy Holly and the Two Tones, a name derived from shirts they bought in Oklahoma City while on tour. The record company changed the name to Buddy Holly and the Three Tunes, and the first Decca recordings appeared under that name.[46]

Sonny continued playing with Buddy around Lubbock, making only three or four dollars a night. On one occasion they played a long gig at the Sixteenth and J Club and received seventy cents apiece for their efforts. During this lull in Buddy's career, Sonny was offered a job playing guitar with the Norman Petty Trio. Despairing of better things happening, he went to Clovis, New Mexico, to speak with Petty. Buddy implored Sonny, "Man, don't go over and do that. That's not the kind of music you want to play. Man, stick around here, we're going to make it big. I feel it in my bones." Sonny asked Buddy how long it would take. Holly replied, "About as long as it took Elvis." Sonny eventually did leave Buddy and take other playing jobs, although not with Norman Petty.

Norman Petty had had success as a piano and organ player in the pop market. He and his wife Violet Ann and guitar player Jack Vaughn performed as the Norman Petty Trio, playing easy listening music. Guided by his acute business and promotional sense, Petty made a recording of the Duke Ellington composition "Mood Indigo" that became a national hit. With the royalties he made from that record, he opened a recording studio in his hometown of Clovis, New Mexico. Buddy Knox and Jimmy Bowen recorded their hits "Party Doll" and "I'm Sticking to You" at Petty's studio. The success of the Knox and Bowen recordings, engineered and promoted by Petty, attracted Holly's attention. Sonny related, "That's where Buddy got the notion to record at Petty's studio and leave Decca Records."

Drummer Jerry Allison played with Buddy off and on for several years and made one of the trips with Buddy to Nashville to record. Buddy, Jerry, and Lubbock bassist Joe B. Mauldin went to Clovis to cut some demos in hopes of interesting another record label. One of the tunes they cut was a reworking of a song used on one of the Decca sessions, "That'll Be the Day." This time Buddy played his own lead guitar, and the recording caught the feel he wanted.

Norman Petty recognized the talent of Buddy, Jerry, and Joe. With his help, a demo of the song was sent to Brunswick Records in New York City. Buddy, unable to use his name because he was still under contract to Decca, needed a band name. Jerry Allison came up with the name "Crickets" while looking through a dictionary for insect names. "Buddy had always admired the black group the Spiders and came up with the name the Crickets," Sonny Curtis further explained. The Brunswick record executives were impressed with the song and the group and wanted to release the demo just as it was sent. Sonny remembered Buddy's reaction, "No, man, that's just a demo, we want to do that again." Brunswick insisted on using the demo. An ironic turn came when Petty and Holly learned that Brunswick was a subsidiary of Decca Records, so there was no conflict in his Decca contract. "That'll Be The Day" was released under the name The Crickets. Eventually, Holly recorded under his own name, and at one time, Sonny pointed out, "between Buddy Holly [records under his name] and the Crickets [records under the group name], they had four records in the top ten."

COUNTRY
BOY
ROCK
AND
ROLL

131

Buddy Holly went on to have a whirlwind career, beginning with the April 1956 release of his first Decca Record "Blue Days, Black Nights." He split with the band in 1958 and moved to New York City. The Crickets continued to record and perform, and Sonny left the area, going first to Nashville and then, after the army, to California and then back to Nashville, writing hit songs and recording many fine country records along the way.

Holly recorded and toured until his death in an airplane crash in a snow-covered field near Clear Lake, Iowa, February 3, 1959. For composer of "American Pie," Don McLean, Holly's death was the "the day the music died." Sonny Curtis refuted that notion in his song "The Real Buddy Holly Story," and *Vogue* reviewer Daniel Wolf pointed out, "The music, you see, never really died—it just became our leading cultural export," referring to Holly's tremendous popularity and influence overseas.[47]

If Buddy Holly had done no more than copy the music and stage style of Elvis, as many have done, he probably would not have had such a successful and influential career. He used the musical model of Presley to propel him into the fulfillment of his own musical vision. From the years of country and bluegrass musical training and practice he had Holly gained playing around Lubbock and the West Texas area, Holly fashioned a sound and a musical persona that were to have a defining influence on rock and roll.

Holly's recordings demonstrate his forceful rhythm-guitar playing. Elvis, however, had used the acoustic guitar more as a prop than an instrument. The first time Bob Luman saw Elvis perform, he viciously strummed the strings of the guitar to begin the show and immediately broke two strings. With the two broken strings dangling from the peghead of the guitar, he continued to play and completed the show. Luman remembered the performance rather than Elvis's guitar playing.[48] A Lubbock reporter added, "He beats on his guitar. You couldn't say he plays it."[49]

Holly took the precision and drive of bluegrass rhythm guitar with open-string chords, added to it quick pick strokes and chord sequences, and brought that sound to the foreground. Curtis termed it "rhythm solos." On his Fender Stratocaster, Holly could combine those rhythmic picking styles with the relatively new power of the solid-body electric guitar to create a powerhouse of rhythm for his music.

"We used drums and played loud," Curtis offered as a major difference between the rock and rollers and the country musicians. "Being in such a small group, he [Buddy] was forced to get as much out of the guitar as possible. The power of his rhythm-lead delivery, especially on his tasteful solos, was very effective." The guitarist during Holly's final tour, Tommy Allsup, described the volume levels: "We had one microphone up front with two little speakers on the sides of the stage, and you played loud out of necessity, because you couldn't hear yourself and those rock and roll shows back in those days. They'd start screaming and that was it. They never heard the music."[50] Curtis added, "Buddy and J. I. [Jerry Allison] used to play just drums and guitar at the Roller Rink in Lubbock and got so tight and so good, they could feel what each other was doing."[51]

Holly was a rock and roller who played his guitar artfully, wrote his own songs, and had his own way of performing them. With a clear vision of the music and the times, Sonny Curtis described Buddy Holly's appeal: "It was teenage music, simple, appealing, something the guitar player could pick up and play and sing and hum along, with nothing far out, no hard chords, no hard lyrics, simple—'I love you, Peggy Sue, with a love so rare and true'—played with a great feel. They played that singable, pretty, listenable music with such a great feel that it was just magic."[52]

Holly's influence on rock and pop music is staggering. The instrumentation of Buddy Holly and the Crickets provided the popular model for rock groups that were to follow: lead guitar, rhythm guitar, bass, and drums. The British music invasion of the United States led by the Beatles and the Rolling Stones in the early 1960s was built in large part on musical examples set in the vinyl of Buddy Holly records. Even the name "Beatles" is a copy of the bug theme of the Holly group name "Crickets." Daniel Wolf reported that "Paul McCartney . . . admitted, 'At least the first forty songs we wrote were Buddy Holly-influenced.' John Lennon was even more succinct: 'I was Buddy Holly.'"[53]

Ironically, one of Holly's last recordings, Paul Anka's "It Doesn't Matter Anymore," was a move away from rock and roll into the pop sound, featuring an orchestra and lush string arrangements. Holly believed that rock and roll was a passing teenage fad that would be replaced, he hoped, by his brand of soft rock/pop music.[54] One can hear the softer, pop-ballad approach in the underground home recordings of the last Holly sound: "That Makes It Tough" and "Love Is Strange," for example. According to Bill Griggs, Holly recorded them alone at his home shortly before his death. Even with the more laid-back pop-ballad feel, he artfully retained a blues influence in "Tough."[55] For Holly, perhaps rock and roll really did not matter anymore. The rock and roll music Holly had helped to develop, with its raw teenage energy and the power of the solid-body electric guitar and drums, had been diluted by the early 1960s to pop music. The tidal wave of the Beatles washed aside this musical lethargy as they flooded the American music market with their version of Buddy Holly's West Texas-born rhythms and sounds.

Buddy Holly's sound is now very much a part of the country music mainstream. Curtis, who has had an intimate association with both country and rock and roll, saw clearly that "what rock and roll was then [in the late 1950s] is what country is today." In his words, "Waylon Jennings had a really great rock and roll band but with a steel guitar so he could call it country." Curtis expressed his view in his song, "A Whole Lot of Cowboys Are Playing Rock and Roll."[56] He regarded Holly's drummer Jerry Allison as one of the most influential drummers on rock and roll and modern country music with his work on Holly's recordings as well as records by the Everly Brothers and the Crickets.

In Texas, Buddy Holly is looked upon as a state treasure and the patriarch of Texas rock music. A leading music magazine in the Dallas

COUNTRY
BOY
ROCK
AND
ROLL

133

area pays homage to Holly in each issue with its title *Buddy, The Original Texas Music Magazine*. It publishes an "Annual Buddy Holly Memorial Issue," which discusses Holly and the current Lubbock music contributions in an article entitled "Lubbock or Leave It."[57]

Bill Griggs, publisher of the magazine *Rockin' Fifties,* speculated that Buddy moved to New York to serve an apprenticeship with the music business masters so that he could return to Lubbock with the money and expertise to open a recording studio, intending to develop the area into a national music center.[58] Holly took an interest in his friend Waylon Jennings and produced his first record, "Jole Blon," at the Petty Studio in Clovis.[59] Holly drew on writers in the region for his material. In addition to the songs of Sonny Curtis and Holly's cowriter Jerry Allison, he recorded "Rave On" and "Oh, Boy," written by Levelland residents Bill Tilghman and Sonny West. With West Texas artists like Waylon Jennings, Sonny Curtis, Tanya Tucker, the Gatlin Brothers, Mac Davis, the Maines Brothers, Jimmie Dale Gilmore, Butch Hancock, Terry Allen, Joe Ely, and countless others under the direction of Buddy Holly, the area might have been a music center to contend with. Don Caldwell, owner of a Lubbock recording studio, speculated further that if Holly had opened a studio in Lubbock, the Beatles would have wanted to be produced by their mentor and record in his hometown.[60] Lubbock may not have become a New York, Los Angeles, or Nashville in record industry esteem, but it is intriguing to imagine John, Paul, Ringo, and George strolling onto University Avenue during a break from recording to get a hamburger and fries from the Hi-D-Ho drive-in.

West Texas produced another influential rock and roll performer whose greatest music bore a close resemblance to the later pop stylings of Buddy Holly. Roy Orbison was born April 23, 1936, in Vernon, Texas, just south of the Oklahoma border. Roy's father, Orbie Lee Orbison, an oilfield worker, moved the family frequently to follow the available work. He moved to Vernon from Floydada, Texas, and then on to Fort Worth, where he worked in the aircraft and defense plants during World War II. Following the war, Orbie Orbison returned to the oil drilling business, locating in Wink, a small, dusty, out-of-the-way place in far West Texas near Midland and Odessa, not far from the New Mexico border.

Roy's first memories of music were of the country music his family and friends sang and listened to on the radio. As a youth he learned to play the guitar and performed on the radio with Charline Arthur on station KERB.[61] In 1953, while in high school in Wink, Roy joined with other students to form a country group, the Wink Westerners. Following the format of other West Texas bands of the day, the group performed the hardcore hillbilly music of such artists as Webb Pierce and Lefty Frizzell, Bob Wills-style western swing, a sprinkling of pop hits, and big band music.[62] In 1954, while still in high school, the Wink Westerners won a talent contest and were invited to appear on a weekly television show hosted by Bill Myrick and sponsored by Pioneer Furniture of Midland.[63]

After graduating from high school in 1954, Roy and fellow band member Pat Ellis left Wink to attend North Texas State College in Denton, where Roy studied geology. While at college, Roy met fellow student Pat Boone, who was having success as a recording artist covering hits by black artists such as Fats Domino's "Ain't That a Shame" and Little Richard's "Tutti, Frutti." Although Roy was not impressed with his music, he was impressed with Boone's success. He also met students Dick Penner and Wade Moore, who had written the song "Ooby Dooby," which was to become Roy's first hit.

Orbison's geology studies proved to be too difficult, and he returned to West Texas, settling in Odessa and enrolling at Odessa Junior College. He soon formed a band called the Teen Kings with Billy Pat Ellis on drums, James Morrow on electric mandolin, Johnny Wilson on rhythm guitar, and Jack Kennelley on bass. Roy and the group appeared on a weekly television program. In early January 1955, Elvis came through the area as part of the Billy Walker show and appeared on Roy's television program.[64] Although Roy had heard Presley's recordings, it was not until seeing him that Roy could appreciate his talent: "I wanted to put on a show like Elvis." Biographer Ellis Amburn pointed out the continuing influence Presley would have on Orbison's career: "Despite the vast difference in their looks and style, Elvis remained his model."[65]

Roy had ample opportunities to see Elvis during 1955, because he performed many times in the Midland and Odessa area. Presley appeared in Midland on January 7, as part of the Billy Walker tour; on February 16, as one of the "Special Added Attractions" of the Hank Snow show promoted by Keith Ward of Midland radio station KJBC; on April 1, at the Ector County Auditorium in Odessa, sponsored by record store owner Cecil Hollifield; on May 31, as part of a large package show beginning at 7:30 p.m. in Midland and at 8:30 p.m. twenty miles away in Odessa; on October 12, headlining a large package show in Midland, promoted by Cecil Hollifield; and on October 14 in Odessa, for his final appearance of the year in the area.[66]

The Teen Kings performed around West Texas and, with the local popularity of the band growing, a record was sponsored by area business executives Weldon Rodgers and Chester Oliver. In late 1955, the Teen Kings traveled to Norman Petty's studio in Clovis, New Mexico, where they recorded the Moore and Penner song "Ooby Dooby" that Roy had learned at North Texas State College and a song he had heard Presley sing, "Tryin' to Get to You." Released in West Texas on the Je-Wel label, the record drew attention in the region. Local record store owner Cecil Hollifield, impressed with the recording, saw "Ooby Dooby" as a potential national hit. As reported in the Odessa *American*, "Holifield [*sic*] is a firm believer in new talent. 'There's more unknown great singers than there are known,' he said flatly. 'I knew the boys could make a hit if given the chance.'"[67] Hollifield, owner of the Record Shop with locations in Midland and Odessa, was one of the largest record retailers in West Texas, and he booked many big-name country acts into Midland and Odessa. He was a big fan and promoter of Sun artist Elvis Presley.

COUNTRY
BOY
ROCK
AND
ROLL

135

Hollifield called Sun Records president Sam Phillips and played the recording of "Ooby Dooby" over the phone. Phillips was impressed and agreed to take "Ooby Dooby" and sign a recording contract with the Teen Kings, but he wanted to rerecord the song in his Memphis, Tennessee, studio. Bill Myrick, Odessa musician, promoter, and disc jockey during the 1950s and 1960s, added that Hollifield also promised to buy a large quantity of the Teen Kings' records as a condition of Phillips accepting the group.[68]

In early 1956 the Teen Kings recut "Ooby Dooby" and recorded an Orbison original, "Go! Go! Go!" in the Sun studios in Memphis. The record was released in April 1956 and was well received in *Billboard* magazine: "Orbison's spectacular untamed singing quality spells big action for both sides . . . oby [sic] Dooby and Go, Go, Go, are wild swinging country blues."[69] The record sold over two hundred thousand copies, but its success was short lived. As rock historian Colin Escott pointed out, "It would be the biggest hit Orbison would see for four years." During 1956 Orbison and the band divided their time between Memphis, where they recorded, and West Texas, where they lived and worked in clubs when not touring the country as part of package shows. In December 1956 Roy split from the Teen Kings because of growing disputes concerning billing and royalty distributions.[70]

Orbison recorded his last material for Sun in August 1957 with just guitar and voice. He later added the full-band accompaniment when the material was finally released. It was also in 1957 that Roy met and began writing songs with Midland resident Joe Melson.[71] The partnership did not come to fruition until the early 1960s, when they produced some of Orbison's biggest hits, such as "Only the Lonely," "Crying," "Running Scared," and "Blue Bayou."[72]

Although, as a vocal artist Orbison's recordings were not selling well in 1957, he did score a success as a songwriter. The Everly Brothers recorded the Orbison composition "Claudette" as the flip side to their hit "All I Want to Do Is Dream." With the money he made from "Claudette," Roy bought out his contract with Sun and signed with RCA of Nashville for two singles, which were released in 1958 and were even less successful than his last Sun material.[73]

Orbison came home to West Texas discouraged. Guitarist Tommy Allsup, after his return from the final Buddy Holly tour, worked with Orbison during 1959 and remembered the rough times: "We played at Hobbs [New Mexico]. . . . We'd go to Amarillo and [then we] played at his hometown . . . Wink. We had about three or four people that night. We'd play rock and roll stuff. We'd do 'Ooby Dooby,' that was the only hit he had at that time, and he'd just do cover songs, . . . some Buddy Holly, Little Richard, and that's about it." The venues Allsup played with Roy were a departure from the liquor—serving clubs that had been the norm for West Texas country-gone-rock musicians. In response to the popularity of rock and roll among teenagers and their desire to hear and dance to the music, teen clubs developed. As Allsup remembered them, "They let kids in, but they couldn't go out. If they went outside they had to pay to get back in. They did that to keep them from going out and drinking. But there was quite a few of those things [teen clubs] popping up back then."[74]

In 1959 Roy signed with Monument Records, a new label in Nashville. It was with Monument that he developed beyond his early country and rock stylings and had his greatest successes, beginning with his first million-seller in 1960, "Only the Lonely." Roy Orbison eventually moved to Nashville, where his career continued with a string of top-selling songs and a successful touring schedule. In 1987 he was inducted into the Rock and Roll Hall of Fame, and in 1988 a tribute concert with an all-star line-up of contemporary rock stars as backing musicians was filmed at the Coconut Grove in Los Angeles for Cinemax television. As one of the pioneers of 1950s rock and roll, Orbison was invited to join Bob Dylan, Tom Petty, and George Harrison to record a concept album as the Traveling Wilburys. It was not long after this recording that Roy Orbison died on December 6, 1988, at the age of fifty-two of a heart attack in Hendersonville, Tennessee.

Buddy Holly and Roy Orbison were West Texas's most important contributions to rock and roll. Other West Texas rock and roll musicians in the 1950s followed a path similar in several respects. Typically, they learned to play instruments and to sing country music with family and friends. Influenced by music they heard on the radio, these musicians joined with peers to form country music groups and, with Presley as their model, began to play rock and roll. While Holly and Orbison became legendary rock and roll performers, many musicians experienced less spectacular results.

Abilene's Dean Beard, billed as the "West Texas Wildman," recorded briefly for Sun and is best known for his 1956 Atlantic recording "Rakin' and Scrapin.'"[75] Beard also recorded for Atlantic records and Slim Willet's Winston label. His group, the Crew Cats, included Rankin area musicians Jimmie Seals and Dash Crofts. Beard, Seals, and Crofts later joined the Champs, who had a major hit with "Tequila." Seals and Crofts formed a successful pop duo in the 1960s and 1970s. Jimmie Seals's brother, Dan, found similar success in the rock world as "England Dan" of England Dan and John Ford Coley. In the 1980s, Dan Seals continued his music career as a successful country music singer.

Earl Sinks from Lubbock played on some Buddy Holly sessions at the Petty studio and had a few releases under his own name. Terry Noland and Jimmy Peters, also from Lubbock, performed with the Four Teens and recorded on the Challenge record label.[76] Jerry Naylor, who grew up in Abilene, was the lead singer for the California version of the Crickets. Johnny "Peanuts" Wilson, who played mandolin with the Wink Westerners and the Teen Kings, recorded several songs at the Petty studio in Clovis. The Bowmans in Lubbock recorded for Columbia Records and had a tight vocal sound that foreshadowed the styles of later groups such as Alabama and the Gatlin Brothers.[77]

In the late 1950s, country music suffered from the impact of rock and roll. By the early 1960s, however, country music had begun a recovery

COUNTRY
BOY
ROCK
AND
ROLL

137

that has never stopped. By incorporating the very music that once threatened it, country music has attracted the now-aging fans of 1950s rock and roll and has cultivated a new generation of fans to whom the mix of rock and roll and country music seems natural.

The recovery of country music in the early 1960s centered around the organization and planning of the country music business community in Nashville, Tennessee. Even while traditional honky-tonk and western swing music continued to be successful in West Texas, young West Texas country music performers increasingly left the region and headed for Nashville.

The Crickets publicity photo, circa 1960.
Top to bottom: J. I. Allison, Sonny Curtis
and Joe B. Mauldin. Courtesy Sonny Curtis.

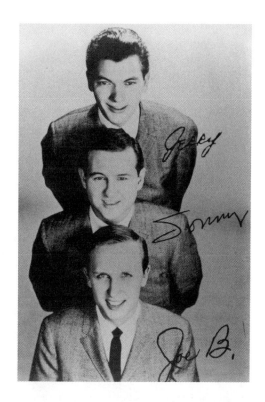

The Everly Brothers with The Crickets, Alma
Cogan Television Program, London, England,
1960. Left to right: Phil Everly, guitar,
vocal; Don Everly, guitar, vocal; Joe B.
Mauldin, bass; J. I. Allison, drums; and
Sonny Curtis, guitar. Courtesy Sonny Curtis.

THE ANNUAL BUDDY HOLLY MEMORIAL ISSUE

BUDDY

Will the Real Buddy Holly please stand?

Buddy Holly to perform at State Fair of Texas

Remembering Doc Pomus and Buster Smith

Autograph Collecting

Eight-page pullout Calendar Section

And much more!

THE ORIGINAL TEXAS MUSIC

FREE

SEPTEMBER

Dallas-based BUDDY magazine, September 1991. Author's collection.

The Rhythm Orchids on the Ed Sullivan show, circa 1957. Courtesy Pete Curtis.

Elvis Presley appearance in Lubbock, April 10, 1956. Courtesy LUBBOCK AVALANCHE-JOURNAL.

Newspaper ad for Elvis Presley's second appearance in Lubbock, February 13, 1955. Courtesy LUBBOCK AVALANCHE JOURNAL.

BY POPULAR DEMAND

ELVIS PRESLEY

The Be-Bop Western Star of the LA. Hayride Returns to Lubbock.

4:00 P.M. MATINEE
TODAY ONLY
FAIR PARK COLISEUM

ALSO ON THE BIG WESTERN SHOW:

DUKE OF PADUCAH—of the Grand Ole Opry "Get On The Wagon, Boys. These Shoes Are Killing Me."

CHARLENE ARTHUR—Miss Dynamite of the Big D Jamboree and Victor Records.

JIMMIE RODGERS SNOW—Son of Hank Snow and Victor Recording Artist

ACE BALL—Okeh Recording Artist

BILL MYRICK and the **RAINBOW-RIDERS**

BUDDY AND BOB

BOXOFFICE OPENS AT 2:30

Newspaper ad for an Elvis Presley promotional appearance prior to a "Grand Ole Opry - Louisiana Hayride show" at the Lubbock Fair Park Coliseum, June 3, 1955. Courtesy LUBBOCK AVALANCHE JOURNAL.

SEE! HEAR! IN PERSON ELVIS PRESLEY
TONIGHT
FRIDAY--7:00 AT
JOHNSON-CONNELLEY
PONTIAC SHOW ROOM
AT MAIN AND Q
(No Admission Charge)

Roy Orbison and the Teen Kings (formerly the Wink Westerners) promoting "Ooby Dooby" and "Go, Go, Go." From the
ODESSA AMERICAN. Left to right, front row: Johnny Wilson, Roy Orbison, Cecil Hollifield (sponsor). Back row: Billy Pat Ellis,
James Morrow, and Jack Kennelley. Courtesy Keith Ward.

Curtis Brothers, 1952. Left to right: Sonny,
Pete, and Dean Curtis. Courtesy Pete Curtis.

7

THE NASHVILLE CONNECTION

In the late 1950s, it became clear that Nashville, Tennessee, was the place to pursue a country music career on a national level. By 1966, country music and Nashville's eminence as the center of that music had earned a cover story in the prestigious *Saturday Evening Post*.[1] Nashville had amassed all the ingredients for success: It was the home of the major record companies, recording studios, musicians, publishing concerns, booking agents, the Country Music Association, and the influential Grand Ole Opry radio show. Additionally, Nashville was strategically located in the populous eastern half of the United States.

Nationally, country music took a back seat to rock and roll music during the 1950s. The Country Music Association, founded in 1958, labored to find new markets for country music. One of its efforts was to sponsor country-format radio stations. During the 1950s only a few stations in the United States programmed solely country music; Lubbock's KDAV was the first of these. It is a testament to the CMA's efforts that by 1968 at least 328 stations broadcast country music on a full-time basis.[2]

Many West Texas country artists who began their careers in the late 1940s and early 1950s relocated to Nashville—"Music City USA"—or at least made it the center for their business endeavors. West Texas singers and musicians Billy Walker, Sonny Curtis, Waylon Jennings, Weldon Myrick, Ben Hall, and many others performed regionally and nationally for several years before finally moving to Nashville. During the 1960s, more West Texas country artists, including Mac Davis, Tanya Tucker, Jeannie C. Reilly, and the Gatlin Brothers, left early in their careers for Nashville and other national entertainment centers.

The career of current Grand Ole Opry star Billy Walker best illustrates the pathways to Nashville taken by West Texas country music performers in the postwar years. Born January 13, 1929, in Ralls, Walker grew up in a family of eight. When Walker was six years old, his mother died. Because of economic hardships and the strain of raising such a large family, his father placed Billy and two brothers in an orphanage in Waco, Texas. Billy remained there until 1939, when his father brought the family back together and moved just over the state line to Portales, New Mexico. In early 1942, the Walker family moved sixty miles north to Clovis, New Mexico. After a brief attempt at finding work in California, the Walker family relocated to Whiteface, Texas, where Billy attended high school.

While living in Portales, Billy, at the age of thirteen, saw a Gene Autry movie and was impressed with the film star's singing and guitar playing.

Walker remembered thinking, "'I gotta do what that guy's doing on the screen.' I got fascinated by Gene Autry. He became my hero."[3] Billy found a cheap guitar and a twenty-five- cent guitar instruction book and taught himself how to play. Walker's first recording was a demo disc he made at the age of fifteen at schoolmate Norman Petty's house. Billy sang in his best Autry imitation Autry's theme song "Back in the Saddle Again."

At fifteen, Walker entered and won an amateur talent contest sponsored by radio station KICA in his hometown of Clovis, New Mexico. As a result of the contest, Billy was given a fifteen-minute spot on the radio each Saturday at 1:00 p.m. The performance was live and featured just Billy and his guitar. Although the Walker family moved to Whiteface shortly after the radio program began, Billy hitchhiked the eighty miles back to Clovis each Friday, spent the night with an uncle, performed on the radio show on Saturday and, immediately following the program, left to make the trek back to Whiteface. While living in Whiteface, Billy attended a Bob Wills dance in nearby Morton and met Wills's guitarist, the legendary Eldon Shamblin, who graciously showed the eager young Walker "some chords and what songs they went to."

In 1946, during the summer break from his junior year in high school, Walker hitchhiked to Abilene. Prompted by a friend, he auditioned there and landed a radio spot on KLBT, performing on two early-morning shows five days a week, for which he received fifteen dollars. On these shows, Walker advertised his upcoming personal appearances, usually a dance held at the American Legion hall, Elks lodge, schoolhouse, or dance hall. Walker had no band of his own and would perform with whatever band was available at the event. Despite his young age, Walker had no problems in these venues. He recalled, "there was no liquor in the dance halls. There was no [legal] liquor in West Texas. If somebody drank, they went out to the pickup and drank and came back in and danced." At these rural West Texas functions, parents would often bring their children; Walker confirmed that "it was sort of a community thing." He played hundreds of dances in schoolhouses around West Texas in these early days of his career. Once, he played in the ranching town of Matador for a dance whose electric power was supplied by a tractor turning the electric generator. At the end of the summer, he returned to his home in Whiteface to begin school.

Following Walker's graduation from high school in 1947, he moved to Lubbock, where he was hired as a vocalist for the Jake Miller band. Miller, a Sears Roebuck employee in Lubbock, led a western swing-style dance band and played drums. Jake Miller and the Mustangs played a dance every Saturday night in Brownfield, an occasional date at the Cotton Club or some other area dance hall and, beginning in November 1946, on a fifteen-minute radio show at 7:45 a.m. on Lubbock radio station KSEL.[4]

After the stint with the Miller band, Walker joined a band led by Columbia recording artist Willie Lawson. As a member of the Lawson ensemble, Billy traveled around the region for a year, with a trip to Illinois and Michigan, and finally returned to West Texas. Billy spent a few months in fall 1948 on radio station KTSR in San Angelo.

Walker's next move was to Waco, where he performed on radio stations WACO and KWTX and worked as the guitar player and emcee for Hank Thompson's band. Thompson, a fine guitarist and singer, had a hit in 1947 with his honky-tonk classic "Humpty Dumpty Heart" and is now a member of the Country Music Hall of Fame.

Early in 1949, at the age of twenty, Billy auditioned for and was given a spot on the most prestigious country music radio show in Texas, the Big D Jamboree, broadcast live on KRLD on Saturday nights from Dallas. As a member of the Big D Jamboree, Walker used the gimmick of wearing a mask and billing himself as "The Traveling Texan, the Masked Singer of Folk Songs." Walker remarked, "The guy on the Big D Jamboree said, 'Well, you sing real good, but nobody knows you, so we're gonna' put a mask on you.'" The gimmick helped get some local coverage, and "it helped me get a record contract with Capitol Records," he added. He continued, "It peaked after about six months, and once I had a local hit, the Jamboree bosses decided we'd have an unveiling. When the mask came off, they announced, 'Billy Walker,' and everybody said, 'Billy who?' I stayed 'Billy Who' for a long time."[5]

After the stint with the Big D Jamboree, Walker moved back to West Texas and performed four times daily on radio in Wichita Falls. One of the programs was a regional network hookup with thirteen stations, five of which were large, fifty-thousand-watt stations. The sponsor of the network portion was Hadacol, a patent medicine tonic, "suspected to be mostly alcohol and used as an all-purpose aches and pains remedy."[6] In addition to sponsoring the radio programs, Hadacol promoted the Hadacol Caravan, a troupe of performers that appeared nationally, traveling by train and featuring big stars such as Hank Williams and Bob Hope. Walker participated in these tours as they came through the region.

In February 1951, Billy Walker began recording for Columbia and in early 1952 had a hit with the song "Anything Your Heart Desires." After Walker had met Webb Pierce in Nashville, Pierce, a regular on the Louisiana Hayride, called the program's management and suggested they use Walker on the show. As a result, Walker performed as a guest on the Hayride and was so well received that he was given a regular spot on the show. In July 1952 Walker moved to Shreveport, Louisiana.

By July 1954, Walker had another hit with "Thank You for Calling" and was performing with fellow Hayride star Slim Whitman and others at the Overton Band Shell in Memphis, Tennessee. Bob Neal, a Memphis radio personality who was promoting a young Memphis talent by the name of Elvis Presley, asked Billy and Slim to put Elvis on the show because he had a local hit with "That's All Right, Mama." Billy and Slim agreed to this, and Walker remembered clearly that "Elvis knocked the crowd out." Walker also reported, "So when we got back to the Hayride, I talked to Horace [Horace Logan, the manager of the Hayride] about him [Elvis] and then Slim talked to Horace."[7] The result was that Elvis came to the Hayride and, just as in Memphis, he "knocked the crowd out."

At that time, although Presley had a hit with "That's All Right, Mama," he was unknown outside Memphis. Walker explained, "People don't realize . . . he got hot in West Texas before he got popular much anyplace else." As a regular on the Hayride, Elvis was accessible to the listeners in West Texas, but he also played a West Texas tour lead by Billy Walker in early January 1955 that coincided with the release of Presley's next record, "Milk Cow Blues Boogie," giving West Texas audiences an early firsthand view of Elvis—and they loved him. The review in the *Lubbock Avalanche-Journal* stated about the new release, "It is a rock-and-roll honey."[8] It was on this tour that many of the soon-to-be West Texas rock and rollers saw Elvis for the first time. Walker described some of these early shows:

> It was me and Elvis Presley and a couple of guys that had a number-one record called Jimmy and Johnny. I booked that show. We played the Ector County Coliseum in Odessa. We did a little free miniconcert at one of the high schools to plug the date. And then we went out to the TV station with Roy Orbison, who was on about 5:00 p.m. for a furniture store. He [Elvis] knocked them out. I closed the show that first night; the second night I let him close the show.[9]

On this tour, the troupe played in Lubbock, and once again Elvis was met with wild enthusiasm.

Walker continued as a member of the Hayride until fall 1955, when he left to join another regionally popular country music radio show broadcast from Springfield, Missouri. The Ozark Jubilee, like the Big D Jamboree, the Louisiana Hayride, and the Grand Ole Opry, was an important outlet for country music talent, and Billy spent the next four years on the show until he moved back to Fort Worth, Texas in late 1959.

In 1960, Walker moved to Nashville at the insistence of Randy Keith, manager of country artist Patsy Cline. Walker related, "Randy insisted, saying you can't make any money except in Nashville. They are the only people making money." It was not an easy decision:

> I never did really want to come to Tennessee. I was from Texas, you know, and that's your home, and Texas is a big state. It seemed like that for a long time I had a western swing band, because I liked Bob Wills music too. . . . West Texas was full of Bob Wills records and he played everywhere out there. So I had a big band and we played all kinds of different places, but the thing about it is, nobody was making any money in the country music business, or serious money, except people out of Nashville.[10]

Walker became a regular member of the Grand Ole Opry and performed the first time on January 4, 1960. He has had many hit records in his career, recording for five major labels: Capitol, Columbia, Monument, MGM, and RCA. His biggest hit was in 1962 with the song

"Charlie's Shoes." Walker is one of a very few artists to have been a regular member of four successful postwar radio jamboree-type programs. He continues to tour and perform as a member of the most successful program of them all, the Grand Ole Opry.

Ben Hall, a West Texas country singer, songwriter, recording engineer, and disc jockey in the 1950s and 1960s, also answered the call to Nashville. His early career in West Texas had an important impact on the country music and artists of the region.

Hall was born in the central Texas community of Alvord on June 13, 1924. Shortly after his birth, Hall's family moved to a ranch near Breckenridge in West Texas, where Ben's father was in the farming and ranching business. During the next few years, the Hall family moved several times within the West Texas region, living on ranches near Matador and Throckmorton.

Although his father was not musical, both sides of Ben's family boasted many musicians: one paternal aunt played guitar, another the banjo, and his mother's family included many singers. Hall noted, "They'd sit around at night and sing . . . and play, and I wanted a guitar real bad from the earliest times."[11] The family music making consisted of "old songs like the Carter family sang," Hall added. Although Ben's grandmother owned a cylinder phonograph record player, it was not until he was ten, when his father bought a wind-up disc record player, that Ben heard the music of country singing legend Jimmie Rodgers. These recordings were purchased at the local drugstore and general store for around twenty-five cents each.

Around 1934, Hall earned the money to buy his first guitar by raising and selling a calf his father had given him. He bought an old Washburn brand guitar from a friend's grandmother, who had originally ordered it from the Sears and Roebuck catalog. She taught Ben how to tune the guitar and to play the G, C, and D chords. Enthusiastically, Hall began to learn Jimmie Rodgers's songs and style: "I could do blue yodels and everything he did. I copied him exactly from the records."

While growing up on the remote ranches of his childhood, Ben played music with family members and the cowhands and construction workers that the ranchers employed. Ben and his aunts played for house dances, where the hosts would clear the furniture out of a room for the dancers and the musicians would stand in one corner and play the old dance tunes like "Rubber Dolly." Several of the ranch workers played music:

> I worked for SMS Ranch there in Throckmorton, Texas. There was a guy who was the straw-boss out there called Poss Murray. He played fiddle and I'd play guitar. . . . There was one old fellow named Uncle Billy Weeks, who was around eighty years old at the time, that I played with around there in Breckenridge, Texas. . . . He would play "Brown-Skinned Girl" and "Rattlesnake Warning." He was one of the greatest ones I'd ever heard.

Hall learned to play a few standard tunes like "Sally Goodin" on a fiddle given to him by an uncle.

Hall also heard music played at the medicine shows that appeared periodically in the area. These shows would usually feature a stringed instrument such as the banjo or guitar in addition to a harmonica or kazoo. "I would go, of course, and listen to them very intently. Anybody that could play, I was always wanting to go and listen to them," Hall said.

Ben remembered the singing of black farmhands as they worked in the cotton fields, especially one instance:

> In the old days we had terrible grasshoppers that would try to eat up the cotton crop, and they [the farmhands] would stretch a long bunch of binder twine and tie papers on it, and a bunch of the black people would get on a long row of that stuff and they'd get in rhythm singing with this thing and work it backwards and forwards, backwards and forwards, and then they'd go to singing to that time, running the grasshoppers . . . out to the pastures and keep them out of the fields. They would start singing and get in time with it, and each one of them would have perfect rhythm across that field.

The first radio programs Ben heard were at his uncle's house in Alvord. During the Depression, the Hall family, who had no automobile, would drive a mule-drawn wagon into town with produce to sell and then stay the evening with Ben's uncle, listening to the Grand Ole Opry from Nashville. Ben heard Opry performers Uncle Dave Macon and Uncle Jimmy Thompson: "That's the first real live country thing [on the radio] that I can recall. We could barely hear it even though [the antenna] was on the garage and [the radio] had a good battery system." By the time Ben was thirteen, the Hall family had purchased a Philco battery-powered radio. With the antenna stretched between two willow poles attached to the top of the ranch house, the few stations they could receive came in the clearest early in the mornings and in the evenings.

Hall first heard the full band sound of Milton Brown and his Musical Brownies and the Light Crust Doughboys featuring Bob Wills on WBAP from Fort Worth. "They were the earliest type band people that I listened to. I liked his [Bob Wills's] type of music with a band, and we began to play that type of music," Hall remembered.

After graduation from high school and a tour of duty in the service during World War II, Hall returned to Breckenridge and in 1945 began performing on station KSTB in Breckenridge. He performed just with his guitar at first and later organized his first band, which played every Saturday on the station. Billed as the Mesa Valley Boys, the band members styled themselves after the Bob Wills band.

The Mesa Valley Boys' radio program was popular, and Ben booked the group for Saturday night dances and personal appearances. Hall also worked at the station as a disc jockey and announcer with an hour-and-a-half program of country music. He explained, "Everybody listened to that program, because we were one of the only country programs around there."

Noting the lack of family entertainment in the area, Ben Hall began a live Saturday night country music show using the American Legion Hall in Breckenridge. Hall promoted the event on his radio program, and from the beginning, the 250-seat hall was full. Admission to the Country Roundup, as the show was called, was twenty-five cents, and it soon became so popular that it was reported in several out-of-town newspapers, and the audience grew even larger.

With this increased exposure, Hall came to the attention of Dave Stone, at Lubbock's KSEL, who hired Hall as a disc jockey. Hall moved to Lubbock in early 1953 and began with a daily program broadcast from 1:00 to 3:00 p.m. During his tenure at KSEL, Ben performed on the live broadcasts of the KSEL Western Jamboree, often using young local musicians in his band. At various times, Hall's band included Sonny Curtis, Buddy Holly, Weldon Myrick, and Hall's wife, Dena, on bass.

In addition to small production studios for the disc jockeys, KSEL had a one hundred-seat auditorium used for broadcasting live musical programs. Hall remembered several occasions when Bob Wills and the Texas Playboys came by the station and performed on the air from this facility to promote a local appearance. Local groups like Tommy Hancock and the Roadside Playboys, Hope Griffith, and the Pickwicks, a gospel family group, also used the studio for their regular programs.

Hall left KSEL in late 1953 and moved to KDAV, the new, all-country format station operated by former KSEL general manager Dave Stone. The move did not work out well for Hall, and he left the station at the end of 1954. Shortly before he left KDAV, Hall wrote "Blue Days, Black Nights," the song that was to become Buddy Holly's first release. Hall described the song's origins: "When we left Lubbock, it was in December, it was real bad weather, and [I] kinda got the idea from not having any money and being broke, and there were blue days and black nights."

After leaving KSEL, Hall spent the next two years working on radio and television in various Texas markets, including Wichita Falls, Vernon, Fort Worth, and Dublin. He made plans during this time to move to Nashville and was waiting for fellow musician Weldon Myrick to graduate from high school. In 1956, Hall was offered a job by a radio station owner in Big Spring who was putting in a television station. Hall stated, "I told him [the station owner] I could be out there for a little while but I was moving to Nashville in about six months. He said, 'Well, that'd be fine, just come and work even that long.' I went out there, and that's when I got bogged down and stayed there ten years." Hall, Myrick on guitar and steel guitar, and Dena Hall on bass performed on the television station as the Circle Four Ramblers. While in Big Spring, Hall built a small recording studio in his garage to record demos of his songs. He named the studio the High Fidelity House, and soon many regional artists were attracted to his garage studio—the first professional recording facility in the area. Hoyle Nix and the West Texas Cowboys, Gene Tabor, Blackie Crawford and the Cherokee Cowboys, Larry Welborn, Troy Jordan and the Cross B Boys, and Hank Harral all made recordings in Hall's studio.[12] Harral's recording of "Hank's Boogie," made for his own Caprock label, was recorded at Hall's studio and received air play in the region. Roy Orbison also recorded song demos at the studio, as did his cowriter Joe Melson.

Ben Hall performed and operated his studio and a sound installation company during the ten years he was in Big Spring. In 1967 he finally made the move to Nashville he had been planning since the mid-1950s. In Nashville, he built a studio, eventually sold it to Roy Orbison, and then built another. Currently, Hall is still operating a recording studio in Nashville. Recent interest in the early days of rock and roll and country boogie music has resulted in the release of some of the music recorded at Hall's Big Spring studio on two compact discs by an English label: *Hep Cats from Big Spring* and *Country Days In Rock and Roll*.

Ben Hall's friend and fellow musician Weldon Myrick has been a top studio steel guitarist since moving to Nashville in 1963 and is one of the most highly respected session players in the country music industry. Myrick was born April 10, 1938, in the ranch country of West Texas in the small town of Jayton. The Myrick household was often filled with the music of family and friends. At an early age, Weldon crawled onto the bed to strum on his older brother Texie Gene's guitar. When Weldon was eight, his brother, who had moved to Lubbock, returned to Jayton prior to his leaving for the Air Force and brought back a steel guitar that he was trying to learn to play. With the few lessons he had received on the instrument at Adair Music in Lubbock, Texie Gene demonstrated the sound of the steel to Weldon, who recalled that "I dearly loved it."[13]

When his brother went into the service, eight-year-old Weldon took up the abandoned steel guitar; as he modestly remembered, he "did pretty good." Texie eventually sold the steel, and Weldon's father took Weldon to Lubbock to buy his own steel—a Rickenbacker brand, similar to that played on record by the nationally known steel guitarist Jerry Byrd.

Weldon played with some friends around Jayton, and by the age of thirteen he was playing with a group from Peacock called the Double Mountain Boys, led by Henley Diggs, who had a once-a-week radio show in Stamford. To pay the radio station for the air time, the band members sold advertising spots for the show to local merchants. If any money was left, the band members would split the profits. "Sometimes it might be three or four dollars apiece, sometimes it wouldn't be anything, or we'd have to pay in a little," Myrick said. "I thought I was in the big-time then."

Despite being underage, Myrick also played dance halls with various pick-up bands and tried to capture the sounds of the popular steel players of the day: Don Helms on Hank Williams records, Bud Isaacs on Webb Pierce recordings, and Elmer Lawrence on radio from Lubbock with the Billy Walker band. Myrick met Ben Hall in Breckenridge and began playing with him, an association that would continue for many years.

After Ben Hall moved to Lubbock in 1953 to work for KSEL, Myrick spent his summer vacations from high school living with Hall and playing music. During these summer vacations Weldon met and played with

Sonny Curtis, Waylon Jennings, Buddy Holly, Bob Montgomery, and other Lubbock area players of the day on the KSEL Western Jamboree and the "Sunday Party" radio broadcasts on KDAV. He also worked on the KDUB television show starring teenage country singer Hope Griffith. In addition to Weldon on steel, Waylon Jennings was the lead guitarist for the television band. Weldon made his first trip to Nashville to record on a demo with Griffith.

At the age of seventeen, Myrick followed Ben Hall to Wichita Falls and found work playing for local disc jockey, songwriter, and performer Bill Mack. After graduating from high school, he moved to Big Spring, once again following Ben Hall to play with him. In Big Spring, Weldon started writing songs on his own and with Hall. Songwriting eventually led Weldon to move to Nashville, although it was his recording studio skills as a steel guitarist, developed at Ben Hall's Big Spring studio, that would bring him his biggest success. Buddy Holly recorded the Hall and Myrick composition "It's Not My Fault," which appeared on Holly's *Reminiscing* album.

In 1958, through their songwriting and contacts with West Coast music promoter Cliffie Stone, Ben Hall, Dena Hall, and Weldon Myrick landed a recording contract with Capitol Records. "They said you can record out in California, or you can go to Nashville. We said we wanted to go to Nashville," Myrick said. Billed as the Benny Hall Trio, the only record released was a duet by Ben and Weldon that had very little success. Weldon returned to Big Spring, where he worked on the police force and continued to write and record at Hall's garage studio.

Myrick's experience in Nashville convinced him that it was where he needed to be: "I had always wanted to make a living in the music business. I'd become twenty-five years old, and if I'm ever gonna try it, I need to go ahead and try it now." In 1963, encouraged by fellow West Texan Sonny Curtis, Myrick and his family moved to Nashville. He wrote songs and placed them with various music publishers in town but had only limited success. He also made an attempt at a singing career, putting out two releases on Dot Records, one on Mega, and a few releases on smaller labels, and singing once as a guest on the Grand Ole Opry. To pay the bills, Weldon took jobs playing steel with comedian Pap Wilson and after three months went to work with emerging singer/songwriter Bill Anderson in his "Po' Boys" band. Working with Anderson gave Weldon an opportunity to record in Nashville as a steel player. He was soon noticed by other artists and producers, who began using him on their productions. In 1966 Myrick was hired as the house steel guitar player for the Grand Ole Opry, a prestigious position he continues to hold.[14] In 1969, Myrick participated in the recording of *Area Code 615,* a historic album featuring the leading Nashville session players of the day. This was possibly the first recording to feature the super talents of Nashville's finest studio musicians. It was a boon to the heretofore uncredited Nashville session musicians; Myrick felt that "it was definitely a help and was a prestigious thing to have done."

Waylon Jennings is perhaps the most recognized country singer to emerge from West Texas in the 1960s. His popular songs and top-selling albums and his association with Willie Nelson as one of the "outlaws" of country music have assured his superstardom. Born June 15, 1937, in the community of Littlefield, Jennings gained his musical experience in much the same way as had other West Texas youth of the period: His father, various family members, and friends played guitars and sang country music; there was music on the radio, with the Grand Ole Opry, Louisiana Hayride, and live local shows like the KSEL Western Jamboree; and he heard the cowboy music of the movies.[15]

Littlefield resident Emil Macha was just out of high school when he first met Waylon. Macha was working at Littlefield station KVOW when Jennings came in and auditioned for a spot on the radio. Macha and station owner J. B. McShan made a tape of Waylon, liked what he did, and put him on the air for a thirty-minute program each week. Waylon needed a band and asked Emil to play bass (he played a washtub bass) and to emcee the show. The Texas Longhorns, Jennings's first band, included Jennings on guitar and vocals, Macha on bass, banjo player Roscoe Taylor, a 390-pound mandolin player called "Tiny," and some other youthful players.[16] To give the group the appearance of notoriety, Macha cut a picture of longhorns off a grease bucket label and wired it to the front of his father's 1937 Chevrolet, which was used as the band vehicle.[17] Macha played bass with Jennings for eight years, many times practicing in Macha's parents' home just north of the KVOW studio.

According to Macha, the Texas Longhorns played a mixture of "country western, bluegrass . . . it all just mixed together." The group was not always well received: "I begged and begged the VFW to let us play a dance for them. Finally they knuckled down. They were going to pay us twenty-five dollars to play that dance, and we had an eight-piece band. We got up and started playing. We played about four songs and they plugged in the juke box." Jennings seemed to have the ambition at this early age to "make it big," Macha recalled. "He was a good ole boy and everything, but he was the guy that played his guitar too loud . . . he was the only one with an amplifier . . . he was a star, so to speak," Macha added. At the age of seventeen, Waylon and the Texas Longhorns went to the KFYO radio station in Lubbock to record a demo. "Stranger in My Home" and "There'll Be a New Day" were cut despite the fact that only four of the band members showed up.[18]

In addition to performing on KVOW, Jennings worked at the station as a disc jockey, billed as "America's Youngest DJ."[19] Waylon next moved to Lubbock, where he worked for Dave Stone at KDAV and later at KLLL. KLLL, owned by Larry Corbin, began broadcasting with an all-country music format in March 1958 in competition with the highly successful KDAV. Corbin related, "We went down a little different track . . . if there was a country station, the air staff would always say stuff like, 'Howdy, friends and neighbors' and 'Aw shucks' . . . all that kind of stuff. We were fast paced; played a lot of jingles. . . . If it was anywhere close to country, say from Ricky Nelson to Roy Orbison, we played it."[20]

With Waylon Jennings and other radio personalities, such as Don Bowman, KLLL and the Corbins gave country radio in the area a new sound and, with the youthful Jennings performing locally, a new look. KLLL promoted the disc jockeys' personalities, and Waylon's brash, ad-lib radio chatter drew attention to him and the station. Emil Macha noted that not everybody liked Waylon's approach: "He was too corny . . . corny jokes, corny remarks. Things that wasn't even funny, over and over and over again. . . . Probably somebody liked it. I felt most of us didn't care for it."[21] Some listeners did like it, and this new, youthful country radio attracted Sonny Curtis and other young Lubbock musicians away from KDAV.[22] The KLLL studios in the Great Plains Building in downtown Lubbock quickly became the hangouts for country enthusiasts.

In 1958, Buddy Holly helped Waylon make his first professional recordings. Holly knew Waylon from the KDAV "Sunday Party" broadcasts of the mid-1950s. Holly, now an established artist, wanted to expand into record production and arranged for Waylon to record at the Petty studio in Clovis on September 10, 1958. The two songs recorded at the session were a new version of the Cajun hit "Jole Blon" and "When Sin Stops (Love Begins)" by Lubbock songwriter Bob Vanable.[23] The recordings featured Holly and Tommy Allsup on guitars and New York saxophonist King Curtis, whom Holly had brought in to be on one of his own sessions. The recording, which saw only limited success, was released in spring 1959 on Brunswick Records, the same label for which the Crickets recorded.[24]

Holly hired Jennings to play bass in his backup band on the Winter Dance Party tour that was to be Holly's last. Tommy Allsup, Holly's lead guitarist on a mid-1958 tour, remembered, "I was working in Odessa at the Silver Saddle, and Buddy came in there the night before New Year's Eve and said, 'I've gotta sign with an agent in New York and he's got another dance party show coming up in February, and Waylon told me to find a drummer.'" Tommy located rock drummer Carl Bunch in Odessa and with Tommy on lead guitar, Waylon on electric bass guitar, and Carl on drums, the band was set for that last, legendary Holly tour. Allsup and Jennings were to have been on the plane that crashed, but they gave up their seats at the last minute.

Less well known is the fact that the tour continued after the crash. Allsup remembered finishing the tour without Holly and his surprise at the singing talent of Jennings: "The only time I heard him [Jennings] sing was when he and I sang harmony with Buddy on a few songs. Waylon, after Buddy got killed, started singing those [Holly's] songs. We finished up two more weeks of that tour . . . and those kids just ate him up. He went over big guns. You could see that he had something . . . I could tell he had it."[25]

At the end of the tour both Allsup and Jennings returned to Texas. Tommy returned to the Saddle Club in Odessa, and Waylon, suffering from the loss of his mentor and somewhat disillusioned by his experiences with big-time music operations, returned to radio announcing at

KLLL and performing music regionally. He recorded briefly for the West Texas-based Trend Records and released "Another Blue Day," which got some local air play.

In 1961 Waylon and his wife and newborn son moved from West Texas to Coolidge, Arizona, where he worked in radio briefly before relocating to the booming Phoenix area. In Phoenix, working regularly at JD's club, Waylon developed his unique, brooding, rock-tempered style of country music, which led to his national success as a one of the "outlaws" of country music. After first looking to Los Angeles and Herb Alpert at A&M Records for guidance, Jennings settled on Nashville and Chet Atkins to provide the hits needed for a national career. In Nashville, however, Jennings experienced the same belittling attitudes towards his music and style as Buddy Holly had years before. Waylon's Nashville producers did not want him to play his own guitar on the recordings or pick the songs he was to record. In short, they felt that they knew better.[26]

By the mid-1960s the country music industry, in an effort to rebound from the rock and roll takeover, had developed a diluted pop form of country music promoted as "countrypolitan," complete with orchestra arrangements. Noticeably absent from these recordings were traditional country music instruments such as the fiddle and steel guitar. The developing country-rock sounds coming from the West Coast would not infiltrate Nashville for several years. Jennings had difficulty finding a place in this Nashville music scene for his earthy, gutsy, straightforward brand of country, and his greatest success was sparked by a music scene far from Nashville.

Texas-born singer and songwriter Willie Nelson had cultivated a youthful market for his country music in Austin, Texas, outside the sometimes crushing control of the Nashville music clique. Nelson's growing success demonstrated a way the country music industry could create and market country-inspired sounds for youthful rock audiences. In alliance with the kindred-spirit Nelson, Jennings, Jessi Colter, and Tompall Glaser recorded the album *Wanted! The Outlaws*. This recording, which featured artists viewed as outsiders by the conservative element within the Nashville music industry, was released in 1976 and became the first country album to be certified platinum.[27] The success of this album pushed Waylon Jennings into the superstar category.

Waylon may be the main successor to Buddy Holly, an artist who, with his distaste with the Nashville musical mindset, found his own unique expressions for country-born rock music. Jennings had the distinct advantage over Holly in arriving in Nashville ten years later, at a time when the music industry was in the process of maturing. The success of *The Outlaws* and other such albums forced the Nashville industry to become more receptive to the innovative, personal approach of artists like Waylon Jennings.

Oklahoma-born guitarist, recording engineer, and record producer Tommy Allsup has played an important role in the careers of many West Texas musicians. Allsup moved to West Texas in 1958 and spent several years in the Odessa area. He led several western swing and honky-tonk bands in the Odessa region, in addition to performing on two tours as part of Buddy Holly's backup group. He also played as a studio musician on a number of recordings made at the Norman Petty studio, including those of Buddy Holly, Earl Sinks, the Bowmans, and others. Allsup left West Texas in 1960 for California and worked for Liberty Records as a producer of such artists as Willie Nelson, Tex Williams, and Little Joe Carson. He performed briefly with Jerry Allison and Joe Mauldin in a version of the Crickets during his tenure in California.

Allsup returned to West Texas in 1965, opened a recording studio in Odessa, and produced a number of local artists, including Hoyle Nix and Edna Lee. In the 1960s, the mystique of Buddy Holly and his West Texas roots attracted a few national rock acts to the region to record. In 1969 Allsup recorded the Zager and Evans hit "In the Year 2525" in his Odessa studio, a song that became the biggest selling record worldwide in that year. "It was quite an accomplishment for West Texas," Allsup said with pride.[28] That year, Tommy left for Nashville to move into the larger music business arena. One of his most notable projects was as producer of the United Artists two-album set "Bob Wills, For The Last Time," which featured, in addition to a number of Wills's alumni and Merle Haggard, West Texas fiddler Hoyle Nix and his son Jody.

Allsup played an important role in the performing and recording career of Edna Lee. Born in Glenwood, Arkansas, in 1931, Edna House and her family moved to West Texas around 1942 and eventually settled in Morton. Edna's first public singing performance outside of church was in 1950 with her sister Billie on the KSEL Western Jamboree in Lubbock. The sisters were soon invited to join Jimmy Johnson and his Melody Five, a group that included talented Lubbock musicians Wayne Maines, Wayne Hill, and Wally Moyers. Edna, who had married Percy Dewbre in 1947, stopped performing in the mid-1950s to raise her family.

In 1959, Edna started performing again and appeared for six months on Bill Mack's Lubbock television program. In 1963, she recorded two original songs, "Devil" and "Until the End of Time" for the Memphis, Tennessee-based Millionare Records label. Edna met Tommy Allsup shortly after he returned to Odessa in 1965, and soon she was performing regularly with Allsup's band and recording in his studio. When Allsup moved to Nashville, he arranged a recording contract for Edna Lee with Metromedia Records. Edna recorded "Full House" and "Men" in 1969 and was nominated for female vocalist of the year. Edna stopped recording in the early 1970s but continued singing in the Lubbock area with Morton's Freddie Lewis until 1984, when medical problems ended her performing career.[29]

Many other West Texas singers and musicians left West Texas beginning in the late 1950s and through the next decades to find success in various national meccas of entertainment, including Nashville. Country entertainer Jimmy Dean of Plainview led the exodus in the 1950s, with a successful career in television based in Washington, D.C., and New York; in 1961, he scored big with the narrative hit "Bad John." Jeannie C. Riley, from Anson, firmly established her stardom with the 1968 hit

"Harper Valley P. T. A.," the first superhit for songwriter Tom T. Hall. Tanya Tucker of Seminole began her Nashville career in 1972 at age fourteen with the controversial hit "Would You Lay with Me in a Field of Stone?" and her sister La Costa landed a Nashville recording contract soon afterward. Larry Gatlin and the Gatlin Brothers from Odessa experienced a long succession of country hits, beginning in 1973 with "Sweet Becky Walker." Country folk vocalist Don Williams, who spent part of his youth in Floydada, was a member of the Pozo Seco Singers before finding a country audience in America and Europe with hits such as the classic "Amanda." In the mid-1960s, Lubbock-born comedian Don Bowman signed with RCA Records and had a major hit with "Chit Atkins, Make Me a Star."[30]

West Texas songwriters had increasing success beginning in the late 1950s. Farwell songwriter Charlie Phillips wrote and recorded "Sugartime," which became a hit for the McGuire Sisters in 1957, while Sonny Curtis of Meadow found success both as a performer and as a writer of such diverse material as "I Fought the Law and the Law Won," "I Love You More Than I Can Say," and the Mary Tyler Moore television show theme song. Mac Davis's hit "Lubbock in the Rearview Mirror" revealed the mixed feelings the writer had about his hometown.

West Texas also spawned some of Nashville's finest country music record producers. Bob Montgomery from Lubbock, Buddy Holly's high school singing partner, now is a leading independent producer in Nashville. Jimmy Bowen, who, along with Buddy Knox, recorded the fifties hit "Party Doll," is the head of Capitol Records in Nashville. Lubbock Walk of Fame inductee Snuff Garrett, who was originally from Dallas and grew up in West Texas, has produced records for major artists in California and Nashville.

Noted West Texas musicians who played with national acts in these years include Levelland native Glen D. Hardin, who played piano with the Crickets, Elvis Presley, Emmylou Harris and others; fiddler Merle David of Childress,with Hank Thompson; and Joe Stephenson of McAdoo, who played fiddle with Johnny Rodriguez.

In 1980, largely through the efforts of former KLLL radio co-owner Larry Corbin, a bronze statue of Buddy Holly was dedicated near the Lubbock Civic Center. Around the base of the statue the "Walk of Fame" was established.[31] The inscription reads:

> "Walk of Fame"
> Lubbock and the West Texas area are rich in heritage and contributions from many gifted people in the field of music and entertainment. To preserve and share this rich heritage, the Lubbock "Walk of Fame" was dedicated September 6, 1980. Civic Lubbock Inc. 1983.

The first plaque was dedicated to Buddy Holly and reads:

> Buddy Holly
> 1936-1959

Buddy Holly contributed to the musical heritage of not only West Texas but the entire world as a musician and composer. It is significant that this first plaque on the "Walk of Fame" be in his name. The citizens of Lubbock pay tribute to and honor their native son. Inducted into the Walk of Fame 1979.

In subsequent years many West Texans have been added to the list. In 1980, Waylon Jennings was inducted, and Mac Davis was added in 1983. Jimmy Dean, Lubbock singer Ralna English, who worked with Lawrence Welk's orchestra, and Lubbock saxophonist Bobby Keys, who toured with the Rolling Stones, were inducted together in 1984. In 1985, two area actors, G. W. Bailey and Barry Corbin, were inducted, while in 1986, four former members of Buddy Holly's Crickets were inductees: Niki Sullivan, Jerry Allison, Joe B. Mauldin, and Sonny Curtis. After another two-year lapse, Tanya Tucker was included in 1988, followed by Lubbock country rocker Joe Ely and Roy Orbison in 1989. Bob Wills and the Gatlin Brothers—Larry, Steve, and Rudy—were inducted in 1990, and in 1991 the sole inductee was Snuff Garrett. In 1994, rocker Buddy Knox and doo-wop singer Virgil Johnson were inducted.

Despite an exodus of entertainers from West Texas that started in the 1960s, the country music scene stayed active. Groups lead by Tommy Hancock, Wilburn Roach, and Larry Trider in Lubbock, Jimmie Mackey in Brownfield, L. C. Agnew in Abilene, and Hoyle Nix in Big Spring, to name only a few, continued to play a combination of classic favorites and new material that has been basis for musical success in West Texas since the 1930s.

As West Texas musicians spread throughout the country in the 1960s and 1970s and built successful careers in the national arena, West Texas earned a reputation for producing talented musicians and singers. In addition, the success of West Texans on the national scene encouraged a new generation of musicians and songwriters within the region.

8

POETS

AND

PICKERS

The youth music culture of the 1960s changed music throughout the world, and West Texas was no exception. Through the work of a young group of musicians and songwriters, influenced by the sounds of folk and rock music, an active blending of musical styles reshaped West Texas country music in the 1970s, just as it had been reshaped in the 1930s by Bob Wills and his contemporaries, in the 1940s with the development of honky-tonk music, and in the 1950s by the rock and roll generation.

West Texas is not unique in its mixing of musical styles. The history of American popular music is one of diverse musical genres blending and influencing one another. Given the creative musical history of the region, however, West Texas musicians may have felt less constrained by categories, especially country and rock, than did artists in other areas of the country in the 1960s and 1970s.

Lubbock musician Tommy Anderson, who has played trumpet with every kind of musical group imaginable since the early 1950s, feels that an openness to many types of music distinguishes the area.[1] An open dialogue among jazz, pop, blues, bluegrass, and country musicians facilitated the development in West Texas of hybrid musical styles such as western swing, rock and roll, and country-rock.

Anderson, primarily a jazz and pop artist, also played regularly with country groups in the Lubbock area. He found Lubbock bandleader Wilburn Roach as quick to hire a good horn player for his country dance band as he was to hire the more common fiddler or steel guitar player. Fiddler Homer Logan taught Anderson the pop standard "Polka Dots and Moonbeams" while the two were performing at a country dance in Lubbock. That a western swing-style country fiddler would teach a pop tune to a jazz musician illustrates the willingness of West Texas musicians of different styles to exchange ideas.[2]

The musical interests of musicians are always several years, if not decades, ahead of the interests of the general public. This was especially true in the 1970s in music communities outside the mainstream recording centers of country music. In areas such as southern California, Austin, and Lubbock, musicians experimented, mixing musical styles resulting in new categories such as blues-rock, folk-rock, and country-rock. The most commercial of these experiments enjoyed economic success and in turn influenced others. Country-rock, for example, once considered an odd fringe subcategory of country music, became a mainstream movement in the country music industry during the late 1980s.

In the 1970s, Lubbock was the town most associated with West Texas music, a perception that continues to the present. Country music was played in cities and towns throughout West Texas during this period, but it was the music that developed in Lubbock that drew attention to the region. Legendary as the birthplace of Buddy Holly, Lubbock owed its reputation to a new generation of singer/songwriter/musicians who further established it as the place to be from, if not necessarily the place to be.

The typical West Texas country music group in the 1960s and 1970s was a "copy band"—a band that played music made popular by other artists. These groups were and continue to be very popular with club owners and their clientele. Employers often encouraged bands to learn the latest songs on the radio to the exclusion of obscure or original material. Lubbock musician Lloyd Maines, for example, remembered Terry Allen and Joe Ely as the first musicians in the area to feature original music prominently, and Maines was amazed that audiences liked this material.[3]

The songwriting of Butch Hancock, Jimmie Dale Gilmore, Terry Allen, Joe Ely, and others became the source of the excitement about Lubbock as a music center for West Texas. The emergence of these performers in the 1970s started music journalists asking, "What is it about Lubbock [or West Texas] that breeds so many talented musicians?" Some of the inspiration for these West Texas songwriters came from the physical environment. Violent storms, flash flooding, hail and wind storms are part of the collective consciousness of West Texans. Most inhabitants of the region have been inconvenienced, sustained property losses, or even suffered injury or death as a result of the weather.[4] Big sky and flat terrain are unavoidable features of the landscape, so it is not surprising that the work of Lubbock's emerging songwriters often concerned the physical environment.

Lubbock songwriter Terry Allen remembered the sound of the wind, particularly the moan of the wind blowing through the weatherstripping in his home as a child: "Always, the wind or the dirt is the first thing people talk about. . . . I think that is etched in all of that music." Allen also felt that geography affected the music of West Texans: "The music is almost as flat as the ground," Allen commented, referring to the lack of contours of the music rather than pitch.[5]

Both Allen and Jimmie Dale Gilmore feel that driving the flat, straight highways of West Texas creates a rhythm that is reflected in many of their compositions. According to Allen, three-quarters of his songs were written in a car on the highway: "There's a rhythm . . . of asphalt and tires and stuff that has something to do with it."[6]

Joe Ely's "Because of the Wind" is an example of music inspired by the physical surroundings:

Do you know why the trees bend at the West Texas border?
Do you know why they bend, sway, and twine?
The trees bend because of the wind across that lonesome border,

The trees bend because of the wind, almost all the time.[7]

Because of the Wind by Joe Ely, ERE Music, ASCAP 1978

In 1971, Ely, along with Butch Hancock and Jimmie Dale Gilmore, formed the nucleus of the Flatlanders, a Lubbock-based acoustic group whose lineup at different times also included Steve Wesson, Tony Pearson, Sylvester Rice, Jesse Taylor, and fiddler Tommy Hancock.[8] In 1972, the group recorded an album in Nashville by producer Royce Clark for Plantation Records that was never released in the formal sense and was available only in eight-track format. The album was not promoted, and shortly after this ill-fated effort, the group returned to Lubbock and performed briefly around town. A highlight of this period was the Flatlanders' performance at the first Kerrville Folk Festival. Later in 1972, discouraged by the lack of work and income, the group drifted apart.[9]

The album, entitled *The Flatlanders*, showcased the early songwriting of Gilmore and Hancock. Included is a song later recorded by Ely and perhaps Gilmore's best known work, "Dallas." After years of being a sought-after collector's item, the Flatlanders album was reissued by Rounder records in 1990 as *The Flatlanders: More a Legend Than a Band*.[10] Although never commercially successful, this music attracted critical acclaim, typified by this newspaper review:

> Twenty years ago—as one of the Flatlanders with Joe Ely and Butch Hancock—Jimmie Dale Gilmore made albums that blew into the music world like a dangerous West Texas sandstorm. The legendary band's recordings didn't blow down all the walls, but the grit off those old LPs seeped into the cracks and wouldn't go away. Like other music from West Texas, the Flatlanders' flavor challenged the critics who really never have nailed down the special appeal and elusive nature of the music that hails from out past Abilene.[11]

Such reviews helped to perpetuate the popular image of West Texas music and musicians. It became almost cliche to compare the work of West Texas musicians to the land from which it came. Gilmore, Ely, and Hancock have all been evaluated in the light of their West Texas roots.

The songwriting is the standout feature of the Flatlanders' album. By contrast, the music, which features several guitars, mandolin, fiddle, dobro, bass, harmonica, and musical saw, is played adequately but not artfully. Compared to other acoustic folk music of the period, the music is quite primitive and has more the sound of a folk jam session than a commercial recording. The vocal style of Gilmore, who sings lead on most of the songs, owes much to early country music singers, such as Jimmie Rodgers and Hank Williams—an anachronism in 1971. Colin Escott, in his notes to the Flatlanders' reissue album, states that the group suffered because of the great disparity between its sound and the commercial country music coming out of Nashville in the early 1970s, and it is surprising that these Nashville recordings were made at all.[12] Country music fans of the 1970s listened to the country-pop music of Ronnie Milsap, Charlie Rich, and Barbara Mandrell, while the young rock audience enjoyed the polished folk-rock of Crosby, Stills, and Nash and the Eagles. The Flatlanders, who were born of both the country and rock music worlds, belonged to neither.

Joe Ely has experienced the greatest fame of this trio. Ely left Lubbock after the Flatlanders disbanded, rambling at various jobs and traveling Europe as a solo performer, often on the street. Returning to Lubbock in 1973, he soon decided to relocate to Austin but had no traveling money. To this end, he formed a band to play two nights only at the Main Street Saloon. The band included Rick Hulett on guitar, Greg Wright on bass, and steel guitarist Lloyd Maines, whom Ely had met while recording harmonica overdubs at Don Caldwell's Lubbock recording studio. Surprisingly, this first group had no drummer. Maines described audience reaction to the group as "mind-boggling" from the first gig. He described the music: "Ely [was] just strumming the acoustic [guitar], no arrangements, we'd never heard the songs. He just got up there and did them and we backed him up the best we could."[13] In fact, audience response was so favorable that Ely continued to play at the Main Street Saloon for the next year. He eventually reformed the group to include some of the best instrumentalists in the Lubbock area.[14] The seeming unlikely combination of Jesse Taylor's blazing, Freddie King-inspired blues guitar style with the equally amazing power of Lloyd Maines's high-energy pedal steel guitar, backed up by Steve Keeton on drums and Greg Wright on bass, created an earthy, energetic ensemble sound that owed as much to rock and blues as it did to country and was one of a kind. A demo tape of this group was passed to MCA Record officials by members of Jerry Jeff Walker's Lost Gonzo band. MCA sent a representative to hear Ely at the Cotton Club in Lubbock, and Ely was signed to MCA.

Ely's first MCA album, simply entitled *Joe Ely*, was released in 1977 and included five Ely originals, five Butch Hancock songs, and one song by Jimmie Dale Gilmore. A critical success, the album seemed to ensure Ely's stardom. Ely featured the musicianship of his impressive group extensively on this and subsequent albums and even more so in live performance. Extended instrumental soloing by the musicians was a hallmark of the Ely band sound, thereby elevating the musician to the level of the singer. Ely's second album, *Honky Tonk Masquerade*, released by MCA in 1978, featured six more Ely originals, three Hancock compositions, and one song penned by Gilmore. Ponty Bone, who played a unique, blues-rock accordion style, was added to the group shortly before this recording, and his unusual contribution made the group even more distinctive and difficult to classify.

Although basically a high-energy country band, albeit an unusual one, Ely's group performed largely for rock audiences. The country world was not yet ready for their rock-influenced sounds, but Ely found acceptance in the rock world for the country nature of his music, just as the Byrds, the Flying Burrito Brothers, Poco, and other experimental country-rock bands of the 1970s did. It was not until the 1980s that groups such as Alabama would successfully introduce heavily rock-flavored music into the country music mainstream.

Ely maintained an extensive touring schedule in the late 1970s and early 1980s, including numerous trips to Europe. Ely was the opening act for important performers such as country-turned-rock singer Linda Ronstadt, English rockers the Clash, and the Rolling Stones. Despite good exposure and critical acclaim, Ely attracted only a small following, by rock music standards.

During this period, Ely produced the celebrated Tornado Jam concerts in Lubbock. The first Tornado Jam was held on May 11, 1980, exactly ten years after the devastating Lubbock tornado it was named for. On May 11, 1970, Lubbock was hit by a massive tornado that left a mile wide by a mile and a half long path of destruction just north of the downtown business district. Twenty-six people were killed, another fifteen hundred were injured, and more than $250 million of property was destroyed or damaged.[15] Conceived by Ely, the Tornado Jam was a large, outdoor music concert held annually in Lubbock's Buddy Holly Park. Described as a "windy West Texas Woodstock," it perhaps did as much as any other event to create the Lubbock music mystique.[16] Although some in the community felt this event was an inappropriate commemoration of the tornado, Ely thought of it simply as a celebration of West Texas music.

The event was tremendously successful from the beginning: the first-year attendance was estimated at from eight to eighteen thousand.[17] The concert was headlined by Ely and Capitol recording artist Jay Boy Adams. Other performers included Joey Allen, Butch Hancock, Jimmie Dale Gilmore, the Maines Brothers, and blues guitar legend Stevie Ray Vaughan.[18] The featured performers were predominantly West Texans, but it was not strictly a country music concert; the music reflected the diversity of interests influencing country music in the early 1980s.

Despite the threat of rain, the second Jam, held on May 3, 1981, was also a success, drawing a larger crowd than the previous year. Many of the same acts returned for the second Jam, and a large souvenir booklet was produced for the event. The third Tornado Jam was held May 3, 1982. Rock singer Linda Ronstadt was a special guest for the concert and performed with Joe Ely's band. Rain throughout the concert was probably responsible for the small crowd.[19]

On the Friday night before the concert, Lubbock's Monterey High School students were pleasantly surprised when Ronstadt and Ely dropped in at their graduation dance, held at the Cotton Club. The Maines Brothers Band was performing for the dance when Ely and Ronstadt joined them for an impromptu jam session, much to the delight of the crowd, although the Cotton Club's manager called the music to an early halt.[20]

The Jam ultimately was stopped when the Lubbock City Council voted not to issue the required permit for the 1983 event. In denying the permit, officials cited their fear that the buffalo grass growing in the park would be damaged by the large crowds.[21] The fact that live music was effectively banned from the park that bore Buddy Holly's name was an irony not lost on the Lubbock music community. In 1985, Ely staged a scaled-down version of the Tornado Jam held indoors at the Civic Center in Lubbock. This concert signaled the death of the idea rather than the desired rebirth. Despite later attempts by the West Texas Music Association to recreate the success of the Jams with their family music festival, the public's interest was never recaptured. Like the tornado it was named after, the Jam dropped down from the clouds, rapidly developed full intensity, and disappeared as quickly as it had appeared.

Ely made a total of six albums with MCA before being released from the label after his 1984 *High Res*. He made two albums with the independent Hightone label, but neither of these efforts resulted in commercial (that is, radio) success for Ely. A hero in West Texas, Austin, and England, Ely was still searching for the elusive hit that would give him a foothold on national success. His problem seemed to be one of labeling. Lubbock newspaper entertainment editor William Kerns put it succinctly: "To be successful—in the business sense—a recording artist has to sell albums. To sell albums, a recording artist has to be played on the radio. And Ely's songs have either been too hardedged for country stations or too, well, West Texas playful for rock n' roll markets. Program directors like to be able to stick an artist into a convenient cubbyhole, and Ely refuses to fit." In a similar vein, *Texas Monthly* writer Joe Nick Potoski commented, "Producing album after album to critical acclaim, country rocker Joe Ely hovers perpetually on the edge of national fame."[22] In 1989, Ely was inducted into the West Texas Walk of Fame, which surrounds the Buddy Holly statue in Lubbock, and in 1991 Ely signed a new contract with MCA and released *Live at Liberty Lunch* in that year and *Love and Danger* in 1992.[23]

Of the Flatlanders, Jimmie Dale Gilmore, after Joe Ely, has received the most media attention. Gilmore was born May 6, 1945, in Amarillo and lived in Tulia until he was six years old, when the Gilmore family moved to Lubbock. Bryan Gilmore, Jimmie Dale's father, played electric lead guitar as a hobby and performed with dance bands around the Tulia area at VFW halls and similar venues. It was at these dances that young Jimmie Dale heard the music of Hank Williams, Lefty Frizzell, and other early 1950s country musicians, as interpreted by his father and the bands. Although he received an offer to perform professionally, Bryan played less and less after the move to Lubbock, where he ran a demonstration dairy at Texas Tech University.[24]

Beginning with a few chords his father showed him, Jimmie Dale learned to play the guitar at sixteen.[25] Jimmie Dale commented, "I think I was at the perfect age for some of the best music that's ever happened because I was . . . in grade school . . . when Elvis came along . . . and then in junior high when Buddy Holly got so popular. . . . And just at the age . . . when you're the most in love with music."[26]

Unlike his classmates, Gilmore continued to like country music while readily embracing rock and roll. Jimmie Dale felt that his open-minded attitude toward music helped to shape his own work: "My career got based, I think, on the fact that I was exposed to these different kinds of music and [I] actually really and truly loved all of them." Gilmore considered himself "basically a folk singer" in his teen years, when he performed solo accompanying himself on acoustic guitar.[27] While he was in high school, two Texas musicians influenced Gilmore's decision to start writing songs: "There's a guy named Terry Allen whom I met in high school. He's a couple of years older than me, and he's a pianist, a songwriter, and also a very accomplished painter and sculptor. We became very good friends, and meeting someone who actually wrote songs turned on a light for me. I realized that you could just do it, you didn't have to wait 'til you were forty years old."[28] A recording of Texas songwriter Townes Van Zandt, loaned to Jimmie Dale by Joe Ely, whom he knew casually from high school, was also an important influence: "It was such a great record. Such simplicity and power. It was a revelation to me, because I heard both worlds, folk music and country music, in the same place."[29]

Gilmore's first major step toward a career in music occurred in 1965 when an English journalist, in Lubbock on a pilgrimage to the birthplace of Buddy Holly, introduced Gilmore to Holly's father. Although they lived in the same town, Gilmore had never met Mr. Holley. Gilmore related that the people of Lubbock were in those years generally unaware of the tremendous impact of Buddy Holly's music around the world. Mr. Holley was impressed with Gilmore's music and offered to pay for a recording session to make demos of Gilmore's songs. Gilmore formed a band for the session with Joe Ely, Jesse Taylor, John Reid, T. J. McFarland, and Al Strehli. Although short lived, the group performed briefly around Lubbock as the T. Nickel House band; as Gilmore remembered, "that band became the framework for . . . a lot of what Joe and I did ever-afterward."[30]

Gilmore, Ely, and Hancock all left Lubbock in the late 1960s to seek their respective fortunes, but by 1971 the three had drifted back to Lubbock. After rediscovering their common musical interests, they formed the Flat-landers. After the Flatlanders group disbanded in 1972, Gilmore stopped playing music to study Eastern philosophy. He lived in Denver for several years, playing music only as a hobby, and moved to Austin in 1980, determined to make a career in music.[31] The 1988 Hightone Records release *Fair and Square* marked his return to music and record-ing.[32] This and his second release on Hightone, *Jimmie Dale Gilmore*, were critical successes and led to a record deal with Elektra. The 1991 release, *After Awhile*, was his first major label recording, followed by *Spinning Around the Sun* in 1993. After many years, Gilmore had found the increased fame that national record distribution and publicity can bring an artist.

By his own choice, Lubbock native Butch Hancock has stayed out of the limelight yet has been the most prolific writer of this group. His songs appear throughout both Gilmore's and Ely's early recordings, and he has been called the "Texas songwriter's Texas songwriter."[33] After the Flatlanders broke up, Hancock moved to Clarendon and later to Austin, working in construction and as an architect. During these years Hancock recorded his music on his own Rainlight label. Also a visual artist, Hancock has made photographs concerning the weather and landscape of West Texas. In the 1980s, several of his photographs were featured in Texas Tech University Museum music exhibits and the accompanying programs.

Hancock's rough vocal style, which he accompanies with guitar and harmonica, is reminiscent of the earthy sounds of Woody Guthrie and Bob Dylan. A reviewer comments, "He . . . calls his musical style—sing-song talking blues with pinched nasal vocals—'tractor music.' To Butch, his songs invoke the rhythms of life on the High Plains, and when you hear him moan 'Wind's Dominion' or chortle through 'West Texas Waltz,' the description makes perfect sense."[34]

In the early 1990s, Hancock ran a business in Austin called "Lubbock or Leave It." This unique establishment offered for sale a variety of items, from Hancock's photographs and recordings to Stubbs's Barbecue Sauce. Despite his renown, Hancock has never been offered a major label recording contract and has instead released eight albums on his own label.[35] "If I were a Bluebird," perhaps his best-known work, was on Joe Ely's first MCA recording and was later recorded by both Jimmie Dale Gilmore and Emmy Lou Harris. Hancock also appeared on the Australian release *Two Roads*, a live recording made in Austin in 1990 featuring Hancock and Jimmie Dale Gilmore. In 1991 Sugar Hill Records released *Own and Own*, a compilation album featuring thirteen tracks taken from Hancock's Rainlight albums recorded from 1978 to 1987 and four songs recorded in 1987 with his group the Sunspots, featuring Lubbock guitarist Jesse Taylor.[36]

Hancock's most ambitious recording project to date has been the 140 original songs he recorded during six nights of performances at Austin's Cactus Cafe. Each month, beginning in September 1990, Hancock released a new cassette tape from this wealth of material. The series, entitled *No 2 Alike*, is duplicated by Hancock himself and is sold at his retail store and through the mail to diehard fans. Hancock remains philosophical about his music and his modest level of success: "I'm gonna go on doing what I'm gonna do, and if people pick up on it, that's wonderful. And if they don't, I can always drive a tractor."[37]

Tommy and Charlene Hancock (no relation to Butch) were part of the early 1970s Lubbock music scene that included Gilmore, Ely, and Butch Hancock. In addition to music making, a growing interest in Eastern philosophy and alternative lifestyles had emerged in this community. Tommy (who has been called "Lubbock's original hippie") and Charlene, although members of the older generation, were involved in a search for self and truth that eventually led them to move their family to an remote spot in New Mexico. Isolated as they were, with no electricity and none of the amenities it brings, the Hancock children learned to sing and play music for entertainment. Before long the desire to perform hit Tommy, and he booked a performance or two with his family band in a local tavern. This was the beginning of several years of travel and music making that took the family around the country and the world.

The Supernatural Family Band consisted of Tommy and Charlene Hancock and their children Traci, Conni, and Joaquin. The group recorded several self-produced albums in Lubbock. This group eventually evolved in the late 1980s into the Texana Dames, an Austin-based group that featured Charlene, Traci, and Conni.[38]

Terry Allen was an influential Lubbock songwriter and musician in the 1970s. Allen was born in Lubbock May 7, 1943. From an early age, Terry was exposed to a wide variety of music while working at his father's performance arena. Terry's father, Sled, had been a professional baseball player and manager. He played briefly with the St. Louis Browns in 1910 and then moved to Houston, where he began a long tenure with different clubs in the old Texas League, first as a player and later as a manager.[39] In the late 1940s, his baseball career over, Sled settled in Lubbock, where he converted an old church building on Thirty-fourth Street into a nightclub and also went into the business of promoting boxing and wrestling events.

After several years at that location, Sled opened the Sled Allen Arena in a more suitable building on Texas Avenue. Used for a wide variety of functions, in 1950 the Arena was the home of the KSEL Western Jamboree. Sled periodically joined with other promoters like Dave Stone of KDAV to bring in national touring groups. The arena was also rented by Hispanic, black, and white groups for dances. In 1956, Sled Allen promoted Lubbock's first multiracial dance, featuring singer Ray Charles and promoted as a "Cosmopolitan Dance." The event was an attempt to bring together Hispanics, blacks, and whites for an evening of dancing and socializing. Terry remembered it as "three paranoid little knots of people."[40]

Working for his father at the Arena and other venues selling concessions, Terry heard a variety of musical artists during the 1950s. In addition to local musicians, he heard many national touring acts, including several of Elvis's early appearances in Lubbock. Terry became interested in rock and roll after hearing Elvis and his rock disciples. Learning to play piano from his mother, Terry wrote and performed songs in high school, mostly out of a desire to get into trouble, according to Allen. One of his early compositions led to a three-day expulsion from school. Allen performed "Roman Orgy" at a school assembly with classmate David Box; as he recalled, "[It was] exhilarating to my peers and highly offensive to the powers that be."[41]

After high school Terry went to Los Angeles to study visual art. While there, he performed with a group called the Black Wall Blues Quintet for three years. During this time, Terry first heard Bob Dylan and was inspired by his writing, although, as Allen remembered, "I had always messed around with writing."

To earn money Terry took a construction job in Hollywood. While on the job, a chance meeting with the director of the rock and roll music television show "Shindig" lead to an appearance on the show. He appeared on the show in 1965 playing a song he wrote, "Redbird." Also on the program was West Texan Jerry Naylor, who had spent a brief time in the Crickets. Naylor helped Terry with the details an amateur needed to get through the show. Nothing came of this performance other than being, as Terry described it, "one of those lessons you learn."

Terry stayed in California during the 1970s, studying art and performing when possible. In 1974, as part of an art piece, Terry recorded his first album, *Juarez*. Terry traded artwork for studio time with his cousin, who was the road manager for the rock group the Jefferson Airplane.

His next and possibly most important album, *Lubbock (on everything)*, was an outgrowth of a meeting with rock musician Lowell George and a concept Allen had for a geographical musical piece. Allen's idea was to record at different locations, including Lubbock, with different artists whom he felt suited the material. George was interested in producing the album, but Terry failed to secure the financial backing. As a result, he abandoned the project until July 1977, when he received a call from fellow artist and Lubbock resident Paul Milosovich. Paul, knowing of Terry's proposed project, suggested he record the entire project in Lubbock and offered that the Don Caldwell studio was available and that Joe Ely's band, including steel guitarist Lloyd Maines and guitarist Jesse Taylor, was in town. Coincidentally, that same day, Terry came into enough money to finance the project.

A week later Terry was in Lubbock to meet with Caldwell, Ely, and Maines and make arrangements for the recording. The recordings were made during July and August of 1977, and it was an eye-opening experience for Allen. Having left Lubbock in the early sixties and only returning for brief periods, he felt some hostility toward his hometown: "Part of me was real freaked about coming back to Lubbock." But after being home and recording, "[it was] such an incredible experience. . . . None of the songs reflected any kind of hatred." He had come to terms with resentment of Lubbock, as he reflected, "You have to leave to see it."[42]

The result was Allen's 1979 two-record set *Lubbock (on everything)*. The musicians came largely from the ranks of the Joe Ely Band and the Maines Brothers Band. This work included several original songs that involve West Texas subjects, like "Amarillo Highway":

> I'm panhandlin'
> Man handlin'
> Post holin'
> High rollin'
> Dust Bowlin' . . . Daddy
> An I ain't got no blood veins
> I just got them four lanes
> Of hard . . . Amarillo Highway

1978, Terry Allen, Green Shoes publishing (BMI).

"Amarillo Highway" was inspired by a day Allen spent with fellow writer David Hickey in 1970 in Idalou during a sandstorm: "We played music . . . all afternoon, and it was a huge, just horrible sandstorm, and there was about two inches of clear space between the door and the floor, and so a lot of dirt was coming in. It was just that thing of . . . playing against the wind. . . . 'Amarillo Highway' kinda came out of . . . that day really."[43]

"Amarillo Highway" became an anthem of sorts for the Maines Brothers, who recorded the song on their *Route 1 Acuff* album. Two other songs written by Allen, "Highplains Jamboree" and "Lubbock Woman," also reveal gritty detail of West Texas life. "The Great Joe Bob (A Regional Tragedy)" tells the bittersweet story of a local football hero gone bad. In 1991 *Lubbock (on everything)* was rereleased on compact disc format by an English label, indicating that interest in this material was still strong thirteen years after its original release.

As a result of the interest created by his fresh, candid view of West Texas and the charm of his music, Allen was able to secure several tour dates for himself and a band. He put together what he labeled the Panhandle Mystery Band, using many of the players featured on the album: Lloyd Maines, Kenny Maines, Richard Bowden, Curtis McBride, Don Caldwell, and Donnie Maines. Working with Allen inspired the Maines Brothers to search out and record original music.

Allen has continued an active involvement in art and music. He recorded two more albums in Lubbock featuring many of the same musicians and following in a similar path as the *Lubbock (on everything)* work: *Smokin the Dummy* and *Bloodline*. Several of Allen's artworks were featured in a 1986 Texas Tech University Museum exhibit, "Honky Tonk Visions." Allen also wrote music for a German documentary about Americans formerly in the armed services living in Southeast Asia. As part of a larger interest in performance art, Allen has created a theater piece based on his *Juarez* recordings. He and his wife, actress Jo Harvey Allen, have written a theater piece entitled *Chippy, The Diary of a West Texas Hooker*. Included in the cast are Jimmie Dale Gilmore, Joe and Sharon Ely, Joe Carol Pierce, and an actor from Snyder, Barry Tubb. A soundtrack album of the production was released in 1994.[44]

The original Maines Brothers Band was a popular Lubbock area dance band in the 1950s and 1960s that featured Wayne, Sonny and James Maines. James is the father of the younger Maines brothers. Musicians regularly gathered in the Maines home, and in this rich environment, James's boys learned to sing and play musical instruments at an early age.

Eldest brother Lloyd, born in 1951, started playing guitar at age thirteen and soon taught Steve, younger by one year, to play rhythm on the instrument to accompany Lloyd's lead guitar playing. When Lloyd was fourteen years old, Kenny, age eleven, started playing the electric bass, and soon the Little Maines Brothers Band, featuring the three brothers, began performing periodically as a part of Maines Brothers performances.

In the mid-1960s, while their schoolmates were listening to the music of the Beatles, the Beach Boys, and the Rolling Stones, Lloyd and his brothers were listening to and performing the music of Buck Owens, Merle Haggard, and other country artists. Lloyd commented, "Our attire was . . . ironed white shirts, these little string ties, black pants, and we had these straw hats. First of all, we all had burr haircuts, 'cause our dad gave us our own haircuts . . . and we all had straw cowboy hats that had those big, huge brims, you know it looks like an airplane. . . . Thinking back on it, I'm not sure if people came to hear us play, or to see how funny we looked."[45]

A year or so after their first performances with their father and uncles, the boys began to work music jobs on their own. According to Lloyd, there were no other "kid" western bands during these years; most young musicians were playing rock and roll. The three Maines Brothers were joined by Joe Stephenson on fiddle and Steve Braddock on drums. Around 1968, Lloyd, now seventeen, started playing a pedal steel guitar given to him by Frank Carter, who played steel for the elder Maines Brothers Band. This instrument was handmade by Carter, and its inclusion gave the Little Maines Brothers Band a traditional country sound. Lloyd would later use the steel in new ways to make decidedly noncountry sounds.

After high school, the brothers headed in several directions. Lloyd eventually went to work with Don Caldwell at Caldwell Studios in Lubbock as a recording engineer and a session steel guitar player. Steve went away to college, and Kenny worked as a bass player with Kenny Vernon's Las Vegas show band. Lloyd met Joe Ely at the Caldwell Studio in 1973 and joined his band that same year.

Although he maintained an active tour schedule with the Ely band, Lloyd continued to work at the Caldwell Studio when he was not on tour and performed periodically with his brothers. With the retirement of the original Maines, Lloyd, Kenny, Steve, and Donnie became the Maines Brothers Band. In 1977, the group released its first album, a self-produced effort entitled *The Maines Brothers and Friends*. The Maines Brothers continued to play for dances throughout the area, becoming one of the leading bands. Lloyd was juggling four jobs in the late 1970s: touring with Joe Ely, performing with the Maines Brothers and Terry Allen's Panhandle Mystery Band, and working at the Caldwell Studio. The schedule proved too demanding, and in 1980 Lloyd left the Ely band.

With Lloyd now a full-time member, the Maines Brothers performed regularly, featuring Kenny's lead vocals and original songs by West Texas and regional songwriters such as Terry Allen, John Hadley, and Kevin Welch. They recorded and released *Route 1 Acuff* in 1980 on Texas Soul, a label created for records produced at the Caldwell Studio. *Hub City Moan* followed in 1981, also on Texas Soul.

Nashville country music producer Jerry Kennedy heard one of these albums and called to pursue a record deal. The Maines Brothers were just finishing their third album on Texas Soul, the 1982 release *Panhandle Dancer*. Kennedy flew to Lubbock, saw the band at Coldwater, a local music club, and signed the band to Mercury Records. At the band's insistence, their first album, *High Rollin'*, was recorded in Lubbock and was released in 1984. Their second album for Mercury, *The Boys Are Back in Town*, was released in 1985, but neither album produced a hit single—a prerequisite for commercial success. "Everybody Needs Love on a Saturday Night" was released as a single in 1986 and received good radio play, but there was no album to follow up the single and, consequently, nothing for the public to buy. Dissatisfied with Mercury's treatment of the band, the Maines Brothers soon left the label.[46]

Back in Lubbock and free of their Mercury contract, the Maines Brothers recorded again on the Texas Soul label and released *Red Hot and Blue* in 1987 and *Windstorm* in 1989. The group experienced continued regional popularity in the early 1990s and maintained a limited performance schedule. Lloyd remained the most musically active member of the group, engineering recording sessions at Caldwell Studio and performing with the Jerry Jeff Walker band on live and televised performances, such as TNN's *Texas Connection* music program.

The Lubbock music scene in the 1970s and 1980s centered around several establishments that featured local music regularly. The Cotton Club, an important site of music for several decades in Lubbock, was operated by Tommy Hancock from the early 1960s to 1980. Hancock was well known as a western swing bandleader in Lubbock during the 1950s. Under Hancock's direction the club attracted an odd mixture of people: some were of Hancock's generation and had been dancing in honky-tonks and clubs for years, while others were a younger group of musicians and others that could have been characterized as "hippies." This unusual mix of "redneck" and "hippie" must have seemed even more improbable in West Texas, whose image was and is conservative. This scene provided musicians a unique test audience on which to try their music. In many ways, the mix of country and rock is the basis of the "Lubbock Sound."

Stubbs' Barbecue Restaurant on East Broadway in Lubbock was another center of Lubbock music activity. Established in 1968, the restaurant, especially its Sunday jam sessions, served as a focal point for Lubbock musicians. Owner C. B. Stubblefield became a guru of sorts to this group of musicians, and his encouragement and offer of a place to play helped them develop and hone their music. Stubbs, as he was known, catered the Tornado Jams and, like the musicians he sponsored, he eventually left Lubbock for Austin. In 1992, Stubblefield returned to Lubbock and reopened Stubbs' Restaurant at a new location.[47] Other local clubs such as Fat Dawg's, Main Street Saloon, and Coldwater provided outlets for the developing talents of Lubbock musicians during the period.

The music performed at these establishments in the late 1970s and early 1980s attempted to balance the inputs of songwriters, singers, and musicians into a cohesive trinity. In direct contrast to the style of commercial country music then produced in Nashville, Lubbock music often featured the band on equal footing with the singer-"star." Influential projects such as Terry Allen's *Lubbock (on everything)* album and the Maines Brothers Band continued to promote this sound—original songs presented in musical arrangements showcasing virtuosic musicianship, rather than simply having the band provide backup music for the singer, as in commercial country music.[48]

In the 1980s, the Museum at Texas Tech University in Lubbock developed two exhibits featuring West Texas music. In 1984, "Nothin' Else to Do" featured artifacts, photographs, and interviews from West Texas musicians. The Paul Milosevich painting "Nothin' Else to Do" was displayed in the exhibit and was used as the cover for the catalog and record jacket produced in conjunction with the exhibit. The attention given West Texas music by project director Future Akins and her staff served as a boost to the West Texas music community.[49] The success of this exhibition resulted in the presentation of another exhibit at the museum in 1986. "Honky Tonk Visions, On West Texas Music: 1936-1986" focused on artworks by or about West Texas musicians and their music. Featured were photographs by Butch Hancock, works by Terry Allen, paintings by Paul Milosevich, and artifacts such as Buddy Holly's guitar and a hat worn by Bob Wills. The touring exhibit also appeared at museums in Corpus Christi, Austin, and Tyler.[50]

Ultimately, the West Texas sound, so successful regionally, was not a national commercial success. Many of the musicians, however, learning from the successes and failures of the 1970s and 1980s, continue to perform and search for a national audience.

Elsewhere in West Texas, traditional country music continued to enjoy popularity. In Abilene, for example, the Ponderosa, featured in Bill Porterfield's book *The Greatest Honky Tonks in Texas*, was operated by L. C. Agnew, a fiddler whose group the Dixie Playboys played there regularly.[51] The Dixie Playboys, originally organized by Agnew's uncles in 1929, played through the 1940s in the Abilene area. In 1963, Agnew adopted the name for his own group, which played at the Cow Palace in Abilene. Later he moved the group to Carpenters' Hall, where he played from 1964 to 1975 before opening the Ponderosa. The Dixie Playboys were also the band for the Cowboy Christmas Ball in Anson for much of the 1970s and 1980s.[52]

Traditional country music continued to attract fans across West Texas during the 1970s and 1980s, but it was the Lubbock scene that garnered media attention. Despite critical acclaim for much of this music, there was little immediate commercial success for the musicians. In the 1990s, some of these artists enjoyed greater exposure and larger audiences.

Ben Hall promotional postcard, 1950s.
Courtesy Jack Douglas.

BEN HALL
THE COUNTRY DRIFTER
I talk and play your Favorite Western Recordings
on "THE WESTERN ROUNDUP"
THE CORRAL CLUB" "WESTERN HIT PARADE"
on K S E L - Lubbock, Texas

Troy Jordan publicity photo, 1950s.
Courtesy Keith Ward.

Backstage photo of performers, Odessa, Texas, 1950s. Left to right: Bill Myrick, Faron Young, and promoter Keith Ward. Courtesy Bill Myrick.

Tommy Allsup and the Southernaires, Odessa, early 1960s. Left to right: Tommy Camfield, fiddle; Bob Wahlen, drums; Buddy Beasley, fiddle; Pete Waller, bass; Tommy Allsup, guitar; Louise Rowe, vocals and bass, and Chuck Caldwell, steel guitar. Photograph by Bill Sorrells, courtesy Tommy Allsup.

Backstage photo at Billy Walker and Elvis Presley concert, Odessa, Texas high school field house, circa 1955. Left to right: Billy Walker, Scotty Moore (Elvis' guitarist), and Bobby Garrett. Courtesy Bill Myrick.

Grand Ol' Opry member Billy Walker publicity photo, 1992. Courtesy Billy Walker.

Publicity photo, circa 1960s.
Courtesy Edna Lee Dubre.

Edna Lee performing in McCamey, Texas, 1969, with Edna Lee and the Lee Riders. Courtesy Edna Lee Dubre.

Benefit show at McCamey, Texas, 1960s. The show featured "AOK Recording Artist" Edna Lee. Courtesy Edna Lee Dubre.

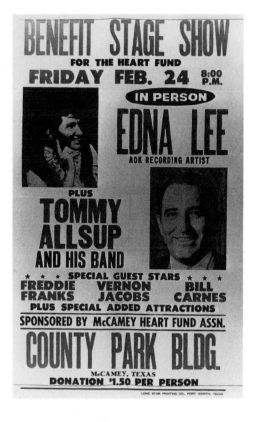

CHARLIE "Sugartime" PHILLIPS

Charlie "Sugartime" Phillips of Farwell, Texas. Publicity photo, circa 1970. Courtesy Charlie Phillips.

Edna Lee Dubre on stage
with Tommy Allsup and the
Tomahawks, December, 1965.
Courtesy Edna Lee Dubre.

Promotional poster, 1966.
Lineup includes Abilene rocker
Dean Beard and Edna Lee.
Courtesy Edna Lee Dubre.

The "Original" Maines Brothers Band, Lubbock Supper Club, 1967. Left to right: Frank Carter, steel guitar; Curley Lawler, fiddle; Sonny Maines, vocal; James Maines, guitar; Gerald Braddock, drums; and Fernie Reed, bass. Courtesy Lloyd Maines.

The "Little" Maines Brothers Band at Cotton Club, Lubbock, Texas, 1967. Left to right: Lloyd Maines, Steve Maines, Kenny Maines, Joe Stephenson, and Steve Braddock. Courtesy Lloyd Maines.

L. C. Agnew at 38th annual Cowboy Christmas Ball, Anson, Texas, 1972. Courtesy ABILENE REPORTER NEWS.

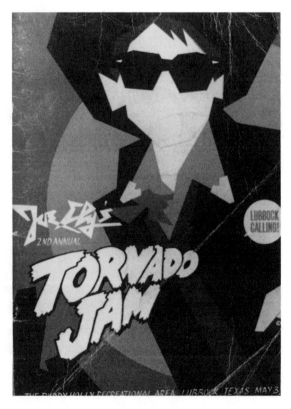

Program cover for Second Annual Joe Ely Tornado Jam, Lubbock, Texas, May 3, 1981.

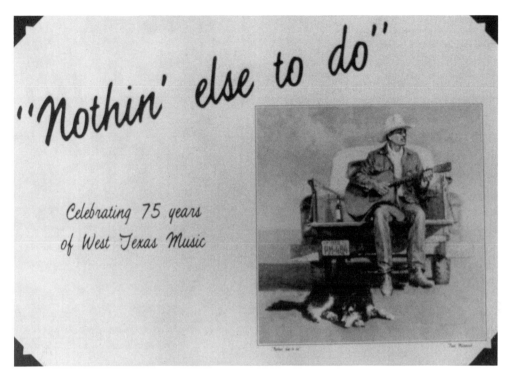

"Nothin' Else to Do," The Museum of Texas Tech University, catalog, Lubbock, Texas, 1984. Author's collection.

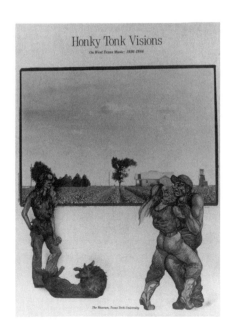

"Honky Tonk Visions—On West Texas Music: 1936-1986," The Museum of Texas Tech University, catalog, Lubbock, Texas, 1986. Author's collection.

Promotional photo for Joe Ely's Tornado Jam, 1985. Lubbock, Texas. Courtesy T. G. Caraway Collection, Southwest Collection, Texas Tech University, Lubbock.

Promotional poster for 1986 W.T.M.A. Family Music Festival, Lubbock, Texas. Courtesy T. G. Caraway Collection, Southwest Collection, Texas Tech University, Lubbock.

Stubb's Bar B-Q restaurant, Lubbock, Texas, circa 1975. This establishment, operated by C. B. "Stubbs" Stubblefield, was the site of much music including the Sunday jams during the 1970s. Courtesy T. G. Caraway Collection, Southwest Collection, Texas Tech University, Lubbock.

The Texana Dames, 1987. Left to right: Connie Hancock, Charlene Hancock, and Traci Lamar. Courtesy Lloyd Maines.

Joe Ely at Fat Dawgs club, Lubbock, Texas, 1977. Courtesy Lloyd Maines.

Tommy Anderson, 1988. Courtesy Lloyd Maines.

Terry Allen and the Panhandle Mystery Band, July, 1982, Santa Fe, New Mexico. Left to right: Richard Bowden, Terry Allen, Joe Ely, Cary Banks, Kenny Maines, Donnie Maines, Lloyd Maines, and C. B. Stubblefield. Courtesy Cary Banks.

Andy Wilkinson, courtesy Nebraska Educational Television.

9

ince the first Anglo settlement of West Texas, people have gathered periodically to share music and fellowship. Gospel sings, ranch dances, fiddle contests and similar events provided important musical and social outlets for the isolated settlers of the newly opened section of Texas. This frontier tradition was reestablished in modern times with the community musical, held weekly at locations scattered throughout West Texas. As totally self-generated social events, these musicals are an interesting facet of West Texas culture and country music at the grass-roots level.

The community dances held in barns, school buildings, and homes beginning in the 1880s and continuing through the 1930s and 1940s were most often family events where community standards of behavior prevailed. Alcohol consumption and overt sexual activity, seen in later honky-tonks, were fringe activities conducted out of the public eye. Bootleggers were common at the these events, but they kept a low profile, and in many cases the entire community cooperated in the public denial of such activities.[1]

Social and legal sanctions against the consumption or sale of alcohol in West Texas stemmed directly from a southern religious and social heritage. The most conservative southern religious and social mores held that alcohol consumption was a sin and that to drink at all, even in moderation, was to put one's soul in jeopardy. Additionally, many religious groups taught that dancing was equally sinful. Throughout the American South, conservative religious groups, especially the Baptists, had a powerful influence on local social and governmental systems. The sphere of influence of this conservative, fundamental religion extended throughout the southern states and into East Texas. The Bible Belt, as this area was called, extended into areas of West Texas, especially the panhandle, because of the influx of settlers from East Texas and the South.

With the emergence of honky-tonks and other meeting and dance places where alcohol was served, the chasm between "nice" church people and "drinkin', dancin'" people grew. Consumption of alcohol became a primary reason to visit one of these establishments, although socializing and dancing were still important attractions. The clientele was generally aware of the conservative community opinion of their activities, and, as the honky-tonk's reputation for drinking, dancing, fights, and sexual misbehavior grew, fewer "nice" folk attended. By the late 1940s, country music fans who attended community dances regularly in their younger years were left with fewer acceptable venues to enjoy live music, other than occasional concerts, radio broadcasts, and package shows.

The advent of local television in West Texas in the early 1950s further hurt the dance tradition. Former Texas Playboys Tiny Moore and Johnny Gimble remember that television adversely affected dance club attendance in the early 1950s.[2] Left with no acceptable place to dance and listen to country music, and offered an alternative in television, many West Texas country music fans stayed home and listened to records and the radio rather than risk the evils of the honky-tonk.

It is unclear when the current form of community musicals first appeared in West Texas, but they provided an acceptable alternative for displaced country music fans. The contemporary popularity and spread of the community musical in West Texas dates to the early 1970s. Today, people gather by the hundreds in community centers, agricultural buildings, and schoolhouses to visit with their neighbors and to enjoy music performed by their peers. Several desired elements from the early days of community music gatherings and dances characterize these musicals: country music, social interaction, and family atmosphere. Absent are the objectionable features of the honky-tonks: dancing, alcohol, and dim lighting. For many, the community musical provides the same social atmosphere as their church activities. The typical West Texas community musical is an amateur music concert held once a month. The term *musical*, universally accepted name for these events among the participants, bears no kinship to Broadway musical productions. Most of the musicals are held in small towns and rural communities. Rural location appears to be an important factor in the success of a musical. George Ashburn, organizer of the Meadow Musical in Meadow, explained, "If you want to have a country music show, you have to have it in the country."[3]

These events are usually held on the same weekend each month, and there is no admission fee. Donations, which may be solicited during the program, cover any incurred expenses. In the case of the Meadow Musical, sizable donations allowed Ashburn to purchase the building, and the funds continue to pay for improvements and maintenance. The voluntary self-funding of these noncommercial events distinguishes them from similar commercial country music concerts, such as Lubbock's West Texas Opry, which charge an admission fee.

West Texas musicals differ significantly from similar events held in north-central and East Texas, where the events, typically called "Oprys," are held on a weekly basis, feature a house band to back up singers, and charge admission fees. Although Oprys feature local talent as do West Texas musicals, there is often an audition process, and the presentation is much more formal than the typical West Texas musical.[4]

The performers on West Texas programs are almost exclusively unpaid amateurs. Some individuals travel as far as one hundred miles one way to perform thirty minutes of music with no renumeration. Some performers call in advance to reserve a place on the program, while others simply show up on the night of the program, with musical instruments in hand, and wait to be worked into the schedule. The performers play a variety of country, pop, early rock and roll, and gospel music to an audience that often includes many of their friends and family. Spontaneous applause often breaks out throughout the audience for skilled performances or in support of young performers. Some performers sell albums and cassettes of their music, but most play only for the enjoyment. Bob Suggs of Welch was a regular performer at many of the musicals on the South Plains in the early 1990s. He and his group, Big Sandy, performed every weekend at different community musicals and spent many other nights performing at nursing homes throughout the region, never expecting payment for their music.[5] A talented fiddler, Suggs played a program of sentimental favorites, classic country music, and fiddle tunes. Suggs's devotion to the community musical format is typical of the musicians who perform.

Bluegrass musicians form a distinct subgroup at these events. Devotees tend to be opinionated about music and often listen only to bluegrass music, to the exclusion of other country music. When bluegrass fans and musicians gather at community musicals in West Texas, they congregate away from the stage and audience areas. At musicals such as Meadow, separate areas are provided for informal jam sessions among the "pickers." Where no special areas are provided, the musicians gather in parking lots, hallways, and foyers. Many musicians attend the musicals solely to participate in these jam sessions and may not perform or otherwise participate in the stage show.

The values of community and family are important at these events, a fact evidenced by the "clean" and noncontroversial nature of the song selection and the performers' commentaries. Testimonials, religious and otherwise, are frequent. These invariably earn a round of applause from the audience in support of the sentiment.

Despite their preference for wholesome material, community musical audiences appear to ignore or otherwise dismiss the real implications of popular honky-tonk type songs presented in the program that deal with promiscuity, infidelity, alcohol consumption, and other behavior normally not condoned by this group of people. These themes have been the staple of country music songwriting. The mixed messages sent by a nine-year-old girl dressed and made up to appear much older, wearing a belt buckle emblazoned with the words "Holy Bible" and singing "You Ain't Woman Enough to Take My Man," illustrate the odd marriage of honky-tonk music and family values at these events.[6]

The success or failure of a community musical depends on attendance. Typically, the audience contains a significant proportion of senior citizens; in many cases this group forms the majority of the audience. Emil Macha, coordinator of the Littlefield musical, described the older audience and one particularly devoted fan:

> It's the only place a lot of these older people can go . . . except to church on Sundays. This one little old lady from Earth [Texas], I'll never forget her, she'd come in and about 9:30 or 10:00 p.m. her husband decided to go back home, and you'd see her start

hopping chairs just to stay [away] from him. He'd be on this side of the building looking for her, she'd be over there. He'd see her and walk over there to get her, she'd be back over here.[7]

In addition to dedicated senior citizens, families attend with small children and teenagers. Lights are left on in the audience area, and children as well as adults wander freely during the evening. Unlike a quiet concert setting, a murmur of conversation drifts throughout the crowd during the performances. Apparently, it is this social factor that draws the audiences month after month, rather than simply a chance to hear live country music. Charlsie Roach, director of the Higgenbotham musical, described her audience: "We're all a big family here. We know everyone, and if we don't see somebody for a while, we ask about them."[8] A sense of community is felt among the audience of these musicals. Stage announcements routinely declare births, sickness, hardship, and death among audience regulars. Prayers are occasionally offered for the needy, and during emergencies, collections might be made to help friends in financial need. The boundaries of a given musical's "community," however, are much larger than the immediate rural area. Regulars may travel as far as one hundred miles one way to attend their favorite musicals, and many attend a different musical each week.

Generally, each musical owes its existence and survival to a single individual who is responsible for all facets of the event, including arranging the location, entertainment, publicity, and concessions. This individual is an unpaid organizer who is often motivated only by a desire to help provide this kind of entertainment to an audience. If donations do not cover operating expenses, musical organizers may make up the difference out of their own pockets.

The musical held on the second Saturday of each month at Littlefield in 1989 is typical of such events. Held in the Lamb County Agricultural Building, the Littlefield musical was one of the most organized events of its type on the South Plains. The West Texas Bluegrass, Country, and Gospel Music Association, which operated the musical, was a legally registered group with an elected board and officers. Emil Macha, who served as the president of the association, owned and operated Macha Brothers Tire and Garden Center in Littlefield and was a Lamb County commissioner.[9]

According to founder George Ashburn, the Meadow Musical at Meadow was the longest continuously running musical on the South Plains, with 268 consecutive monthly shows as of October 1994. The musical began as weekly jam sessions held in Ashburn's home in Meadow. The event became so popular that it was moved to a empty grocery store in town. Through donations, the building was eventually purchased and improvements made. A local farmer donated five thousand dollars toward an eleven-thousand-dollar steel add-on building, which housed the stage and front section of the audience area. Ashburn, who installed irrigation equipment for a living, was largely responsible for the growth and success of the Meadow Musical. He missed only a few of the programs and once drove back from a job in Nevada to be in Meadow for the musical. The facility's pine siding was installed, sanded, and varnished by Ashburn and his wife. This ambitious project took over four years to complete, an example of the Ashburns' commitment to the musical. The Meadow Musical's success and longevity made it a model for many of the more recent musicals in the region.[10]

Several factors contribute to the success of community musicals. The performers are supportive and plentiful, so that the directors have no problem filling their programs each month. This may be the only outlet for many performers, because they never work in commercial situations and have never been paid for their music. The open-door policy encourages individuals who may not have played music in years to get on stage. The audiences are tolerant of mistakes and supportive of new or marginal talent.

Social interaction is the single most important factor contributing to musicals' appeal. The social group includes the audience and the performers. Unlike more formal musical concerts, the performers mingle freely with the audience and even become audience members themselves before and after their performances. For the participants, musicals provide a safe family environment in which they can socialize and enjoy good music. This situation may be the only acceptable alternative for the individual who does not want to frequent an establishment that serves alcohol or otherwise condones behavior deemed unacceptable. Further, Meadow's George Ashburn felt that the musicals give people a chance to get "out from in front of the TV."[11]

Not all West Texas musicals had the success and staying power of Meadow or Littlefield. Events at Ropesville, Petersburg, Sundown, Tahoka, and Brownfield all enjoyed a period of activity before dying from lack of audience or organization. Despite these failures, new events of this type develop periodically across the region. The persistence of the idea is testimony of its appeal to the people of the West Texas. Clearly, these musicals address a need unfulfilled by any commercial venue. Not motivated by financial gain, the promoter and the performers volunteer their time and resources for their own satisfaction; for the audience, the community musical serves as an important social outlet. Although a relatively new phenomenon, the community musical is only the current manifestation of the ageless desire of rural Texans to gather to share music and fellowship.

10

LUBBOCK
AND
BEYOND

The Texaco gas station in Guthrie serves as the local bus stop. A simple, handwritten sign lists daily arrivals and departure times for the two possible bus routes out of Guthrie. Eastbound buses are identified as "Wichita Falls, Lawton, Oklahoma, and Dallas/Fort Worth," while westbound destinations are identified simply as "Lubbock and Beyond."

After the flurry of West Texas music activity in the 1970s and early 1980s centering around Lubbock, one can only speculate about what lies ahead for the country music of the region. Country music continues to be popular here, and bands play regularly at VFW halls, clubs, rodeos, and honky-tonks. Regardless of national or international attention, country music enjoys an active life in West Texas.

West Texas musicians still contribute to country music on a national scale. Country songwriter Royce Porter from Sweetwater has written numerous hit songs, including the 1990 ASCAP song of the year, "What's Going on in Your World," recorded by Texas singer George Strait. Porter has written 250 songs that have been recorded by a who's who of country music singers, including Reba McIntire, Merle Haggard, George Jones, Tanya Tucker, Ricky Van Shelton, Doug Stone, Ray Charles, Keith Whitley, and Tammy Wynette.[1]

Lubbock fiddler Ricky Turpin has worked with the western swing group Asleep at the Wheel and with country singer Rick Trevino. Ricky is the son of Weldon Turpin, a respected fiddler who has performed in contests and with most of the major country bands in the Lubbock area since the 1950s. In bluegrass music, two West Texas women have leading roles in dynamic new groups: Laura Lynch of Dell City with the Dixie Chicks and Lynn Morris of Lamesa with the Lynn Morris Band. Austin's Texana Dames, featuring Charlene Hancock and her daughters Conni Hancock and Traci Lamar, attract international attention, while on the regional level, artists such as Lubbock's Andy Wilkinson continue the West Texas songwriting tradition. Wilkinson's original epic *Charles Goodnight,* which traces the life of the Texas legend, debuted in Palo Duro Canyon during Michael Martin Murphy's WestFest and received critical acclaim. Country singer Darron Norwood of Tahoka enjoyed commercial country radio success in the early 1990s.

West Texas country music radio programming in the 1980s and early 1990s was for the most part identical to that found elsewhere in the country. Little or no local country music was played on regional radio stations. A notable exception was the "West Texas Music Hour," a weekly Sunday night program broadcast since 1987 on Lubbock's KLLL radio.

Hosted by Lloyd and Kenny Maines and Cary Banks, all of the Maines Brothers Band, this program was the only radio outlet for many contemporary local artists as well as historically important regional artists such as Bob Wills.

Numerous special music events draw media attention to the region. Bob Wills Day is held annually on the last weekend of April in Wills's hometown, Turkey. The event was established in 1971, and Wills was in attendance that year. Each year many of the former Texas Playboys gather to play a dance on Friday night and a reunion concert on Saturday afternoon. Thousands of dedicated western swing fans as well as casually interested people attend the concert and the dances, and they tour the Bob Wills Museum. Hoyle Nix and his band performed each year for the Saturday night dance until his death in 1985. Jody Nix has continued the tradition since his father's death.

For many, a special excitement is associated with these concerts, which reunited former Bob Wills musicians for the first time in many years. For example, in 1987, Herb Remington, Tiny Moore, and Eldon Shamblin played together for the first time since the 1940s. At present this event is still quite successful, but a problem looms for the event organizers: the advanced age of the musicians threatens to end the show. In 1992, only one original member of the Playboys remained, the great guitarist Eldon Shamblin.

Another music event in West Texas, the Cowboy Christmas Ball, is held annually at Anson. First held in 1885 at Anson's Morning Star Hotel, the event was immortalized in "The Cowboys' Christmas Ball," a poem by Larry Chittenden published in the early 1890s. After a lapse of many years, an association was formed in Anson in 1934 to recreate and stage the annual event, which is primarily a country dance. Through the years, many bands have played for the ball, including Arch Jefferies and his band in 1954, Bob Burks and the West Texas Wranglers in 1965, and Leon Rausch and the Texas Panthers in 1982. Abilene's L. C. Agnew and the Dixie Playboys performed at most of the balls in the 1970s and 1980s and were replaced by Vernon Willingham and the Texas Rhythm Boys in 1990.[2] For many years, the ball was the only exception to an Anson ordinance that prohibited public dancing, inspiring the popular slogan, "no dancin' in Anson."

A renewed appreciation of cowboy music has accompanied the popularity of cowboy cultural gatherings throughout the Southwest. One of the largest events is the National Cowboy Symposium and Celebration, held annually in Lubbock. Begun in 1989, it features cowboy poets, musicians, writers, artists, authors, and scholars sharing cowboy lore in seminars, exhibitions, and concerts. As a result of this interest in cowboy culture, the early cowboy music of West Texas and the Southwest is finding a growing audience. While much of the music played at such events is of the Hollywood cowboy variety, the authentic music is finding a wider audience.

Musicians such as Amarillo's Buck Ramsey perform traditional cowboy music, including many songs collected by Thorp and Lomax. A beneficial effect of cowboy events and other musical happenings in the Southwest, such as the Bob Wills celebration at Turkey, is that they feature older musicians who have made significant contributions in their earlier careers, providing them an appreciative audience for their unique talents. Singer Buck Ramsey and fiddler Frankie McWhorter are two such performers.

The 1950s tradition of country music stage shows continues with the West Texas Opry, staged several times a year at the Lubbock Coliseum Auditorium. Established in 1977 by David House, Don Caldwell, and Larry Corbin of KLLL, it was originally called the KLLL West Texas Saturday Night Opry. The first cast of performers included Kenny and Lloyd Maines, Terry Sue Newman Caldwell, Cecil Caldwell, David House, Jim Fullingim, Johnny Ray Watson, Roma Haley, Zelda Ellison, Clarence Neiman, Tommy Anderson, and a host of other Lubbock area perform-ers.[3] Today, the Opry draws large crowds and features local amateur talent and an occasional guest star, such as fiddler Johnny Gimble. Since 1983, the event has been organized by Cecil and Maxine Caldwell. Cecil's unique fiddling and dance act has become a symbol of the Opry itself.

National attention was focused on West Texas music in October 1992, when the U. S. Postal Service announced plans to issue a series of stamps commemorating American popular music figures, including Buddy Holly and Bob Wills. Buddy Holly has also been the subject of several film and theater projects, including the feature film *The Buddy Holly Story,* Paul McCartney's documentary film *The Real Buddy Holly Story,* and a musical entitled *Buddy.*

Bob Wills had been a member of the Country Music Hall of Fame in Nashville since 1968. In 1990 he was inducted into the West Texas Walk of Fame in Lubbock. Largely through the efforts of organizer Lloyd Maines, nearly forty fiddlers came together at the induction ceremony. Under the direction of former Texas Playboy Johnny Gimble, they played Wills's "Faded Love" together. It was an inspired idea, and all the fiddlers enjoyed the opportunity to participate in this memorable event. In many ways, the occasion and those present symbolized the spirit of West Texas music. The group included seasoned professionals, such as Gimble and Lubbock's Curley Lawler, Weldon Turpin, and Cecil Caldwell; a large group of adult fiddle hobbyists; at least one classical violinist; and a small but important group of young fiddlers. It is through the music of this last group and young people like them that the legacy of West Texas music will continue. The young musicians of West Texas will no doubt carry on the traditions of the past while adding innovations of their own, as long as there are people to dance and listen.

Slaton Canyon Sunday Concert, May 1976. Joe Ely performs for dancers. Photograph by Karin Wikstrom-Miller.

Slaton Canyon Sunday Concert, May 1976. Left to right: Elyse Gilmore, vocal; Jesse Taylor, guitar; Joe Ely, guitar, vocal. Photograph by Karin Wikstrom-Miller.

Don Caldwell, Austin, Texas, 1976. Photograph by Karin Wikstrom-Miller.

Joe Ely watching Bob Wills Day
Parade, Turkey, Texas, 1976.
Photograph by Karin
Wikstrom-Miller.

C. B. "Stubbs" Stubblefield, near
Acuff, Texas, 1977. Photograph
by Karin Wikstrom-Miller.

Bluegrass musicians in the backroom,
Meadow Musical, 1989. Left to right:
Gaylord Coe, banjo; unidentified, guitar;
Jayson Jones, fiddle (back to camera)
Wes Perry, mandolin; Karen Perry, bass.
Author's collection.

Larry Buchanan Band at Littlefield
Musical, 1989. Left to right:
Unidentified, drums; Wayne Buchanan,
guitar; Crystal Finley, bass; and Larry
Buchanan, guitar. Author's collection.

Crowd at Littlefield Musical, 1989. Author's collection.

Bob Suggs group, "Big Sandy" performing at Littlefield Musical, 1989. Left to right: Clovis Branum, mandolin; Bob Suggs, fiddle; Tylene Suggs (behind Bob), piano; Darrell Batten, guitar; and Tempie Branum, mandolin. Author's collection.

Performing group and crowd, Higgenbotham Musical, 1989. Author's collection.

Performing group and crowd, Meadow Musical, 1989. Author's collection.

Lamb County Agriculture Community Center, Littlefield, Texas. Site of Littlefield Musical, first Saturday of the month. 1988. Author's collection.

Organizer Emil Macha at soundboard, Littlefield Musical, 1989. Author's collection.

Buddy Holly statue, Lubbock, Texas. Author's collection.

Third Annual National Cowboy Symposium and Celebration poster, Lubbock, Texas, 1991. Author's collection.

Higgenbotham Musical,
Higgenbotham, Texas, 1989.
Author's collection.

Lubbock fiddler Ricky Turpin
photographed on the occasion of
winning the Hale Center fiddle
contest, Hale Center, Texas,
1980s. Courtesy HALE CENTER
AMERICAN.

Fiddlers at 1990 Walk of Fame induction ceremony, Lubbock, Texas. Courtesy Lloyd Maines.

Bandleader Arch
Jeffries talks to
unidentified couple
at Cowboy Christmas
Ball, Anson, Texas,
1954. Courtesy
ABILENE REPORTER NEWS.

Hank Thomson (left), with Lubbock bandleader/fiddler Tommy Hancock, Glassarama Club, Lubbock. Courtesy Tommy Hancock.

Tommy Hancock and the Roadside Playboys, late 1950s. Left to right standing: Guy "Tex" Brooks, drums; J.B. Westbrook, rhythm guitar and vocals; Tommy Hancock, fiddle; Bill Clark, bass. Seated: Charlene Condray, vocals; Alex Martinez, steel guitar; Louis Martinez, lead guitar.

NOTES

Introduction

1. "Anglo" refers to white, English-speaking people who settled West Texas, largely from East Texas and the southern United States.

2. Liner notes to *Bob Wills Roundup,* Bob Wills and His Texas Playboys, Columbia C-128, 1947.

3. Bill C. Malone, *Country Music U.S.A.,* rev. ed. (Austin: University of Texas Press, 1985), 145; Linell Gentry, *A History and Encyclopedia of Country, Western, and Gospel Music* (Nashville: Clairmont, 1969), 430-31.

Chapter One

1. Donald Emmet Worcester, *The Chisholm Trail: High Road of the Cattle Kingdom* (Lincoln, Neb.: University of Nebraska Press, 1980), xiii-xiv.

2. Nathan Thorp, *Songs of the Cowboys,* and variants, commentary, notes and lexicon by Austin E. Fife and Alta S. Fife (New York: Clarkson N. Potter, 1966), 6.

3. N. Howard Thorp and Neil M. Clark, *Pardner of the Wind* (Caldwell, Idaho: Caxton Printers, 1945), 43.

4. Thorp and Fife, *Songs of the Cowboys,* 12.

5. Walter Prescott Webb, ed., "John Lomax," *The Handbook of Texas,* Vol. II (Austin: The Texas State Historical Association, 1952), 74.

6. John Lomax, *Cowboy Songs and Other Frontier Ballads* (New York: Macmillan, 1927), introduction to original 1910 edition by Barrett Wendell.

7. Thorp and Fife, *Songs of the Cowboys,* 24-25.

8. John Lomax and Alan Lomax, *Cowboy Songs and Other Frontier Ballads* (New York: Macmillan, 1938), 91.

9. Irvin Stambler and Grelun Landon, *Encyclopedia of Folk, Country, and Western Music* (New York: St Martin's Press, 1969), 176.

10. Notes to booklet accompanying *Cowboy Songs, Ballads, and Cattle Calls from Texas,* Library of Congress Folk Recordings L 28, 1952. Recorded by John A. Lomax and others.

11. Thorp and Clark, *Pardner of the Wind,* 29-30.

12. Lomax, *Cowboy Songs.*

13. Guy W. Logsdon, *The Whorehouse Bells Were Ringing* (Urbana and Chicago: University of Illinois Press, 1989). This pioneering work includes a good historical overview of bawdy cowboy songs.

14. Ross Edwards, *Fiddle Dust,* (Denver: Big Mountain Press, 1965), 13.

15. Ibid., 14, 20.

16. W. C. Holden, *The Spur Ranch* (Boston: Christopher Publishing House, 1934), 152.

17. Jim Laning and Judy Laning, eds., *Texas Cowboys* (College Station: Texas A&M University Press, 1984), 210, 212. Note that spellings of fiddle tunes often vary, because the tunes were originally part of oral tradition. Throughout, we use the spellings dictated by informants and record labels; hence, Sally/Sallie, Gooden/Goodin/Goodwin, etc.

18. Harry H. Campbell, *The Early History of Motley County* (Wichita Falls: Nortex Offset Publications, 1971), 61. The practice of "beating wires" on the fiddle strings was not uncommon in the fiddle traditions of the eastern U.S. Also called "beating the straws," it consisted of the fiddler playing in the normal fashion while a second person beat rhythmically on the strings over the upper fingerboard of the fiddle (between the fiddler's left hand and the bow) with a pair of straws, knitting needles, or sticks. For a recorded

example, listen to "Durham's Bull" on the New Lost City Ramblers album, *Rural Delivery No. 1*, Verve Folkways FV 9003.

19. Bill Green, *The Dancing Was Lively: Fort Concho, a Social History 1867 to 1882* (San Angelo: Fort Concho Sketches Publishing), 110.

20. "Old Cox Charms with Fiddle Yet," *San Angelo Standard* (40th edition), May 3, 1924, section 3, 8.

21. W. C. Holden, *Rollie Burns* (Dallas: The Southwest Press, 1932), 89-90.

22. Wayne Gard, *Rawhide Texas* (Norman: University of Oklahoma Press, 1965), 109.

23. John Hendrix, *If I Can Do It Horseback* (Austin: University of Texas Press, 1964), 158.

24. Bob Suggs, interview with authors, Littlefield, Texas, January 7, 1989.

25. Earl V. Spielman, "The Texas Fiddling Style," *Devil's Box* 14, no. 3 (Sept. 1980): 24.

26. Thorp and Clark, *Pardner of the Wind,* 27. The first chapter, entitled "Banjo in the Cow Camps," is an excellent essay on cowboy music and Thorp's efforts to collect cowboy songs.

27. William Ranson Hogan, *The Texas Republic: A Social and Economic History* (Norman: University of Oklahoma Press, 1946, 1969), 116-17. Originally published in *New Orleans Daily Picayune*, March 11, 1843.

28. J. R. Craddock, "The Cowboy Dance," in *Coffee in the Gourd*, ed. J. Frank Dobie (Austin: Texas Folklore Society Publications II, 1923, 1935 reprint), 32.

29. W. C. Holden, *The Espuela Land and Cattle Company* (Austin: Texas State Historical Association, 1970), 162. Revised edition of *The Spur Ranch*.

30. Craddock, "Cowboy Dance," 35.

31. Listen to *Texas Farewell*, listed in discography, for examples.

32. Speilman, "Texas Fiddling Style," 24.

33. Some people call this style "long bow," but this name is misleading. The best players of the style are able to play long phrases of notes, changing bow direction subtly, therefore giving the impression of long bow strokes. This conclusion was drawn from discussions with numerous Texas fiddlers, especially Texas Shorty, who thinks the term is used by non-Texas fiddlers.

34. Peter Feldman, "Biodiscography," booklet accompanying *Eck Robertson-Master Recordings*, Sonyatone Records STR 201, 2.

35. J. B. Cranfill, "Dr. Cranfill Writes About Old-Time Fiddlers and Gives History of Some Tunes That Are Famous Over South," *Houston Chronicle*, August 8, 1926. Reprinted in Charles Wolfe, "Dr. Cranfill and Pioneer Texas Fiddlers," *Devils Box* (Winter 1983):7.

36. Feldman, "Biodiscography," 2.

37. J. B. Cranfill, in Wolfe, "Dr. Cranfill," 7.

38. Jack Shaw, "He's 'Fiddled Away' All his Life," *Amarillo Sunday News Globe*, May 1, 1949, 21.

39. Bill C. Malone, *Country Music U. S. A.*, rev. ed. (Austin: University of Texas Press, 1985), 35.

40. J. B. Cranfill, in Wolfe, "Dr. Cranfill," 6.

41. Raymond Brown, interview with Joe Carr, Lubbock, Texas, December 11, 1990.

42. Michael Mendelson, illustrated booklet accompanying *The Farr Brothers: Texas Crapshooter*, JEMF-107.

43. J. B. Cranfill, in Wolfe, "Dr. Cranfill," 6.

44. Raymond Brown, interview with Joe Carr, Lubbock, Texas, December 11, 1990.

45. Notes to booklet accompanying *Cowboy Songs....*

46. Lillie Mae Hunter, *Book of the Years* (Hereford: Pioneer Book Publishers, 1969), 111-12. Dallam County history.

47. Ibid.

48. "Louis Franklin of Wilbarger Wins Old Fiddlers Contest," *Amarillo Daily News*, March 21, 1928; "Rusk of Canyon Wins Old Fiddlers' Contest," *Amarillo Daily News*, March 2, 1931.

49. A high bounty had been placed on wolves to help remove them as a threat to ranching. A wolfer killed wolves and collected bounty on the pelts. When the owner of the ranch and the county simultaneously offered bounties, the wolfer could collect twice for each pelt.

50. Jess Morris to Copyright Office, Library of Congress, Washington, D.C., April 15, 1943; Jess Morris reference file, Southwest Collection, Texas Tech University, Lubbock.

51. Jess Morris to Pioneer Editor, Fort Worth *Star-Telegram*, Fort Worth, Texas, July 18, 1940; Morris to James R. Record, Editor, Fort Worth Star Telegram, Fort Worth, Texas, July 24, 1940. Jess Morris reference file, Southwest Collection, Texas Tech University, Lubbock.

52. John A. Lomax, *Adventures of a Ballad Hunter* (New York: The MacMillian Company, 1947), 70-71.

53. Jess Morris, quoted in booklet accompanying *Cowboy Songs* . . . . Texas fiddlers also use this tuning, DDAD, for "Bonaparte's Retreat" and "Midnight on the Water."

Chapter One Discography

Eck Robertson, *Eck Robertson-Master Recordings*, Sonyatone STR 201. This album contains all of Robertson's commercial recordings and includes a "bio-discography" by Peter Feldmann.

John A. Lomax and others, collectors, *Cowboy Songs, Ballads, and Cattle Calls from Texas*, Library of Congress L 28. This album includes Jess Morris's performance of "Goodbye, Old Paint", recorded in Dalhart, Texas in 1942.

Louis H. Propps and others, *That's My Rabbit, My Dog Caught It: Traditional Southern Instrumental Styles*, New World NW 226, 1978. This album includes a recording of "Lost Indian" by Texas fiddler Propps in 1936.

Texas fiddlers, *Texas Farewell*, County 517. Recorded between 1922 and 1930, this album presents an overview of early Texas fiddling including Robertson, Gilliland, and Solomon.

Chapter Two

1. Sonny Curtis, interview with authors, Levelland, Texas, January, 27, 1990. Lubbock area musician Curtis was born near Meadow, Texas, in 1937 while his family was still living in a dugout.

2. *Texas Almanac 1952-53* (Dallas: A. H. Belo Corporation, 1951), 75-78.

Population and county organization of selected West Texas cities, 1890 and 1920. Compiled from *Texas Almanac 1952-53* (Dallas: A. H. Belo, 1951), 75-78.

City	County	Organized	1890 pop.	1920 pop.
Abilene	Taylor	1878	3,194	10,274
Amarillo	Potter	1887	482	15,494
Big Spring	Howard	1882	no report	4,273
Lubbock	Lubbock	1891	no report	4,051
Midland	Midland	1885	no report	1,795
Pecos	Reeves	1884	393	1,445
San Angelo	Tom Green	1875	no report	10,050
Sweetwater	Nolan	1881	614	4,307
Wichita Falls	Wichita	1882	1,987	40,079

3. Henry Lester, interview with Joe Carr, Idalou, Texas, December 11, 1990.

4. Michael Mendelson, essay accompanying *The Farr Brothers: Texas Crapshooter*, JEMF-107, 1978.

5. Bob Kendrick, interview with Joe Carr, San Angelo, Texas, March 19, 1991.

6. For a history of fiddle contests in the United States, see Stacy Phillips, *Contest Fiddling*, a Mel Bay publication.

7. Bill C. Malone, *Country Music U.S.A.* (Austin: University of Texas Press, 1985), 42.

8. "Best Fiddlers of Nation to Compete in Program Here," *Amarillo Daily News*, March 18, 1928.

9. "Louis Franklin of Wilbarger Wins Old Fiddlers Contest," *Amarillo Daily News*, March 21, 1928. The Franklin family name is quite well known in Texas fiddle circles.

10. Earl V. Speilman, "An Interview with Eck Robertson," *John Edwards Memorial Foundation Quarterly* 8, no. 28 (Winter 1972):82; Hubert Cole, "Oklahoma Fiddler Touches Hearts of Veteran Officers," *Amarillo Sunday News,* April 29, 1928, 2.

11. "Fiddlers Gather in Amarillo for Contest Tonight," *Amarillo Daily News,* April 27, 1928.

12. "Southpaw from New Mexico is Champ Fiddler," *Amarillo Daily News,* April 28, 1928, 2.

13. Cole, "Oklahoma Fiddler," 2.

14. "Lubbock Man is Winner of Fiddler Prize," *Amarillo Daily News,* March 8, 1929.

15. "Winners' List in Fiddlers' Contest Given," *Amarillo Daily News,* March 6, 1930.

16. Henry Lester to Joe Carr, November 20, 1990.

17. Henry Lester, interview with Joe Carr, Idalou, Texas, December 11, 1990.

18. Ibid.; Charles R. Townsend, *San Antonio Rose: The Life and Music of Bob Wills.* (Urbana: University of Illinois Press, 1976), 31.

19. Henry Lester, interview with Joe Carr, Idalou, Texas, December 11, 1990.

20. "Winners' List in Fiddlers' Contest Given," *Amarillo Daily News,* March 6, 1930.

21. "61 Fiddlers To Play Here on Saturday," *Amarillo Daily News,* February 25, 1931; "Rusk of Canyon Wins Old Fiddlers' Contest," *Amarillo Daily News,* March 2, 1931.

22. "Fiddler Entertainer Tonight," *Amarillo Daily News,* April 3, 1931; "Eck Robertson of Borger Carries Off First for Fiddlers," *Amarillo Daily News,* April 4, 1931.

23. Townsend, *San Antonio Rose,* 30. Robertson also used this technique of singing with the fiddle and in fact was quite well known for it. Listen to *Eck Robertson: Famous Cowboy Fiddler.* Modern bluegrass fiddler Byron Berline remembered Robertson's use of this trick, and Berline himself recorded "Lost Indian" using the technique on Country Gazette, *A Traitor in Our Midst,* United Artists, 1972.

24. Peter Feldmann, "Eck Robertson, A Bio-discography," booklet accompanying *Eck Robertson-Master Recordings,* Sonyatone STR 201, 1976, 4.

25. Charles K. Wolfe, "What Ever Happened to Country's First Recording Artist? The Career of Eck Robertson," *Journal of Country Music* 16, no. 1 (1993): 34. Excerpt from 1924 Victor catalog.

26. John Cohen, "Fiddlin' Eck Robertson," *Sing Out!* 14, no. 2 (April-May 1964), reprinted in *Devil's Box* 11 (Jan. 1970):7.

27. Malone, *Country Music U.S.A.,* 37-38.

28. Wolfe, "Career of Eck Robertson," 35.

29. Feldmann, "Bio-discography," 5; Wolfe, "Career of Eck Robertson," 39-40.

30. Wolfe, "Career of Eck Robertson," 41.

31. Recordings made during this 1963 visit are available on County 202, *Eck Robertson, Famous Cowboy Fiddler.*

32. Michael Price, "Amarillo Profiles," *Amarillo Globe-Times,* 1976; Mike H. Price, "Pioneering Sound," *Texas Country-Western Magazine* (Jan. 1977):20.

33. Jim Chancellor, "Texas Shorty," conversation with Joe Carr, Richardson, Texas, March 12, 1988.

34. Charles Farout, liner notes for *Texas Farewell: Texas Fiddlers 1922-1930,* County Records 517.

35. Tom Bean [Colquitt Warren], "Lewis Family Enjoys Fiddlin' and Horsin' Around," *New Mexico Magazine* (Feb. 1990):18.

36. Farout, liner notes for *Texas Farewell.*

37. Bean, "Lewis Family," 18.

38. *2nd Annual Old Lincoln County Cowboy Symposium,* Glencoe, New Mexico, souvenir program, October 3-6, 1991.

39. Bill Rattray with Jack Cartwright, "The Cartwright Brothers' Story," *Old Time Music* 9 (Summer 1973): 10-14.

40. Ibid.

41. Nolan Porterfield, *The Life and Times of America's Blue Yodeler Jimmie Rodgers* (Urbana: University of Illinois Press, 1979), 433-36.

42. Bill C. Malone, *Country Music U.S.A.* (Austin: University of Texas Press, 1985), 77; Porterfield, *Jimmie Rodgers,* 202.

43. *Stars of Country Music,* 125, 133.

44. A picture from this period shows Rodgers posed in front of a wall of posters promoting his May 4, 1930, appearance in Borger; see Burt Goldblatt and Robert Shelton,

The Country Music Story: A Picture History of Country and Western Music (Secaucus: Castle Books, 1971), 54.

45. Porterfield, *Jimmie Rodgers*, 436.

46. *Stars of Country Music*, 135.

47. Townsend, *San Antonio Rose*, 31, 45; Raymond Brown, interview with Joe Carr, Lubbock, December 11, 1990.

48. Cliff Bruner, telephone conversation with Joe Carr, Houston, September 19, 1991.

49. Bob Wills was once asked to challenge the medicine show fiddler in his home town of Turkey; Townsend, *San Antonio Rose*, 31.

50. Bob Kendrick, interview with Joe Carr, San Angelo, Texas, March 19, 1991. Kendrick's experience with medicine shows was an unexpected and welcome addition to his interview.

51. Ibid.

Chapter Two Discography

Country Gazette, *A Traitor in Our Midst*, United Artists USA 5596, 1972. This modern recording features fiddler Byron Berline playing the version of "Lost Indian" he learned from Eck Robertson.

Eck Robertson, *Eck Robertson*, "Famous Cowboy Fiddler," County 202, 1992. John Cohen, Mike Seeger, and Tracy Schwarz recorded these tunes in 1963 in Amarillo.

Chapter Three

1. Bill C. Malone, *Country Music U.S.A.*, rev. ed. (Austin: University of Texas Press, 1985), 93.

2. Woody Guthrie, *Bound for Glory* (New York: E. P. Dutton, 1968), 231.

3. Joe Klein, *Woody Guthrie: A Life* (New York: Alfred A. Knopf, 1980), 43-74. Chapter 2 of this biography concentrates on Guthrie's years in Pampa.

4. Ibid., xiv.

5. Nessye Mae Roach, correspondence with authors, January 11, 1991.

6. Robena Stevenson Watts, interview with Joe Carr, Idalou, Texas, November 1, 1992.

7. Robena Watts scrapbook. Letters from C. H. Hutto dated October 4, 1936 for Lamesa; November 4, 1936 for Floydada; September 6, 1937 for Littlefield; October 6, 1937 for La Mesa; September 9, 1938 for Brownfield; and October 4, 1938 for La Mesa.

8. Ibid., C. H. Hutto form letter, November 10, 1936.

9. Ibid., C. H. Hutto to Nathan Stevenson, October 11, 1936.

10. Robena Stevenson Watts interview, Ibid.

11. John Brooks, "Missing: Centennial Fair Song Writer from Today's State Fair Reunion," *Castro County News*, October 2, 1986, 12.

12. Dutch LaRue to Joe Carr, October 23, 1990.

13. Brooks, "Missing," 12.

14. Listen especially to "Garbage Man Blues," which includes a conversation in "black" dialect.

15. Charles R. Townsend, *San Antonio Rose: The Life and Music of Bob Wills* (Urbana: University of Illinois Press, 1976), 73.

16. Ibid., 76.

17. Ibid., 9-10, 12-13.

18. Ibid., 194.

19. Johnny Gimble, conversation with Joe Carr, Lubbock, July 20, 1991.

20 Hugh Cherry and Lawson Warren, *The Bob Wills Story*, Great Empire Productions, KFDI, Wichita. Executive producers Mike Lynch and Mike Oetusu, associate producer Keith Besher. This series of six one-hour taped radio programs draws largely from the Townsend biography.

21 Jimmie Meek, interview with authors, Amarillo, January 6, 1990.

22. Gary Ginell, liner notes, *Sons of the West*, Texas Rose Records TXR 2708, 1982.

23. Jimmie Meek, interview with authors, Amarillo, January 6, 1990.

24. Ginell, *Sons of the West*.

25. Jimmie Meek, interview with authors, Amarillo, January 6, 1990.

26. Cliff Bruner, telephone conversation with Joe Carr, Houston, August 19, 1991.

27. Johnny Gimble, conversation with Joe Carr, Lubbock, July 20, 1991.

28. Bob Kendrick, interview with Joe Carr, San Angelo, Texas, March 19, 1991.

29. Bob Kendrick to Joe Carr, July 13, 1991.

30. E. E. Oberstein to Bob Kendrick, 1937.

31. Tony Russell, comp., *Bob Skyles and his Skyrockets*, unpublished discography.

32. Ibid.

33. Bob Kendrick, interview with Joe Carr, San Angelo, Texas, March 19, 1991.

34. Russell, *Bob Skyles*.

35. Bob Kendrick, interview with Joe Carr, San Angelo, Texas, March 19, 1991.

36. Henry Lester, interview with Joe Carr, Idalou, Texas, December 11, 1990.

37. Henry Lester, interview with Elizabeth Shrank, May 1980, Southwest Collection, Texas Tech University, Lubbock, Texas.

38. Nancy F. Bredenburg, liner notes to *East Texas Serenaders 1927-1936*, County Records 410.

39. Henry Lester, interview with Joe Carr, Idalou, Texas, December 11, 1990.

40. Ken Griffis, *Hear My Song: The Story of the Celebrated Sons of the Pioneers* (John Edwards Memorial Foundation, Special Series #5, 1974), 10-11.

41. Velma Spencer, interview with Lannie Fiel, Lubbock, Texas, April 6, 1991.

42. Ibid.

43. John Julian, conversation with Joe Carr, Lubbock, June 18, 1992; Roy Rogers, interview with Rusty Hudelson, Los Angeles, March 17, 1992.

44. Griffis, *Hear My Song*, 13-14.

45. Michael Mendelson, *The Farr Brothers: Texas Crapshooter*, illustrated booklet accompanying recording, JEMF-107, 1978.

46. Lawrence Graves, *A History of Lubbock* (Lubbock: West Texas Museum Association, 1962), 614-615.

47. Ross Edwards, *Fiddle Dust* (Denver: Big Mountain Press, 1965), 81.

48. Frank P. Hill and Pat Hill Jacobs, *Grassroots Upside Down* (Austin: Nortex Press, 1986), 297.

49. Burt Goldblatt and Robert Shelton, *The Country Music Story*, (Secaucus: Castle Books, 1966), 121

50. Ronnie Pugh, Country Music Foundation, Nashville, TN, to Joe Carr, June 4, 1991. CMF researcher Bob Pinson found that the group may have appeared in the 1935 Universal film "Stormy."

51. Joe Bob Tinsley, comp., *For a Cowboy Has to Sing* (Orlando: University of Central Florida Press, 1991), 98, 99, 234, 235. Louise Massey Mabie died in San Angelo, Texas, on June 22, 1983.

52. Goldblatt and Shelton, *Country Music Story*, 55.

53. Russ Parsons, "Beyond a Doubt," *Honky Tonk Visions* (exhibition catalog) (Lubbock: Texas Tech University Museum, 1986), 17, 19.

Chapter Three Discography

Milton Brown, *Milton Brown and his Musical Brownies 1934*, Texas Rose TXR-2706, 1982. This album includes "Garbage Man Blues."

Cliff Bruner, *Cliff Bruner's Texas Wanderers*, Texas Rose TXR 2710, 1983. This album includes three selections featuring J. R. Chatwell.

East Texas Serenaders, *East Texas Serenaders 1927-1936*. County 410. This recording includes the selections recorded with Henry and Shorty Lester.

The Farr Brothers, *Texas Crapshooter*, JEMF 107, 1978.

Woody Guthrie, *Dust Bowl Ballads*, Rounder, 1940.

Woody Guthrie, *Library of Congress Recordings*, Rounder CD1041, 1988. This impressive set contains three hours of songs and conversation recorded in 1940 by Alan Lomax.

The Sons of the Pioneers, *Empty Saddles*, MCA MCAC 1563, 1983. This is a compilation of the group's recordings from the 1930s and 1940s.

The Sons of the West, *Sons of the West: 1938-1941*, Texas Rose TXR 2708, 1982.

Various artists, *Operators' Specials*, String STR 807, 1979. This British release includes "Rubber Dolly" and "Jump and Jive" by Bob Skyles and his Skyrockets, "Panhandle Shuffle" by the Sons of the West, "A Big Ball's in Cowtown" by Hoyle Nix and his West Texas

Cowboys, and "Sometimes" by Adolph Hofner and his San Antonians featuring J. R. Chatwell on fiddle.

Various artists, *Under the Double Eagle: Great Western Swing Bands of the 1930s, Vol. 1,* RCA 2101-4-R, 1990. This cassette features Milton Brown and his Musical Brownies and Bill Boyd and his Cowboy Ramblers and includes "Garbage Man Blues."

Bob Wills, *Bob Wills and his Texas Playboys Anthology 1935-1973,* Rhino R2-70744, 1991. This is a two-disc "best of" compilation.

Bob Wills, *Bob Wills/Fiddle,* Country Music Foundation P20156, 1987.

Chapter Four

1. Bill Malone, *Country Music U.S.A.,* rev. ed. (Austin: University of Texas Press, 1985), 199.

2. Tommy Hancock, interview with authors, Lubbock, December 11, 1990.

3. Malone, *Country Music,* 187; see also "Factfile," *Close Up Magazine* 26, no. 11 (November/December 1991): 31. Chet Hagan considers this story fictitious; see Chet Hagan, *Grand Ole Opry* (New York: Henry Holt, 1989), 90. See also Monte Montejoy, liner notes, *The Tiffany Transcriptions, Volume 6: Sally Goodin,* Bob Wills and his Texas Playboys, Kaleidoscope Records, C-27, 1987.

4. Hagan, *Grand Ole Opry,* 90.

5. Malone, *Country Music,* 157.

6. Ibid., 154.

7. Johnny Gimble, conversation with Joe Carr, Lubbock, July 20, 1991.

8. R. T. Fry, interview with Alan Munde, Amarillo, September 16, 1991. After the war, many small rural schoolhouses, which had often served as community centers, were closed as schools were consolidated. The loss of the community schoolhouse as a dance place may have contributed to the emergence of clubs.

9. Rich Kienzle, liner notes to *Columbia Country Classics: Honky Tonk Heroes Volume Two,* CK 46030, 1990.

10. Even today in West Texas, when unscheduled musicians show up, the authors hear members of the audience ask not "Are we going to hear some music?" but "Are we going to have a dance?"

11. Tommy Allsup, interview with Alan Munde, Nashville, October 10, 1991.

12. *Lubbock Avalanche-Journal,* September 19, 1953 and various Amarillo newspaper advertisements.

13. Jody Nix, interview with authors, Big Spring, Texas, June 6, 1989. In 1991, Hoyle Nix was inducted into the Texas Western Swing Hall of Fame for his impressive contributions to western swing music.

14. Joe W. Specht, "An Interview with Hoyle Nix, The West Texas Cowboy," *Old Time Music,* no. 34 (Summer-Autumn 1980): 9.

15. Jody Nix, interview with authors, Big Spring, Texas, June 6, 1989.

16. Many old-timers refer to this method as "playing over the bass" since the bass strings of the fiddle are closest to the bowing hand in this position. In Specht, "Interview with Hoyle Nix," Nix refers to this style as "over the bass."

17. Cary Ginell, liner notes, *Sons of the West: 1938-41,* Texas Rose TXR 2708, 1982.

18. Weldon Allard, interview with Joe Carr, Amarillo, May 24, 1992.

19. Ginell, *Sons of the West.*

20. Leon Gibbs, interview with Joe Carr, Wichita Falls, Texas, November 25, 1991. In the 1970s the Gibbs brothers performed in the motion picture "The Last Picture Show," which was filmed in Archer City. They were cast as a country dance band playing for a Christmas party. In the early 1990s, Leon Gibbs taught several days a week at Sam Gibbs's music store in Wichita Falls.

21. Charles R. Townsend, *San Antonio Rose: The Life and Music of Bob Wills* (Urbana: University of Illinois Press, 1976), 269.

22. Lanny Fiel, *The Bob Wills Fiddle Legacy* (Lubbock: Mel Bay and Texas Tech University Press, 1992); afterword by Buck Ramsey, 52-56. McWhorter's life as a cowboy is related in *Horse Fixin': Forty Years of Working with Problem Horses,* and his fiddling is documented in *Cowboy Fiddler,* both published in 1992 by Texas Tech University Press.

23. Tommy Hancock, interview with authors, Lubbock, December 11, 1990.

24. Lubbock musician Henry Lester verified this practice. Lester tried his hand twice at the club business in Lubbock and was twice burned out within the first year of operation. Henry Lester, interview with Joe Carr, Idalou, Texas, December 11, 1990.

25. Tommy Hancock, interview with authors, Lubbock, December 11, 1990.

26. In 1962, he sold out to his partner and moved to Colorado Springs, Colorado, to operate KPIK. He eventually retired to Las Vegas, Nevada.

27. Dave Stone, interview with Alan Munde, Las Vegas, Nevada, August 21, 1991.

28. KSEL Western Jamboree program, Saturday, July 15, 1950.

29. Dave Stone, interview with Alan Munde, Las Vegas, Nevada, August 21, 1991.

30. KSEL Jamboree Program.

31. Ray Price made his professional debut on Willet's program. See William Whitaker, "Ray Price still singing it his way," *Abilene Reporter News*, morning edition, November 30, 1985.

32. Slim Willet reference file, obituary, *Abilene Reporter News*, Abilene.

33. John Turner, interview with Joe Carr, Abilene, July 1991.

34. Keith Ward to Joe Carr, November 22, 1990.

35. Wally Moyers, *Thirty-Four Years of Country Music in Lubbock, Texas*, unpublished manuscript, author's collection, July 23, 1990, 4. Courtesy Wally Moyers, Jr.

36. Ibid., 9, 14, 15, 25, 27.

37. Wally Moyers, Jr., interview with authors, Lubbock, August 18, 1992.

38. Unidentified 1949 article, presumably from a Lubbock newspaper, included as liner notes to *Tank Town Boogie*. See discography.

39. *Tank Town Boogie* liner notes.

40. Phillip J. Tricker, "Hank Harral 'Tank Town Boogie,'" *Roll Street Journal* (London; n.d.): 4.

41. *Tank Town Boogie* liner notes.

42. Tricker, "Hank Harral," 5.

43. Phillip J. Tricker, "The Caprock Records Story," *Roll Street Journal* no. 7 (London; n.d.): 1-5.

44. "Durwood Haddock," *Country Music Parade*, April 1989, 26.

45. Ibid.

46. Ibid., 27.

47. "KDUB To Sign On Tonight," *Lubbock Evening Journal*, November 13, 1952, section 2.

48. *Plainview Evening Herald*, May 13, 1953, 14.

49. Moyers, *Thirty-Four Years*, 12.

50. Program listing, *Lubbock Morning Avalanche*, November 13, 1953, section 3, 7.

51. Charlene Condray Hancock, interview with Joe Carr, Austin, August 21, 1992.

52. Ellis Amburn, *Dark Star: The Roy Orbison Story* (New York: A Lyle Stuart Book, Carol Publishing, 1990,) 17.

53. Bob Allen, "Charline Arthur," *Now Dig This* no. 60 (March 1988):3-4.

54. Ibid.

55. Jim Chancellor (Texas Shorty), interview with authors, Richardson, Texas, February 22, 1988.

56. Bryant Houston, interview with Texas Tech University students, Rising Star, Texas, February 12, 1980. Southwest Collection, Texas Tech University, Lubbock.

57. "450 Titles Won by Cisco Fiddler," *Abilene Reporter News*, May 20, 1973, p. 2-B.

58. Bryant Houston, interview with Texas Tech University students, Rising Star, Texas, February 12, 1980. Southwest Collection, Texas Tech University, Lubbock.

Chapter Four Discography

Charline Arthur, *Welcome to the Club*, Bear Family BFX 15234.

Wally Moyers, *Wally Moyers Plays West Texas Steel Guitar*, Broadway Studios, Lubbock, 1990.

Jody Nix, *New Road Under My Wheels*, Brooke Records and Tapes, Big Spring, Texas.

The Sons of the West, *Sons of the West: 1938-41*, Texas Rose TXR 2708, 1982.

Various artists, *Boppin' Hillbilly vol. 14*, White WLP2814, Holland, n.d. This album contains singles from the 1950s on the Dallas-based Star Talent label and includes selections by Hank Harral, Hoyle Nix, and Slim Willet.

Various artists, *Hank Harral and Caprock Records*, White WLP8831, Holland, n.d. This Dutch release includes 1950s recordings by Harral, Hoyle Nix, Ace Ball, and Durwood Dailey.

Various artists, *Hillbilly Houn' Dawgs and Honky-Tonk Angels*, Detour 33-008. This English album contains two RCA cuts by Charline Arthur, 1989.

Bob Wills, *Bob Wills and His Texas Playboys: For the Last Time*, United Artists, 1973. UA-LA 216-J2, 1973.

Chapter Five

1. Chet Hagan, *Grand Ole Opry: The Complete Story of a Great American Institution and Its Stars* (New York: An Owl Book, Henry Holt, 1989), 10.

2. Neil V. Rosenberg, *Bluegrass: A History* (Urbana: University of Illinois Press, 1985), 95-131.

3. Alvie Ivey, interview with Alan Munde, Lubbock, May 17, 1989.

4. Herb Mayfield, interview with authors, Dimmitt, Texas, March 29, 1989.

5. Alvie Ivey, interview with Alan Munde, Lubbock, May 17, 1989.

6. Bill Myrick, interview with Alan Munde, Odessa, Texas, February 3, 1991; for the band's title, see the KSEL Western Jamboree Program, Saturday, May 6, 1950.

7. Sonny Curtis, interview with authors, Levelland, Texas, January 27, 1990; Dave Stone, interview with Alan Munde, Las Vegas, Nevada, August 26, 1991. In the early 1950s, bluegrass was still a part of mainstream country music, and to find bluegrass on a country music program was not unusual. Jack Douglas, a Lubbock High School student at the time, walked after school to U. V. Blake's record store to buy the latest releases of the bluegrass artists of the day-Bill Monroe, Reno and Smiley, Flatt and Scruggs-in addition to the current country artists. All those artists' records were found in the same country music bin. Jack Douglas, interview with authors, Littlefield, Texas, April 6, 1990.

8. *Shreveport Magazine*, April 1951, 32-33.

9. Bill Myrick, interview with Alan Munde, Odessa, Texas, February 3, 1991.

10. Larry Richardson, interview with Alan Munde, Lake Butler, Florida, June 1, 1989.

11. Bobby Hicks, taped interview with Doug Hutchens for Mayfield Brothers Tribute, South Plains College, Levelland, Texas, May 6, 1989.

12. Doug Hutchens, "Edd Mayfield: The Mystery Man of Bluegrass," *Bluegrass Unlimited* 18, no. 2 (August 1983):26-30.

13. John Hartford, taped interview with Doug Hutchens for Mayfield Brothers Tribute, South Plains College, Levelland, Texas, May 6, 1989.

14. Neil V. Rosenberg, *Bill Monroe and His Blue Grass Boys: An Illustrated Discography* (Nashville: Country Music Foundation, 1974), 61.

15. Herb Mayfield, interview with authors, Dimmitt, Texas, March 29, 1989.

16. Ibid.

17. Rosenberg, *Bill Monroe*, 65, 66.

18. Herb Mayfield, interview with authors, Dimmitt, Texas, March 29, 1989.

19. Rosenberg, *Bill Monroe*, 68-69.

20. Hutchens, "Edd Mayfield," 30. The serious illness was totally unsuspected. Herb related that several others who had served in the infantry with Edd in the Pacific died of the same disease; Herb Mayfield, interview with authors, Dimmitt, Texas, March 29, 1989.

21. Hutchens, "Edd Mayfield," 26.

22. David Grisman, conversation with Alan Munde, Owensboro, Kentucky, September 1992. Peter Rowan's knock on his guitar to imitate a door knock, the key of his arrangement, and the falsetto vocal on the opening all seem to be copied from the Edd Mayfield recording.

23. Sonny Curtis, interview with authors, Levelland, Texas, January 27, 1990.

24. Tex Logan, interview with authors, Colorado City, Texas, July 28, 1989.

25. Tex Logan, interview with Alan Munde, Morristown, New Jersey, January 15, 1993.

26. Ibid.

27. Liner notes, *Early Days of Bluegrass Volume 1*.

28. Robert Cogswell, "We Made Our Name in the Days of Radio: A Look at the Career of Wilma Lee and Stoney Cooper," *John Edwards Memorial Foundation Quarterly* 11, no. 38 (Summer 1975): 89-90.

29. Tex Logan, interview with Alan Munde, Morristown, New Jersey, January 15, 1993. In 1955 Tex wrote a song describing the sound of the bluegrass instruments called "Down

in the Bluegrass." It was not until 1974 that it was finally recorded by the West Coast bluegrass group Country Gazette, featuring Byron Berline on fiddle. Tex also wrote additional lyrics and music to the folk song "Diamond Joe." Tex related, "'Come and get me Diamond Joe' was a metaphor lamenting the impossibility of reliving the past with old friends"; Tex Logan, interview with Alan Munde, Morristown, New Jersey, January 15, 1993. His reworking of this old song was first recorded by Wilma Lee and Stoney Cooper in 1957 and more recently by Grateful Dead leader Jerry Garcia with David Nelson.

30. Tex Logan, interview with authors, Colorado City, Texas, July 28, 1989.

31. Rosenberg, *Bluegrass*, 153-54.

32. Ibid., 203.

33. Tex Logan, interview with authors, Colorado City, Texas, July 28, 1989.

34. Roger Mason, interview with Lannie Fiel, *Roots Music*, KOHM radio, Lubbock, August 1992.

Chapter Five Discography

Country Gazette, *Country Gazette, Live,* Antilles/Island AN-7014, 1975. This recording features the Tex Logan composition "Down in the Bluegrass" with Byron Berline on fiddle and Alan Munde on banjo.

David Grisman and others, *The David Grisman Rounder Album,* Rounder 0069, 1976. This album includes Ricky Skaggs singing "I Ain't Broke, But I'm Badly Bent," a song learned from a tape of Bill Monroe featuring Edd Mayfield's singing.

Bill Monroe and the Bluegrass Boys, *Bill Monroe Bluegrass 1950-1958,* Bear Family BCD 15423, 1989. This four-compact disc set contains all of Monroe's recordings for Decca Records between 1950 and 1958, including all of the Edd Mayfield sessions. It also includes "Christmas Time's a-Coming," written by Tex Logan.

Peter Rowan, *Peter Rowan,* Flying Fish FF-071, 1978. Tex Logan appears on "When I Was a Cowboy" and "Panama Red."

Peter Rowan, *The First Whippoorwill,* Sugar Hill SH3749, 1985. On this tribute album to Bill Monroe, Rowan sings and selects for the title cut "The First Whipoorwill," the first song Edd Mayfield recorded with Monroe.

Various artists, *Bluegrass at Newport, Recorded Live at the Newport Folk Festivals 1959, 1960, and 1963,* Vanguard VCD 121/32. Tex Logan performs "Jordan Am a Hard Road to Travel."

Various artists, *Mountain Music, Bluegrass Style.* Smithsonian/ Folkways CD SF 40038, 1959. Tex Logan appears on this release performing "Katy Hill" and "Natchez under the Hill."

Various artists, *Early Days of Bluegrass,* Rounder 1013, 1989. This release contains two cuts by Red Belcher featuring Tex Logan.

Chapter Six

1. Nelson George, *The Death of Rhythm and Blues* (New York: Pantheon Books, 1988), 26. George points out that in 1949, *Billboard,* the most influential music magazine in the industry, changed the name of its black pop-music chart from "race" to "rhythm and blues," and that disc jockey Allan Freed used the term *rock and roll* because it did not connote just black music but portrayed a more universal image that could be marketed to a white audience. George sees the term *rock and roll* as "perhaps the perfect emblem of white Negroism."

2. Lubbock musician Terry Allen recalled about the rock and roll song "Blue Suede Shoes," "It was the first time I was conscious of a song that wasn't about family or church or institutions or school. It was directed at you." Terry Allen, interview with authors, Santa Fe, November 27, 1993.

3. Sock rhythm is achieved when all strings of the guitar are fretted or depressed to form the chord and then released slightly to stop the strings from sounding, creating a percussive, harmonic sound.

4. Bill C. Malone, *Country Music U.S.A.,* rev. ed. (Austin: University of Texas Press, 1985), 247, 199-243. Disc jockey Allan Freed actually coined the term in 1951, and Bill Haley and the Comets had their first national hit with "Crazy, Man, Crazy," in 1953 and

released "Rock Around The Clock" in 1955. See also Colin Escott and Martin Hawkins, *Sun Records: The Brief History of the Legendary Record Label* (New York: Quick Fox, 1980), 3.

5. Bill Griggs and Larry Holley, presentation about Buddy Holly, Goedeke Library, Lubbock, November 27, 1990.

6. Sonny Curtis, interview with authors, Levelland, Texas, January 27, 1990.

7. John Goldrosen and John Beecher, *Remembering Buddy: The Definitive Biography of Buddy Holly* (New York: Penguin Books, 1987), 13. Buddy Holley changed the spelling of his last name to Holly in 1956 because it was misspelled without the "e" on his first Decca contract.

8. Larry Holley, *The Buddy I Knew* (Lubbock: Larry Holley, 1980), 2.

9. Griggs and Holley, Lubbock, November 27, 1990.

10. In a photograph from 1955, Bob plays the guitar and Buddy the tenor banjo; see Holley, *Buddy*, 5.

11. Ben Hall, interview with Alan Munde, Nashville, October 17, 1991.

12. Ibid.; Jerry Coleman, interview with Alan Munde, Lubbock, October 1991. Lubbock disc jockey Jerry Coleman, host of the late-night radio program "Hi-D-Ho Hit Parade" on station KSEL, remembers Buddy Holly hanging out at the station and going off into an unused production room to listen to the new recordings of the black artists. Ben Hall's first meeting with Holly occurred when Holly stopped by the KSEL studios to speak to him.

13. Bill Griggs, "Spotlight On Sonny Curtis," *Rockin' 50's* (April 1990): 11.

14. Lubbock *Avalanche-Journal,* advertisement for Hi-Hat Club, 1953.

15. Sonny Curtis to authors, October 7, 1993. Sonny related, "Charles Brown's guitarist came into Adair's where I was working and invited me to the show that night at the Cotton Club. He had a chair put on stage for me, right next to him, and I sat there all through the performance. It is true that I was the only white person there, but the racial aspects of the situation never crossed my mind. I was only eighteen . . . I don't remember being made to feel uncomfortable once that evening. What impressed me most was the abandon exhibited by the performers. That was all quite new to me. It was a great show and a memorable experience."

16. Goldrosen and Beecher, *Remembering Buddy*, 36.

17. Albert Goldman, *Elvis* (New York: McGraw-Hill, 1981), 110.

18. Nelson George offers his view of Elvis in *Death of Rhythm and Blues,* pp. 62-63: "On stage he [Elvis] adopted the symbolic fornication blacks had unashamedly brought to American entertainment. Elvis was sexy: not clean-cut, wholesome, white-bread Hollywood sexy but sexy in the aggressive earthy manner associated by whites with black males. In fact, as a young man Presley came closer than any other rock and roll star to capturing the swaggering sexuality projected by so many R and B vocalists."

19. Maurine Garton, conversation with Alan Munde, Norman, Oklahoma, 1985.

20. Peter Guralnick, *Lost Highways: Journeys and Arrivals of American Musicians* (New York: Vintage Books, 1982), 119.

21. Chet Hagan, *Grand Ole Opry: The Complete Story of A Great American Institution and Its Stars* (New York: Henry Holt, 1989), 181-82.

22. Lee Cotten, *All Shook Up: Elvis Day by Day* (Ann Arbor: Pierian Press, 1985), 27.

23. Pete Curtis, interview with authors, Levelland, Texas, January 27, 1990.

24. Slim Richey, interview with Alan Munde, Levelland, Texas, November 11, 1991. See also Webb Pierce's introduction of Roy Hall on "Classic Country" television program, mid-1950s.

25. Goldman, *Elvis*, 121; "Elvis Presley, Folk Music Fireball," *Country Song Roundup* 1, no. 40 (September 1950):14; Guralnick, *Lost Highways*, 129.

26. Slim Richey, interview with Alan Munde, Levelland, Texas, November 11, 1991.

27. Sonny Curtis, interview with authors, Levelland, Texas, January 27, 1990; Dave Stone, interview with Alan Munde, Las Vegas, Nevada, August 26, 1991.

28. Hagan, *Grand Ole Opry*, 182.

29. There is some confusion over the exact date of Elvis's first appearance in Lubbock. We conclude that he appeared on the show during the time frame cited, based on the cross-checking of the recollections of Sonny Curtis, Billy Walker, and Dave Stone with an article in the Midland *Reporter-Telegram*, January 6, 1955, entitled "Western Show Here Friday to Feature Hayride Stars."

30. It was common for artists appearing on a stage show in Lubbock in the early evening to perform later the same night at the Cotton Club. Steve Lewis, current director of the South Plains Fair Association, relates an example found in the minutes of the Association board meeting following the 1954 South Plains Fair. The Fair Park Coliseum was newly completed, and the Association had booked a large country music package show featuring the Wilburn Brothers, Rose Maddox, Slim Whitman, Webb Pierce, Jimmy and Johnny, and others. Apparently, during their daytime Fair performances, many of the acts announced that they would be appearing at the Cotton Club and openly urged people to leave the Fair and come to the club. Fair director A. B. Davis, quite upset with the artists, withheld five hundred dollars of the entertainer's fee from their agent for damages. Steve Lewis, interview with Alan Munde, Lubbock, January 1993.

31. Bill Wilkerson, "Red Foley, Tex Ritter Highlight Program: Near Capacity Crowd Turns Out For Folk Music Frolic," *Lubbock Avalanche-Journal*, December 5, 1954.

32. Goldman, *Elvis*, 117.

33. Griggs and Holley, Lubbock, November 27, 1990.

34. John Tobler, *The Buddy Holly Story* (London: Plexus Publishing Limited, 1979), 14-15.

35. Joel Selvin, "Ricky Nelson: I'm Walkin'," *Journal of Country Music* 13, no. 2 (1990): 9.

36. Colin Escott, liner notes to cassette, *The Best of Buddy Knox*.

37. Norman Petty is a important figure in the story of country and rock music in West Texas of the 1950s and the early 1960s. Many of the artists in this book recorded at his Clovis, New Mexico, studio, and Petty was the conduit for a large number of West Texas performers to the record companies and bookers located in the North and Northeast. Vi Petty, following her husband's death, continued to operate the studio and eventually turned into a museum, which she operated until her death in 1992.

38. Neil V. Rosenberg, *Bill Monroe and His Blue Grass Boys: An Illustrated Discography* (Nashville: Country Music Foundation, 1974), 29.

39. *Lubbock Avalanche-Journal*, February 13, 1955.

40. These dates and locations were gathered and confirmed from ads in the Lubbock *Avalanche-Journal* and with additional help and guidance from Bob Pinson of the Country Music Foundation, Nashville, and Cotten, *All Shook Up*, 35-60.

41. Goldrosen and Beecher, *Remembering Buddy*, 31.

42. *Lubbock Avalanche-Journal*, October 14, 1955.

43. Curtis said that at the session, "They didn't even let Buddy play. Don Guess [bassist] and I were Buddy's band, and Mr. Bradley hired two of Nashville's session greats to join us. Grady Martin, Red Foley's guitarist, played rhythm, and Buddy Harman played drums. I played lead. The mixture was a little weird, and we felt that we came out sounding more country than rock 'n' roll. We were disappointed." Sonny Curtis to authors, October 7, 1993. Sonny added about his last trip to Nashville with Buddy, "We were unable to overcome their country influence. We were young and inexperienced and didn't know how to communicate our thoughts and feelings. We couldn't make it work."
To illustrate how green they were on this first trip to Nashville, Sonny related, "We were in the motel room and thinking, 'We're not in the union. I wonder if we ought to mention that.'" When this was brought to the attention of Jim Denny just minutes before the session, his shocked response was, "Oh my goodness, that's important. You can't go into a studio in Nashville and not be in the musicians' union." Denny hurriedly called the union in Amarillo and worked out a deal, and the session went on. Sonny made forty-two dollars for playing on the session, and that money went to pay his new union dues. Sonny Curtis, interview with authors, Levelland, Texas, January 27, 1990.

44. Sonny Curtis, interview with Alan Munde, Dickson, Tennessee, November 11, 1991.

45. Sonny Curtis to authors, October 7, 1993. "The first two nights of the tour, Carl Perkins and his group was on the shows. He had a navy blue Cadillac and we thought he was really cool. He also played and sang great. We were blown away by him."

46. Sonny Curtis, interview with authors, Levelland, Texas, January 27, 1990.

47. Daniel Wolf, "Theater," *Vogue* 180, no. 10 (October 1990):274. This is a review of the musical "Buddy: The Buddy Holly Story" by Paul Hipp.

48. Guralnick, *Lost Highways*, 119.

49. Ken Kennamer, "Thousands Hear Elvis Presley: Teen-Agers Mob Rock 'n Roll Singer in Appearance Here," *Lubbock Avalanche-Journal*, April 11, 1956.

50. Sonny Curtis to authors, October 7, 1993; Tommy Allsup, interview with Alan Munde, Nashville, October 10, 1991.

51. Sonny Curtis, interview with authors, Levelland, Texas, January 27, 1990.

52. Ibid.

53. Wolf, "Theater," 274.

54. Buddy Holly, interview with Red Robinson, Vancouver, BC, October 23, 1958, on the phonograph picturedisc, *The Unforgettable Buddy Holly: Live.*

55. Bill Griggs, two-part interview with Lanny Fiel on "Roots Music" radio program, KOHM-FM, Lubbock, September 8 and 22, 1991.

56. Sonny Curtis, interview with authors, Levelland, Texas, January 27, 1990.

57. *Buddy Magazine* 19, no. 3 (September 1991):15-16.

58. Bill Griggs, presentation about Buddy Holly, Goedeke Library, Lubbock, November 27, 1990.

59. Bill Griggs, "A Who's Who of West Texas Rock 'n' Roll Music," *Rockin' 50's* (1994).

60. Don Caldwell, conversation with Alan Munde, Levelland, Texas, February 21, 1991.

61. Ellis Amburn, *Dark Star: The Roy Orbison Story* (New York: A Lyle Stuart Book, Carol Publishing Group, 1990), 17.

62. Larry Willoughby, *Texas Rhythm, Texas Rhyme: A Pictorial History of Texas Music* (Austin: Tonkawa Press, 1990), 85.

63. Bill Myrick, interview with Alan Munde, Odessa, Texas, February 3, 1991.

64. Billy Walker, interview with Alan Munde, Nashville, October 28, 1991.

65. Amburn, *Dark Star*, 29, 33.

66. Midland promoter and long-time disc jockey Keith Ward recalled that it was not uncommon to book the same show in both Midland and Odessa on the same night, with different starting times. He reported that this arrangement was referred to as a "bicycle show" because the artists had to hurry or "bicycle" back and forth between locations. The six hundred dollars Ward made on the February 16, 1955, Hank Snow and Elvis concert, he lost on a later Maddox Brothers and Rose bicycle concert. The dates of Elvis Presley's performances were gathered from interviews with Billy Walker and Keith Ward, ads in the *Odessa American* and the *Midland Reporter-Telegram,* and with additional help from Bob Pinson of the Country Music Foundation, Nashville, and Cotten, *All Shook Up*, 35-60.

67. Tracy Byers, "Teen Kings Foresee Nationwide Success," *Odessa American*, May 20, 1956.

68. Bill Myrick, interview with Alan Munde, Odessa, Texas, February 3, 1991.

69. Byers, "Teen Kings."

70. Colin Escott, liner notes to recorded collection *The Legendary Roy Orbison.*

71. Amburn, *Dark Star*, 68, 69.

72. Dave Marsh, *The Heart of Rock and Soul: The 1001 Greatest Singles Ever Made* (New York: New American Library, 1989), 19, 75, 227, 274.

73. Escott, liner notes, *Legendary Roy Orbison.*

74. Tommy Allsup, interview with Alan Munde, Nashville, October 10, 1991.

75. *Roots and Rhythm* (record catalog) no. 90 (September/October 1992):22.

76. Bill Griggs, "Spotlight on the Four Teens (and the Ad-Libs)," *Rockin' 50s* (April 1991):9-13.

77. Tommy Allsup, conversation with Alan Munde, Nashville, December 1, 1992.

Chapter Six Discography

Dean Baird, *Rakin' and Scrapin'*, Revival 3008.

The Crickets, *The Liberty Years*, EMI E4-95845, 1991. These recordings, made after Holly's death, include Sonny Curtis, Jerry Allison, Jerry Naylor, and Glen D. Hardin.

Buddy Holly, *Buddy Holly*, MCA MCAD 5540.

Buddy Holly, *The Unforgettable Buddy Holly: Live* International Foundation of Picture-disc Promotion, early 1980s.

Buddy Knox, *The Best of Buddy Knox*, Rhino R4 70964, 1990.

Roy Orbison, *The Legendary Roy Orbison*, CBS A4T 46809, 1990. This set covers most of the important Orbison material, including his first hit, "Ooby Dooby."

Elvis Presley, *Elvis: The King of Rock 'N' Roll, The Complete 50's Masters*, RCA 666050-2, 1992.

1. *Saturday Evening Post*, February 12, 1966.

2. Bill C. Malone, *Country Music U.S.A.*, rev. ed. (Austin: University of Texas Press, 1985), 264-65.

3. Billy Walker, interview with Alan Munde, Nashville, October 28, 1991.

4. Advertisement in the *Lubbock Avalanche-Journal*, November 1, 1946.

5. A portion of the Big D Jamboree was broadcast by the CBS network, and it helped launch the careers of Walker, Sonny James, and Ray Price. Walt Trott, *The Nashville Musician* (Dec. 1991-Feb. 1992):17.

6. Anne Solomon, interview with Alan Munde, Levelland, Texas, March 29, 1992.

7. Billy Walker, interview with Alan Munde, Nashville, October 28, 1991.

8. *Lubbock Avalanche-Journal*, January 30, 1955.

9. Billy Walker, interview with Alan Munde, Nashville, October 28, 1991. This concert was apparently in nearby Midland; see *Midland Reporter-Telegram*, January 6, 1955, p. 2.

10. Ibid.

11. Ben Hall, interview with Alan Munde, Nashville, October 17, 1991.

12. *Hep Cats from Big Spring . . . Texas Rock 'n' Roll from the 50s and 60s.* Roller Coaster 1991, liner notes by John Ingram.

13. Weldon Myrick, interview with Alan Munde, Nashville, November 23, 1991.

14. At one point in the interview with Weldon Myrick, he read a "partial list" of artists he has recorded with–he read for ten minutes. The list is practically a who's who of country and popular music. Here is an abbreviated list: Bill Anderson, Connie Smith, the Wilburn Brothers, Chet Atkins, Floyd Cramer, Tex Ritter, Webb Pierce, Faron Young, Jim Reeves, Patsy Cline, Tammy Wynette, George Jones, Elvis Presley, Fess Parker, Dolly Parton, Steve Wariner, Willie Nelson, Hank Snow, Roy Orbison, Johnny Cash, Waylon Jennings, the Oak Ridge Boys, Roy Acuff, Porter Wagoner, the Ozark Mountain Daredevils, Tom T. Hall, Wayne Newton, Marty Robbins, Loretta Lynn, Ronnie Milsap, Linda Ronstadt, Alan Jackson, Ricky Skaggs, Olivia Newton-John, Ray Stevens, Brenda Lee, Ray Charles, Slim Whitman, the Pointer Sisters, Charley Pride, Vern Gosdin, Merle Haggard, Billy Walker, Reba McIntyre, Area Code 615, the Carpenters, Freddy Fender, and Bobby Goldsboro.

15. R. Serge Denisoff, *Waylon: A Biography*, (New York: St. Martin's Press, 1984), 37.

16. Emil Macha, interview with authors, Littlefield, Texas, December 28, 1988.

17. Sue Swinson, "Waylon: The Early Years, Emil Macha Recalls Musical Roots of Littlefield Legend," *West Texas Sound* (June 1991): 6.

18. This demo was recorded on tape and from that two acetate discs were cut.

19. Swinson, "Waylon," 6.

20. Shane West, "The Conversation: A Visit with Larry Corbin," *West Texas Sound* 2, no. 3 (September 1991):1.

21. Emil Macha, interview with authors, Littlefield, Texas, December 28, 1988.

22. Jennings performed often with Sonny Curtis. On several occasions, Jennings and Curtis performed during intermissions in a Lubbock movie theater or with other KLLL personalities on live broadcasts from local businesses. Sonny Curtis, interview with authors, Levelland, Texas, January 27, 1990.

23. John Goldrosen and John Beecher, *Remembering Buddy: The Definitive Biography of Buddy Holly* (New York: Viking Penguin, 1987), 181.

24. Jerry Osborne, *Country Music: Buyers and Sellers Reference Book and Price Guide* (Tempe: Osborne Enterprises Ltd., 1984), 131.

25. Tommy Allsup, interview with Alan Munde, Nashville, October 10, 1991. Holly, Ritchie Valens, J. P. Richards (known as the Big Bopper), and pilot Roger Peterson were killed in a plane crash during a snowstorm as they were leaving Clear Lake, Iowa, for a date in Fargo, North Dakota.

26. Bob Allen, *Waylon and Willie* (New York: Quick Fox, 1979), 31.

27. Osborne, *Country Music*, 131.

28. Tommy Allsup, interview with Alan Munde, Nashville, October 10, 1991.

29. Edna Dubre, interview with Alan Munde, Lorenzo, Texas, December 11, 1992.

30. Malone, *Country Music U.S.A.*, 272, 285, 304, 306, 380, 383; Irvin Stambler and Grelun Landon, *Encyclopedia of Folk, Country, and Western Music* (New York: St. Martin's Press, 1969), 33.

31. West, "Larry Corbin," 4.

Chapter Seven Discography

Tommy Allsup, producer, *Bob Wills: For the Last Time*, United Artists UA-LA216-J2, 1974.

Area Code 615, *Area Code 615*, Polydor 24-4002, 1969 (with Weldon Myrick).

Area Code 615, *A Trip In The Country*, Area Code 615, Polydor 24-4025, 1970 (with Weldon Myrick).

Sonny Curtis, *Rollin'*, Elektra 6E-349, 1981.

Mac Davis, *Lubbock in My Rearview Mirror*, Casablanca 7239, 1980.

Mac Davis, *Greatest Hits*, Columbia JC-36317, 1979.

Jimmy Dean, *Big Bad John (& Other Fabulous Songs and Tales)*, Columbia CS-8535, 1961.

Larry Gatlin and the Gatlin Brothers, *Greatest Hits*, Columbia JC-36488, 1980.

Larry Gatlin and the Gatlin Brothers, *Greatest Hits Vol.2*, Columbia FC-38923, 1983.

Waylon Jennings, *The Outlaws*, with Willie Nelson, Jessi Colter, and Tompall Glaser, RCA APL1-1321, 1976.

Waylon Jennings, *Greatest Hits*, RCA 850-2-R, 1979.

Jeannie C. Riley, *Harper Valley P.T.A.*, Plantation PLP-100, 1968.

Jeannie C. Riley, *Greatest Hits*, Plantation PLP-13, 1971.

Tanya Tucker, *Greatest Hits*, MCA 37225, 1984.

Billy Walker, *Greatest Hits*, Columbia CS 8735, 1963.

Billy Walker, *Charlie's Shoes*, Harmony HS-11414, 1970.

Various Artists, *Hep Cats from Big Spring; Texas Rock 'n' Roll from the 50s and 60s*. Roller Coaster, RCD 3003, 1991.

Chapter Eight

1. Tommy Anderson, conversation with Joe Carr at Jazz Restaurant, Lubbock, November 22, 1992.

2. Ibid.

3. Lloyd Maines, interview with authors, Lubbock, December 20, 1989.

4. For Lubbock inhabitants, the devastating 1970 tornado was a harsh reminder that the illusion of safety provided by modern urban surroundings can be shattered in a moment by the sometimes volatile physical realities of West Texas.

5. Terry Allen, interview with authors, Santa Fe, November 27, 1993.

6. Ibid.

7. Joe Ely, "Because of the Wind," from *Honky Tonk Masquerade*.

8. Jimmie Dale Gilmore, quoted in Ben Sandmel's notes to *After Awhile*, Elektra Nonesuch Records, American Explorer Series, 1991.

9. Jimmie Dale Gilmore, interview with Alan Munde, Austin, December 1, 1993.

10. The Flatlanders, *The Flatlanders: More a Legend Than a Band*, with Jimmie Dale Gilmore, Joe Ely, Butch Hancock and others. Rounder SS34 1990, Sun International 1990.

11. Steve Satterwhite, "Snap Shots, Texas Singer Jimmie Dale Gilmore," *Houston Press*, September 19, 1991, 10.

12. Colin Escott, liner notes to *Flatlanders*, 1990.

13. Lloyd Maines, interview with authors, Lubbock, December 20, 1989.

14. Ibid.

15. *Joe Ely's 2nd Annual Tornado Jam*, souvenir program, the Buddy Holly Recreational area, Lubbock, May 3, 1981, 1. This is a forty-eight-page program with articles on Holly, Ely, the tornado, and performance information.

16. Russ Parsons, "Beyond a Doubt," in *Honky Tonk Visions* (Lubbock: Texas Tech University Museum, 1986), 15.

17. William Kerns, *Lubbock Avalanche-Journal*, May 3, 1981; *Joe Ely's 2nd Annual Tornado Jam*, 1981 souvenir program, 48.

18. Ibid.

19. The Lubbock *Avalanche-Journal*, May 3, 1982, estimated the crowd at twelve thousand.

20. Alan Fogg, "Ely, Ronstadt Surprise Monterey Graduation Party," Lubbock *Avalanche-Journal*, May 2, 1982.

21. William Kerns, "Plans Finalized For Ely's Jam," Lubbock *Avalanche-Journal*, May 1985.

22. William Kerns, "Ely's Recordings Defy Labels," Lubbock *Avalanche-Journal*, "Around Town" section, March 9, 1990, 2; Joe Nick Potoski, "Goodbye Kenny Rogers, Hello Wagoneers," *Texas Monthly* 16, no. 10 (October 1988):118-19.

23. Kerns, "Ely's Recordings," 1.

24. Jimmie Dale Gilmore, interview with Alan Munde, Austin, December 1, 1993.

25. Jimmie Dale Gilmore, quoted in Sandmel, *After Awhile*.

26. Jimmie Dale Gilmore, interview with Alan Munde, Austin, December 1, 1993.

27. Ibid.

28. Jimmie Dale Gilmore, quoted in Sandmel, *After Awhile*.

29. Ibid.

30. Jimmie Dale Gilmore, interview with Alan Munde, Austin, December 1, 1993.

31. Ibid.

32. Escott, *Flatlanders*.

33. John Morthland, "Plains Song," *Texas Monthly* 19, no. 11 (November 1991):94.

34. Ibid., 112.

35. Ibid., 94, 114.

36. Thomas Goldsmith, liner notes to *Butch Hancock Own and Own,* Sugar Hill SH-C-1036, 1991.

37. Morthland, "Plains Song," 114.

38. Charlene Hancock, interview with Joe Carr, Austin, August 21, 1992.

39. *The Baseball Encyclopedia: The Complete and Official Record of Major League Baseball* (New York: Collier Macmillan, 1976), 665. Born in West Plains, Missouri, on August 23, 1886 Fletcher Manson "Sled" Allen played in fourteen major-league games, twelve as a catcher, one as a first baseman, and one as a pinch-hitter. He died in Lubbock on October 16, 1959.

40. Terry Allen, interview with authors, Santa Fe, November 27, 1993.

41. Ibid.

42. Ibid. See Elizabeth Skidmore Sasser, *Out of the Ordinary: The Art of Paul Milosevich* (Lubbock: Texas Tech University Press, 1991), 88. This volume includes portraits of several West Texas music figures, including Ely, Allen, and Stubbs, as well as many West Texas-related works.

43. Terry Allen, interview with authors, Santa Fe, November 27, 1993.

44. Ibid.

45. Lloyd Maines, interview with authors, Lubbock, December 20, 1989.

46. Ibid.

47. Parsons, "Beyond a Doubt," 24.

48. Perhaps the music of West Texas in the 1970s and 1980s suffered the same fate as other earthy musics when they are presented to the American public. Blues, zydeco, bluegrass, folk, and even traditional jazz have been pushed out of the American public ear by the omnipresent top 40 radio format, which appeared by the late 1950s. This format is used by rock, pop, and country music radio stations and effectively excludes music that lies outside the mainstream. Some musics have found an outlet in public radio and university stations. The audiences for these stations are smaller; therefore, the availability and sales of records are smaller. Ultimately, the artist draws fewer people to concerts and makes less money.

49. *Nothin' Else to Do: Celebrating 75 Years of West Texas Music* (Lubbock: Texas Tech University Museum, 1984).

50. *Honky Tonk Visions: On West Texas Music: 1936-1986* (Lubbock: Texas Tech University Museum, 1986).

51. Bill Porterfield, *The Greatest Honky Tonks in Texas* (Dallas: Taylor, 1983), 80.

52. J. T. Smith, "Folks Jam Dance Floor For L. C. Agnew's Music,"Abilene *Reporter News,* July 7, 1977, morning edition.

Chapter Eight Discography

Terry Allen, *Lubbock (on everything)*, Fate 1979; reissue 1991, Special Delivery/Topic SPDCD 1007.

Joe Ely, *Joe Ely*, MCA MCAC 10219, 1977. This was Ely's major label debut.

Joe Ely, *Honky Tonk Masquerade*, MCA MCAC 10220, 1978. This is perhaps the best recording of Ely's early period.

Joe Ely, *Down on the Drag*, MCA MCAC 10221, 1979.

Joe Ely, *Musta Notta Gotta Lotta*, MCA MCAC 815, 1981.

Joe Ely, *Dig All Night*, Hightone HCD 8015, 1988.

Joe Ely, *Live at Liberty Lunch*, MCA MCAD 10045, 1990.

The Flatlanders, *The Flatlanders: More a Legend Than a Band*, Jimmie Dale Gilmore, Joe Ely, Butch Hancock and others. Rounder SS34, 1990, Sun International 1990.

Jimmie Dale Gilmore, *Spinning Around the Sun*, Elektra, 1993.

Jimmie Dale Gilmore, *After Awhile*, Elektra/Nonesuch, 1991.

Jimmie Dale Gilmore, *Jimmie Dale Gilmore*, Hightone HCD 8018.

Jimmie Dale Gilmore, *Fair and Square*, Hightone HCD 8018, 1988.

The Texana Dames, *Texana Dames*, Amazing AM-1018, 1990.

Butch Hancock, *Own and Own*, Sugar Hill SH-C-1036, 1991.

Butch Hancock and Jimmie Dale Gilmore, *Two Roads, Live in Austin*, Virgin VOZCD 2036, 1990.

Tommy Hancock and the Supernatural Family Band, *Lubbock Lights!* Volume 1, SNF 1009C Akashic 1986.

Tommy Hancock and the Supernatural Family Band, *Supernatural Honky Tonk Alive at the Shorthorn Lounge*, Akashic 1006.

The Maines Brothers Band, *Red, Hot and Blue*. Texas Soul TSA 71687, 1987.

The Maines Brothers Band, *Hub City Moan*, Texas Soul TSA 61581, 1981.

Jesse Taylor, *Last Night*, Bedrock, 1990.

Various Artists, Chippy: The Diary of a West Texas Hooker, Hollywood HR-616092, 1994.

Chapter Nine

1. A bootlegger in West Texas did not manufacture alcohol as a general rule. His business was reselling alcohol he had purchased legally in a "wet" area of the state, or perhaps New Mexico, to customers in "dry" areas. This illegal practice sidestepped the local liquor laws and saved the customer a long drive to a "wet" area.

2. Johnny Gimble, conversation with Joe Carr, Lubbock, July 20, 1991; Tiny Moore, videotaped workshop, South Plains College, Levelland, Texas, 1980.

3. George Ashburn, interview with authors, Meadow, Texas, January 14, 1989.

4. Marilyn Johnson Chase, "All About Oprys," *Dallas Morning News*, July 19, 1991, "Guide" section, 26-28.

5. Bob Suggs, interview with authors, Littlefield, Texas, January 7, 1989.

6. The described performer appeared on the Meadow Musical, January 14, 1989.

7. Emil Macha, interview with authors, Littlefield, Texas, December 28, 1988.

8. Charlsie Roach, interview with authors, Higgenbotham, Texas, January 13, 1989.

9. Emil Macha, interview with authors, Littlefield, Texas, December 28, 1988.

10. George Ashburn, interview with authors, Meadow, Texas, January 14, 1989.

11. Ibid.

Chapter Ten

1. Royce Porter to Joe Carr, December 12, 1990.

2. "Cowboy Christmas Ball, Anson, Texas," reference file, Library, Abilene *Reporter News*.

3. Don Caldwell, interview with authors, Lubbock, Texas, June 13, 1989.

Chapter Ten Discography

Dixie Chicks, *Little Ol' Cowgirl*, Crystal Clear CCR 9250.

Frankie McWhorter, *Tunes Bob Wills Taught to Me*, Maverick 1988.

The Lynn Morris Band, *The Lynn Morris Band*, Rounder CD 0276, 1990.

The Lynn Morris Band, *The Bramble and the Rose*, Rounder CD 0288, 1992.

Buck Ramsey, *Rolling Uphill from Texas*, Fiel Productions 51192, 1992.

Bluegrass; Western Swing; Gospel Favorites; Country Caravan, South Plains College, cassettes featuring student talent, various years.

Andy Wilkinson, *Dollars to December*, Adobe 1990.

Andy Wilkinson, *Deep in the Heart*, Adobe 1008, 1992.

Andy Wilkinson, *Charlie Goodnight*, Grey Horse, 1994

INDEX

A

B

C

D

H

N

O

P

Q

R

S

T

INDEX

243